The Story of the
Chippewa Indians

The Story of the Chippewa Indians

From the Past to the Present

Gregory O. Gagnon

The Story of the American Indian

An Imprint of ABC-CLIO, LLC
Santa Barbara, California • Denver, Colorado

Copyright © 2019 by ABC-CLIO, LLC

All rights reserved. No part of this publication may be reproduced, stored in a retrieval system, or transmitted, in any form or by any means, electronic, mechanical, photocopying, recording, or otherwise, except for the inclusion of brief quotations in a review, without prior permission in writing from the publisher.

Library of Congress Cataloging-in-Publication Data

Names: Gagnon, Gregory O. (Gregory Omer), 1942– author.
Title: The story of the Chippewa Indians : from the past to the present / Gregory O. Gagnon.
Description: Santa Barbara, California : Greenwood, [2019] | Series: The story of the American Indian | Includes bibliographical references and index.
Identifiers: LCCN 2018034243 (print) | LCCN 2018044055 (ebook) | ISBN 9781440862182 (ebook) | ISBN 9781440862175 (hard copy : alk. paper)
Subjects: LCSH: Ojibwa Indians—History—Juvenile literature.
Classification: LCC E99.C6 (ebook) | LCC E99.C6 G34 2019 (print) | DDC 977.004/97333—dc23
LC record available at https://lccn.loc.gov/2018034243

ISBN: 978-1-4408-6217-5 (print)
      978-1-4408-6218-2 (ebook)

23 22 21 20 19   1 2 3 4 5

This book is also available as an eBook.

Greenwood
An Imprint of ABC-CLIO, LLC

ABC-CLIO, LLC
130 Cremona Drive, P.O. Box 1911
Santa Barbara, California 93116-1911
www.abc-clio.com

This book is printed on acid-free paper ∞

Manufactured in the United States of America

Contents

Series Foreword	vii
Preface	ix
Introduction	xv
Timeline	xxi
1 Chippewa Country—Anishinaabewaki	1
2 Traditional Foundations of Chippewa Worldview	21
3 Securing Chippewa Country, 1600–1736	41
4 Expanding Chippewa Country	61
5 American Incorporation and Colonization	85
6 The Nadir of Chippewa Country	105
7 More Pieces of the Story of the Chippewa	129
8 Self-Government and Threatened Termination, 1935–1960s	151
9 Self-Determination and Civil Rights	165
10 The Story of the Chippewa Continues	185
Bibliography	201
Index	207
About the Author	221

Series Foreword

Historical Native Americans find a place in history books but often as relics of the past. Exploring American Indian history and learning about their struggles, contributions, and cultures, both in the past and present, is vital to truly understanding the American story. American Indians and Alaska Natives have a long and varied history and continue on as vibrant, contemporary peoples comprising more than 6.6 million people living in the United States.

Of the 573 federally recognized American Indian tribes, each has its own history and complex relationship with the United States. *The Story of the American Indian* explores the diverse and wide range of American Indian peoples. Books in the series focus on the histories of individual tribes and encourage readers to break down stereotypes and resist the urge to lump all indigenous people into one group. Unlike many reference books on Native Americans, books in this series share histories from tribal perspectives rather than from traditional colonizers' viewpoints. Authors are tribal members and scholars who have extensive firsthand knowledge of their tribe.

Each volume focuses on a particular group or related groups of American Indians and presents historical chapters about the events, homelands, language, and community; cultural and social traditions; contributions to the larger society; and the tribe's current status. Volumes include a timeline of historical events, chronological narrative chapters, brief biographies in a Notable Figure section, and a bibliography. These richly detailed books provide readers with a holistic picture of the tribe from the past to the present.

Preface

The Story of the Chippewa Indians is a synthesis that offers a narrative with interpretations based on a large body of scholarly work, oral histories, and exchanged information about my tribe. The multiple communities of the Chippewa have ebbed and flowed into various cultural and political configurations over the centuries. Much of this narrative is impressionistically focused on different places, times, and events in order to convey one person's sense of key elements in the story. This means that I sometimes offer an emphasis on one community or one area to amplify the overall Chippewa experience and at other times revert to generalizations applicable to the overall story. This is what a storyteller does.

Events and people external to Chippewa Country are an integral part of the story. Chippewa Country has been buffeted and even cosseted by the French, the English, the United States, and individuals. Sometimes the realities of the outside world are emphasized while the continuing Chippewa story is embedded within the narrative of what others do. Most obviously this applies to U.S. Indian policy and actions that incorporated Chippewa into reservations, court decisions, laws, and forced a struggle to survive as separate, Chippewa sovereignties within an American context.

Reaching out beyond Chippewa Country is part of the story, too. Throughout history, Chippewa people and their governments chose to partner with other Native Americans. For instance, the American Indian Movement was founded by the Chippewa, but it soon became a Pan-Indian organization. Chippewa governments share a history with other Native American governments because they share similar goals, ambitions, and experiences.

This story begins in the Misty Past, an indeterminate time when the world was created, and people came together in northern Michigan to construct Chippewa identity as the Three Council Fires. They called themselves Anishinaabeg (Original Men or Original People). Over time, the Three Fires separated into distinct Chippewa, Ottawa, and Potawatomi tribes. By the 18th century, Chippewa communities stretched from Sault Ste. Marie in Michigan where the three Great Lakes of Huron, Michigan, and Superior are connected, westward across the Great Lakes to Wisconsin, and on to northern Minnesota and even beyond the Red River of the North into North Dakota and Montana. There are Chippewa reservations in each of these states today. The Chippewa numbered 170,742 in the 2010 Census. In combination with Chippewas in Canada, the Chippewa are the largest tribe north of the Rio Grande and the fourth largest in the United States.

I am a citizen of the Bad River Band of Lake Superior Chippewa. My reservation is within the boundaries of Wisconsin along Lake Superior and bordered by Michigan and the Bad River. It includes what was called the La Pointe Band and includes a miniscule part of Madeline Island in the Apostle Islands—where the crane led migrating Chippewa to the land where food grew on the water according to Chippewa oral tradition.

My background includes earning a doctorate from the University of Maryland in history, years as a tribal college administrator and consultant for many organizations and, particularly to tribal colleges throughout Indian country, and a tenured position at the University of North Dakota. In retirement, I teach American Indian law at Loyola University of New Orleans; but that is another story. I have written scholarly works and have drawn on my years of teaching and researching Chippewa history and the narratives passed on to me by my grandmother for this narrative.

The story presented conforms to the standards of academia and is indebted to the quality works of other scholars. It reflects a Chippewa-centric narrative. Many other storytellers have given knowledge to me. Over the years I have absorbed what others have related and added them to the developing narrative. The story of the Chippewa is offered to all in a good way, and I beg understanding and forgiveness for any errors I have made.

Chapter 1, "Chippewa Country—Anishinaabewiki," describes the Chippewa societies that developed in the upper Great Lakes area of the United States and Canada and extended westward. I summarize the academic conclusions about the arrival and development of Native American societies, including the migrations of peoples eventually called Chippewa. It anchors the Chippewa in their environment and emphasizes traditional Chippewa society, its life styles, governance, and worldview. It establishes what Chippewa society was like in its core homeland in Michigan by about 1600.

Chapter 2, "Traditional Foundations of Chippewa Worldview," provides a partial description of the Chippewa origin traditions during genesis in the Misty Past, including the creation of humans and the earth, the migration narrative, the Great Flood, common stories about the Chippewa culture hero, Nanabozho, and the place of Chippewa humans in the world. I summarize traditional Chippewa aspirations and values and explain how some of these are realized in traditional life.

Chapter 3, "Securing Chippewa Country 1600–1736," describes the challenges to Chippewa sovereignty and Chippewa posed by challenges from the Iroquois Confederation and the Fox from about 1640 to about 1736 when wars with these tribes had ended. Interactions with the French and English and the development of the commerce and alliances of the fur trade thread their way through the story. By 1736 challenges to the core homeland were no more, and the Chippewa were the dominant pivot in the upper Great Lakes. A confident, secure, coordinated Chippewa expansion westward accelerated.

Chapter 4, "Expanding Chippewa Country," describes a golden age of Chippewa history from the Dakota Wars beginning in 1736 to the replacement of Chippewa hegemony with American expansion to control Chippewa Country by the 1830s. During the century Chippewa communities absorbed others into their societies, fought glorious wars against the British in Pontiac's War and the Dakota Sioux, and ruled the fur trade connections of French and British commerce with Native Americans. The Chippewa cultural center moved from the Mackinaw Straits in Michigan to Madeline Island in western Lake Superior to western Minnesota by the 19th century.

In Chapter 5, "American Incorporation and Colonization," I describe the American absorption of Chippewa Country through treaties, laws, population expansion, and force. I emphasize that Chippewa societies responded with consistent efforts to survive and maintain their Chippewa identity despite American actions. This chapter covers roughly from 1815 to the 1880s when all Chippewa had been limited to reservations and were subject to American Indian policy. The Chippewa were incorporated into the political realm of the United States. Historical markers for Chippewa history like the Tragedy of Sandy Lake, the land cession treaties guaranteeing

Chippewa rights in reserved portions of Chippewa Country, and efforts in defense of their people by Chippewa leaders are described.

Chapter 6, "The Nadir of Chippewa Country," describes continuing loss of land, American policy attempts to erase Chippewa culture through assimilation policies like boarding schools, land allotment, and laws prohibiting Chippewa religion, and the consequences of imposed poverty for health and well-being. American despoliation of the land and extraction of lumber, copper, and fishing access are included. Finally, the Indian Reorganization Act's restoration of tribal governments introduces another chapter in the story.

In Chapter 7, "More Pieces of the Story of the Chippewa," I examine narratives of Chippewa survival in different settings throughout Chippewa Country: the vigorous nationalism of Red Lake Reservation, Turtle Mountain Reservation established, Rocky Boy created, and Little Shell Band's continuing struggles. The Indian Reorganization Act created a new possibility with tribal governments restored and functioning within federal laws and policies.

Chapter 8, "Self-Government and Threatened Termination, 1935–1960s," describes Chippewa governments adapting to the Indian Reorganization Act by developing constitutional republics and the impact of the New Deal. I offer pieces of the story through an examination of Indian Service (later Bureau of Indian Affairs) data for Bad River Reservation, part of the Lake Superior Chippewa and within Wisconsin. I describe the challenge amid Chippewa efforts to achieve self-government when suddenly Chippewa were faced with termination threats, saw jurisdiction transferred to Wisconsin and Minnesota, and were faced with federal efforts to relocate Chippewa to cities. They also pursued claims with the Indian Claims Commission.

In Chapter 9, "Self-Determination and Civil Rights," I examine the increasing efforts to assert treaty rights, practice tribal government, and rejuvenate tribal religion by the Chippewa after World War II. The radical approach of the American Indian Movement, Chippewa activists, artists, and writers receive attention. I conclude with a description of the impact of the 1975 Tribal Self-Determination and Education Assistance Act that restored even more power to sovereign Chippewa governments.

Chapter 10, "The Story of the Chippewa Continues," is a fluid story. The Chippewa story never ends. This concluding chapter describes the function of casinos in contemporary Chippewa Country, cultural challenges faced by Ojibwe communities, and many of the issues which Chippewa reservations individually and collectively face. It concludes with a return to traditional narrative.

Author's note: General histories are comprised of summaries and interpretations of the work of many scholars who painstakingly assembled pieces of the mosaic from primary sources that a generalist draws upon for synthesis. Although the interpretations, choices, and inevitable errors are mine alone, I owe a great debt to those who have written about each aspect of the Chippewa story and to the Manitos who created and inspired a people to survive. Although works are listed in the bibliography and I have acknowledged my debt in a sidebar, the book would not have been possible without their compilations leading to common knowledge. I have also drawn on contributions of the Chippewa and other Native American peoples to my knowledge about my culture and history. My relatives were instrumental in my education. Chi-miigwetch to all of them.

Introduction

The Chippewa Nation is a significant participant in the history of North America. It played a pivotal role throughout the Great Lakes, in Canada, and the states of Michigan, Wisconsin, and Minnesota particularly. Its impact resonates in loan words to English in both countries. The Chippewa language (Ojibwemowin) was the language of the fur trade that brought wealth to Native Americans and to European economies and to the nascent United States and Canada. Collective Chippewa decisions affected the French, British, and American empires.

Chippewa Country's resources in copper, iron ore, timber, fish, quarried stone, and furs enriched the growing nation states and provided the basic building blocks for the Midwest and some Canadian provinces. In the 21st century, Chippewa individuals and sovereign nations continue as significant actors in history.

VOCABULARY OF THE STORY

The term "Chippewa" is not what they called themselves. Chippewa emerged from what the English heard when Chippewa identified themselves. The United States has continued the use of Chippewa in treaties and other interactions with the nation. Anishinaabe is the self-identifying term used by the Chippewa, and the plural is Anishinaabeg. The language developed by the Chippewa societies is Ojibwemowin and its derivative, Ojibwe, is commonly used by the Chippewa to identify themselves today.

In Canada, the Chippewa are designated as Ojibwe or Saulteurs or Mississaugas. Most scholars have substituted Ojibwe for Chippewa in the past few decades, but Chippewa remains the legal, recognizable term for the nation.

Two other tribes, the Ottawa and Potawatomi, also are Anishinaabe and speak dialects of the same language, Ojibwemowin. The three Anishinaabe tribes had a common origin and only separated in historical times. They have retained a confederated common sense of identity originally referred to as the Three Fires. In traditional cultures, fire was an important symbol of unity. Many Ojibwemowin words are scattered throughout this narrative and are interspersed with more familiar and contemporary terms like Michigan, Sault Ste. Marie, Wisconsin, Madeline Island, Minnesota, etc.

Native American has become the most widely used collective term for America's indigenous peoples since the 1970s in the United States. In Indian country, the terms used depend on context. Most prefer their tribal names but use Indian or Native American almost interchangeably. American Indian, tribal names in either English or the indigenous language, and Native American are all acceptable when they are used respectfully.

The term "Chippewa Country" is not commonly used in political histories, but I coined it from the Chippewa use of the term "Anishinaabewki" (the land of the Chippewa). Chippewa Country encompassed many other tribes, and historians are not comfortable with calling the entire area Chippewa Country. I assert that most of the area was controlled by Chippewa during the prereservation period, and the term is useful for understanding the scope of Chippewa dominance. American Indians did not draw rigid boundaries, but they recognized tribal territories and shared usage according to protocols familiar to all. Chippewa Country describes a vast area the way most Chippewa understood it.

Chippewa Country is a bit of a misnomer because it implies that there was a single entity, the Chippewa Tribe, which ruled all of Chippewa Country as the king ruled France. This is not true. There has never been a single Chippewa sovereign polity. Each band was autonomous and made decisions through consensus within the band. Cooperative ventures among bands were negotiated and agreed upon and binding only on those that agreed. Today, the 20 reservations have separate governments. Some, like the Minnesota Chippewa Tribe, which includes six Chippewa reservations, operate jointly in many areas and independently in others. Various other collective arrangements exist as with the treaty rights of hunting and fishing, but these are intergovernmental, limited agreements. This is as it was before the reservations.

Chippewa is used in this book to describe all of the tribe as it is well understood throughout the world as denominating a large subdivision, a tribe, of the Algonquian language family. We all generally know what Chippewa means. Chippewa politics and population are spread widely in Canada from Western Quebec to Saskatchewan and in the United States from Michigan to Montana. In 2010, Canada recorded a population of 163,290. The Chippewa in the United States numbered 170,142.

Canada has 125 band reserves, and the United States has 20 reservations. Some Chippewa are part of their nation without being citizens because of the political laws established by Canada and the United States, which were based on arbitrary race definitions. The place and history of Chippewa within Canada are beyond the scope of this book.

Chippewa people are also citizens of either Canada or the United States, and many have moved; it is estimated that more than half of all Chippewa live beyond the boundaries of their reservations or reserves. Being American or Canadian citizens and being Chippewa citizens are not mutually exclusive statuses.

Another term, "American," is often used in this narrative as a contrasting term with Chippewa. Throughout history Americans interacted with the Chippewa, and the Chippewa did their best not to be Americans. Racist exclusions during much of American history as part of federal Indian policy also worked to make Chippewa different from Americans (whites). Clearly, the Chippewa are today American citizens. For purposes of easing the narrative, American is often used to distinguish between Chippewa and the U.S. population and governments. Readers should have no problem and should realize that no insult is intended.

Spelling Ojibwemowin is a difficult task. French, English, and American lexicographers as well as merchants, government officials, and Ojibwe individuals have evolved multiple spellings based on one of the several dialects. In the past few decades, those who wish to standardize Ojibwemowin have developed an orthography called "double vowel" and scholars try to follow it. Meanwhile the reader is confronted with generations of "it sounds like" spelling in the historical literature. Dialectical differences can confuse, too. For instance, the Chippewa culture hero Nanabozho is rendered many other ways. As with any storyteller, I choose Nanabozho because it was what I was taught, but I accept that there are many variations in pronunciation for our culture hero.

The Place of Stories

The Story of the Chippewa Indians is an apt title for this narrative because stories or oral traditions are a vital part of Chippewa existence. Traditionally, stories conveyed the essence of being Chippewa from generation to generation and are vital parts of enculturation. Basil Johnston, a preeminent explicator of Chippewa culture pointed out: "It's through story, fable, legend, and attitudes toward life and human conduct and quality and their diverse life forms are embodied and passed on" (quoted in Doerfler, 2013, p. xix). Chippewas understood their world through stories and continue to tell them.

Stories are transmitted in two forms: Adizookaanag (traditional-sacred) and Debaajimowinan (histories). The lines separating the categories are not clear, as stories readily move back and forth as the creation narrative does. Stories vary depending on context and narrator as they evolve, but they all contain the same essential elements. The "correct" version is the one or portion of one that is needed when it is told.

The oral traditional stories have been augmented by scholarship in the western tradition. Empirical studies have taken their place in the body of the Chippewa stories. Both Chippewa scholars and non-Indians have contributed valuable portions.

A composite history of the Chippewa from a Chippewa perspective is hampered by the variety of Chippewa band experiences traditionally and within five different states today. It is also difficult because early Chippewa sources are limited. Government officials and non-Chippewa individuals naturally described what affected them. Their perceptions were colored by various prejudices and assumptions.

Although there are early Chippewa pictograph scrolls, they are not narratives in a western sense. With explication, the Mide scrolls, sacred religious texts of the Midewiwin or Grand Medicine Society of some indigenous peoples, present a widely used version of the creation story. During the 19th century, western-educated Chippewa wrote histories based on oral traditions, but these are necessarily limited in focus to their regional communities and by what non-Natives were willing to publish. William Warren's *History of the Ojibway People* (written in the 1850s), George Copway's *The Traditional History and Characteristic Sketches of the Ojibway Nation* (1850), Francis Assikinack's *Legends and Traditions of the Odahwah Indians* (1858), and Peter Jones's *History of the Ojibway Indians* (1861) flesh out the oral traditions collected by many non-Indian scholars like Ruth Landes, Peter Pond, and Frances Densmore.

Since the 1950s a large number of non-Indian scholars have pieced together large portions of the story of the Chippewa primarily through studies of Chippewa within particular areas or communities. More recently, a number of Chippewa scholars have emerged from graduate school and focused their research on culturally informed scholarship, often about their own reservation communities.

The Themes of the Story

Throughout the development of the Chippewa story, one theme emerges most obviously. Chippewa bands and individuals were determined to control their own lives through their own governments and according to their own values and traditions. From the Misty Past to the present, the Chippewa have seen many challenges to meeting their goal. This part of the story continues.

Timeline

Misty Past BCE
The timeless past when the world and all living things were created and given their functions and identities by Manitos. Chippewa people created. Manitos teach Chippewa the customs and beliefs they need to be Chippewa. Sometimes the Misty Past overlaps with chronological time and events, but usually things just happen as they need to exist.

c. 10,000 BCE–1200 BCE
Proto-Chippewa Algonquian language speakers migrate from the east to western Ontario–Great Lakes–Western Michigan area where several bands evolved their common cultural roots and created Chippewa Country. The core homeland of the Chippewa centers around the Sault Ste. Marie-Boweting and Mackinac Straits area of Michigan where Lakes Huron and Michigan meet and Lake Superior is accessible via St. Mary's River. The Three Council Fires as they call themselves separate into Chippewa, Ottawa, and Potawatomi but retain their sense of common origin.

c. 1200 BCE–1600 CE
The traditional historical progression of the story of the Chippewa continues. Traditional cultural foundations are laid, a traditional annual cycle is established, and Chippewa Country is defined and defended. Independent Chippewa towns and bands emerge. Non-Chippewa tribes in the same general areas experience their genesis, and trade contacts extend throughout Chippewa Country and adjacent areas. These tribes include the Dakota (Sioux), Winnebago, Fox, Iroquois Confederation, and Huron, among others. Some become competitors, and some

become allies of the Chippewa. The Chippewa note the changes the Dutch and English bring to the eastern seaboard areas and establish tentative interactions with the French.

1621
Etienne Brule paddles the St. Mary's River to Sault Ste. Marie, Michigan, and is, probably, the first European in Chippewa Country.

1640–1701
The Chippewa-Iroquois Wars. The Iroquois Confederation launches annual expeditions that devastate much of the areas around Chippewa Country initially and cause ebbing and flowing of populations. The French, Dutch, and English participate and encourage the continuing warfare. The Chippewa win the war and secure hegemony in Chippewa Country. Later historians call the war the Beaver Wars.

1641
French visitors, Jogues and Charles Rayambault, map part of Chippewa Country and name Sault Ste. Marie and the St. Mary's River as well as calling the Chippewa Saulteurs (people who live at the Sault, rapids, in French).

1661
Battle of Iroquois Point reverses initial Iroquois gains as Chippewa and their allies defeat a large Iroquois invading force at present-day Bay Mills Reservation within Michigan. It is one of several major defeats of the Iroquois that force Iroquois retreat, leaving an enlarged Chippewa Country.

1665
Father Claude Allouez establishes a mission on what will be called La Pointe, Madeline Island. The Chippewa have their own names for the island and its communities just off the western shore of Wisconsin. The island is a major Chippewa town and the starting point for more westward expansion. French trading posts and missions allowed by Chippewa.

1671
Sieur Duluth representing the French government conducts a ceremony at Sault Ste. Marie, where he asserts French sovereignty over all of the land touched by the Great Lakes. Chippewa leaders attend the ceremony and attach their clan symbols to the cross Duluth raises. Probably Chippewa leaders see the ceremony as a declaration of alliance and friendship, certainly not an acceptance of French sovereignty in Chippewa Country.

Chippewa leaders permit a Catholic mission called St. Ignace at the Mackinac Straits in Michigan. Along with Sault Ste. Marie, it is the trading entrepôt for eastern Chippewa Country.

1683
The French permitted to establish Fort Baude with 150 soldiers at St. Ignace. A mixed French-Chippewa community grows as intermarriage and commerce expands.

1690–1736
Chippewa-Fox Wars. Chippewa and Ottawa leaders initiate war to drive Fox from Chippewa Country. French forces join the Chippewa. The Fox retreat to Illinois and Iowa by 1736 when the Chippewa end the wars.

1701
The Peace of Montreal hosted by the French brings together major combatants in the Chippewa-Iroquois War. The Iroquois agree to allow the Chippewa into Iroquois Country to trade with the English and to abandon their former lands in Ontario. The Iroquois threat is over.

Detroit is established with Native American leaders' tolerance by Sieur Cadillac. He encourages bands from several tribes, principally Ottawa, to relocate to Detroit. Foolishly, his successor invites Fox Bands to Detroit, and the Fox-Chippewa-French war ensues. Chippewa leaders do not want enemy-competitors.

1710
Chippewa westward expansion is noted by the French when bands move into Dakota areas in Lake Superior islands and eastern shores. Dakota leaders encourage Chippewa presence initially.

1715
Fort Machilimackinac is established as a trade center in the heart of Chippewa Country at the Straits of Mackinac, Lake Michigan. The French see it as blocking any English designs on Chippewa Country.

1736
The Dakota Wars begin and last until the 1860s. They result in Chippewa Country extending from its core in Michigan across northern Wisconsin and Minnesota and to northeastern North Dakota. Canadian Chippewa round northern Lake Superior and extend Chippewa Country into the Winnipeg, Manitoba, area.

1745
The Battle of Kathio forced Dakota to remove southward in Minnesota, surrendering their historical homeland in northern Minnesota to the Chippewa. Oral tradition describes hundreds of Dakota killed.

1754
The Battle of Pickawillany, Ohio, triggers the French and Indian War. Charles Langlade, an Ottawa war leader and fur trader, leads an Ottawa-Chippewa alliance force against a new Miami city that seeks to replace Chippewa control of the fur trade and expand English influence. Soon thereafter, George Washington's exploratory expedition was captured by an Ottawa-Chippewa-French force. Most historians date the French and Indian War from Washington's defeat at Fort Necessity, Pennsylvania.

1760
Fort Michilimackinac surrendered to the English by Charles Langlade, the Ottawa war leader and French officer. English officials claim that the Chippewa are now

their subjects. The Chippewa laugh as they had when the French said the same thing. The Chippewa metis remain and continue as fur traders working with English companies. The French government's departure is lamented.

At Battle River, Minnesota, hundreds of Chippewa and Dakota fight an all-day battle with so many deaths that the river ran red into Red Lake according to oral history. This was the last major Dakota effort to reclaim their homeland from the Chippewa. The Chippewa name for the site is Gaa-danapananiding, a place of slaughter.

1760s–1815

The British Northwest Company replaces French companies throughout Chippewa Country. It establishes a new trading center at Grand Portage and continues operations at Michilimackinac and La Pointe with several subsidiary centers elsewhere in the wake of Chippewa expansion. After the War of 1812, the company shifts posts to Fort William, Ontario, and is replaced in 1835 by the American Fur Company.

1762

Pontiac, an Ottawa war leader, lays siege to Detroit and Native American leaders throughout Chippewa Country and in the Ohio Valley unite against British refusal to obey Native protocols. The British call it Pontiac's Rebellion, but he was just one of many war leaders. Before it ends, the war drives English out of most of the forts, and settlers flee back to the colonies.

The Battle of Michilimackinac results in the expulsion of the British from Chippewa Country. The Chippewa captured the fort by staging a baggataway (lacrosse) game, then killing or capturing British onlookers who had left the fort open. The Chippewa killed only British traders and military, not the French descent traders. Charles Langlade brought the captives to British Montreal, where they were ransomed.

1764

British government issues Proclamation Act that forbids settlement by colonists west of the Appalachians and declares the area west of the mountains is Indian country. It establishes that only the British government can buy land from Indians, a principle later adopted by the United States. The government in effect affirmed an Indian victory in the Pontiac Rebellion. Colonists are angered, and their anger contributes to the causes of the Revolution.

Green Bay, Wisconsin, is established by Charles Langlade, the retired Ottawa-French-British war hero and fur trader. He is considered the first settler in Wisconsin. Ironically, Langlade is often called the "Father of Wisconsin."

1776–1781

The American Revolution involves Chippewa Country marginally. No major engagements involve the Chippewa, but the British loss will change the balance of power in Chippewa Country. Fort Michilimackinaw was captured by the Chippewa yet again.

1795
After the Battle of Fallen Timbers, Native American alliance members sign Treaty of Greenville, which cedes most of Ohio Valley to the United States. American settlers move closer to Chippewa Country. This is the first Chippewa treaty with the United States.

1800–1820
The American Fur Company (AFC) begins displacing the British Northwest Company. American experiment in creating government trading posts is abandoned, and AFC achieves near monopoly South of Canadian border. AFC hires the same traders that the British had used and that earlier French companies had employed. A few Americans are added to the mix, and they learn that Chippewa and other Native Americans control the trade. Michel Cadotte, a Chippewa mixed blood, becomes AFC manager at La Pointe, Madeline Island. Cadotte's sons expand fur trade to Minnesota Chippewa communities.

1805
Michigan Territory encompassing Wisconsin and Minnesota is created by Congress.

1809–1811
The Shawnee Prophet brings a revitalization prophecy to Chippewa Country, and many embrace his doctrine, particularly at Madeline Island. Some Chippewa join Tecumseh in a military alliance but, due to intervention by Michel Cadotte and other leaders, most do not join the war which segues into the War of 1812.

1813
Death of the pan-Indian war leader, Tecumseh, at the Battle of the Thames brings the last pan-Indian alliance against the United States to an end. Chippewa leaders must decide whether to move to Canada or remain in their homelands to deal with the United States. Most stay. Treaty of Paris in 1815 ends the war, and Indians east of the Mississippi are left to deal with the United States on their own.

1818
Lawrence Taliaferro is appointed Indian agent for Minnesota and Wisconsin to supplement the agency already at Sault Ste. Marie. Fort Snelling becomes the military pivot of U.S. presence west of Lake Superior in 1819. Taliaferro tries to broker an end to the Chippewa-Dakota War and negotiates several treaties.

1819
Saginaw Treaty is first cession of any Chippewa Country. Chippewa and Ottawa relinquish 6,000,000 acres but retain hunting and fishing rights. Treaty establishes the southern boundary of Chippewa Country.

1821
Treaty of Chicago includes Chippewa selling land south of the Grand River in Michigan. Other tribes like Potawatomi surrender even more land.

1822

Stockbridge-Munsee, some Oneida, and Brotherton bands are moved to Wisconsin from New York and placed on Menominee land.

1825

Treaty of Prairie du Chien includes multiple tribes such as the Chippewa and Dakota. Terms create a buffer zone between the Chippewa and Dakota in Minnesota and Wisconsin while delineating boundaries for the Dakota and Chippewa Nations. The United States insists that each tribe should have exclusive use of their own land, a principle contrary to traditional tribal laws.

Treaty with the Chippewa acquired signatures of Chippewa band leaders who had not signed at Prairie du Chien. It demonstrates that the United States understands that each Chippewa band is independent and not bound by commitments from other bands.

1830

The Indian Removal Act authorizes the president to negotiate removal of all tribes from east of the Mississippi to Indian Territory or at least to west of the Mississippi. Indian Territory is created by a separate act. Forced removal and forced land sales to the United States are the dominant U.S. Indian policy. The Chippewa would be threatened with removal from their homelands until the late 19th century. Some Ottawa are removed to Indian Territory.

1832

Ozwandib, a Chippewa, guides Indian agent Henry Schoolcraft and others to the source of the Mississippi in Minnesota. Schoolcraft concludes he discovered the source of the Mississippi.

1836

Treaty with the Ottawa and Chippewa, also called the Treaty of Washington, is signed in Washington, DC, by Chippewa and Ottawa leaders. It ceded approximately 37 percent of Michigan (14,000,000 acres). Tribal leaders insisted on language retaining "the rights of hunting on the lands ceded, with other usual privileges of occupancy, until the land is required for settlement." These treaty stipulations are insisted upon by Chippewa in subsequent treaties, too.

Territory of Wisconsin established.

1837

Michigan becomes a state and begins a consistent pattern of insisting on Michigan jurisdiction and control of resources over Chippewa and Ottawa Country. The pattern of encroachment is usually countenanced by the United States and is repeated by other states as they are admitted to the union.

Treaty with the Chippewa, also known as the Pine Tree Treaty, is signed at St. Peters, Minnesota. Timber companies had demanded access to both Dakota and Chippewa forests, and they begin a century-long pattern of clear-cutting forests and leaving devastated resources behind. Lumbering floods rice fields, drives away animals, pollutes streams, removes habitats for fur-bearing animals, and makes the Chippewa cycle of life nearly impossible to maintain. The Chippewa insist on hunting and fishing rights even in land ceded as part of treaty.

1842
Treaty with the Chippewa, also called the Copper Treaty, ceded lands in Michigan's Upper Peninsula and northeastern Wisconsin. The Chippewa and Ottawa, surrounded by the Americans, surrender Michigan to the United States but stipulate retention of hunting, fishing, and gathering rights. Another provision allows them to remain in Michigan on the peripheries of American communities. "Half-bloods" receive payments, thus recognizing their Indian status. Traders are paid for alleged individual debts from tribal funds.

Copper mining begins on Michigan's Keeweenaw Penninsula and spreads to Wisconsin.

1847
The non-Indian population of Wisconsin reaches 210,546 and then is augmented by German immigrants following the 1848 attempted revolutions in the Germanies. Chippewa population within Wisconsin is about 3,000.

1848
Wisconsin becomes a state. State officials ignore treaty stipulations protecting Chippewa rights and demand more control of Chippewa land and resources. Some citizens of Wisconsin attempt to support justice for tribes and engage in lobbying on behalf of the Chippewa.

1850
President Zachary Taylor orders Chippewa leaders and government agents to prepare for removal. Minnesota Territory officials and subagent at La Pointe John Watrous plot to force Chippewa removal from Michigan and Wisconsin to Minnesota.

1851
Sandy Lake Tragedy. Although treaty payments were usually issued at Madeline Island, Chippewa leaders were ordered to Sandy Lake, Minnesota Territory, for 1851 annuities. Many refused, but many others went with their families during hunting season in October. Provisions and shelter were promised but not available when Chippewa arrived. Rotten provisions arrived, and partial payments were not made until November. Winter set in, and hundreds of Chippewa died trying to return home. No one is held responsible for the deaths.

The removal order is rescinded because many American businessmen and community leaders joined Chippewa protests against the inhumane treatment of the Chippewa. Payments were resumed at La Pointe, Madeline Island, by 1854.

1852
Buffalo, the most prominent Chippewa leader, goes to Washington. Apparently, he meets with the president despite efforts by the Office of Indian Affairs to ignore

him and send him home. Buffalo and his delegation receive a commitment to exempt the Chippewa from removal and for a new treaty.

1854
Treaty with the Chippewa at La Pointe abandons idea of removing the Chippewa and creates permanent reservations. The Americans receive more land including most of Madeline Island, but both Michigan and Wisconsin Chippewa bands now have designated, permanent reservations not subject to capricious plots.

1855
Another Treaty with the Chippewa is signed in Washington, DC, and establishes additional Minnesota reservations by consolidating several bands into Leech Lake and Mille Lacs reservations.

1858
Minnesota enters the union with a non-Indian population of about 150,000. Governor Henry Sibley continues a territorial policy of trying to force all Chippewa into a single reservation and taking lands from Dakota and Winnebago tribes in southern Minnesota. Minnesota and federal efforts continue through the 19th century as does Chippewa resistance.

1862
The Dakota Conflict pits desperate Dakota against Minnesota and the United States in a bloody, short war. The Chippewa observe what happens to the Dakota at the hands of a vengeful Minnesota American population. Even the Winnebago are forced to leave the state, and the Dakota are forbidden to live in Minnesota. Thirty-eight Dakota are hanged. The Chippewa do not join the Dakota, although Hole in the Day, a primary Chippewa leader, does threaten war to gain negotiating advantages.

1863
Old Crossing Treaty with the Pembina and Red Lake Bands cedes the Red River Valley to the United States (really to Minnesota and Dakota Territory). It provides payments to the bands, accepts Red Lake Reservation as permanent, and promises the Pembina Band a reservation in Dakota Territory.

1867
Creation of White Earth Reservation by treaty. Reluctant band leaders accept a reservation that will consolidate their bands on one reservation. American officials envisioned a sizable reservation, finally completing consolidation of bands and leaving the rest of Minnesota for the Americans. The Dakota and Winnebago were already gone.

The Dakota give the big drum ceremony to the Chippewa to help them in healing the problems inflicted by the United States. The Dakota indicated that all Indians are suffering, so all should have the healing ceremony. The 150-year war between the tribes ends, and the Chippewa incorporate the big drum into their sacred ceremonies.

1887
Congress passes the Allotment Act (also known as the Dawes Severalty Act). Its intent is to force all Indians to become private landowners by dividing Indian lands into allotments. After 25 years of learning to be farmers, allottees will receive fee simple deeds and be awarded U.S. citizenship. They will be able to sell their lands. It is an act of U.S. faith that Indians will assimilate. Allotment is a disaster for Indian communities, and some Chippewa reservations lose much of their land to the Americans. Nationally, about two-thirds of all Indian lands remaining in 1887 are lost by 1932.

1889
The Nelson Act extends allotment to Chippewa reservations in Minnesota and opens the door for rapid dispossession of Indian-owned allotments and timber rights. Today, 97 percent of White Earth Reservation is non-Indian owned, and similar dispossession occurs in other Chippewa reservations.

Red Lake Reservation leaders refuse to accept allotment. In return for being exempted, they capitulate to demands that they sell 2,900,000 acres. A congressional act that exempts Red Lake but forces other Chippewa reservation allotment is named, "An Act for the Relief and Civilization of the Chippewa."

1913
Rocky Boy Cree Chippewa Reservation is formed in Montana. Currently, this is the westernmost Chippewa reservation.

1924
The United States extends American citizenship to all Indians, including reservation Indians. About half of all Indians in the United States are already citizens.

1934
Passage of the Indian Reorganization Act (IRA) initiated a restoration of tribal governments through reservation-wide constitutions. Allotment was halted, Indian religious freedom was restored, and tribal-reservation Native Americans were able to vote on constitutions that established representative governments if they chose. Modern tribal governments evolved from this change in government policy. Statutes and federal court decisions confirm that American law recognizes that tribal sovereignty is inherent and derives from the people of the tribe. The United States did not give tribes sovereignty; they have had it since the Misty Past.

1930s
Chippewa reservations within the states of Minnesota, Michigan, and Wisconsin choose tribal constitutions by referendums on each reservation. The Minnesota Chippewa Tribe (MCT) is organized as a confederation of equal reservations with separate constitutions, while other Chippewa reservations maintain entirely independent governments. Only Red Lake Reservation voted against the IRA in favor of keeping a 1918 tribal government constitution that included the seven hereditary chiefs. All tribes work on learning and practicing self-government under American control.

1953

Congress passes PL 280, which delegates civil and criminal jurisdiction over reservations to Minnesota and Wisconsin, a reversal of federal Indian law. Treaty rights, trust land, and taxation are not included in the transfer. Red Lake is excluded. The law is seen as one step in terminating all reservations by moving Native Americans to complete state control. Another phase of the termination plan includes funding individual Native American migration to urban areas.

1959

Bad River Reservation's tribal government declares nonviolent war on the state of Wisconsin. The declaration is symbolic of continuing battle by reservation governments against state usurpation of treaty rights by arresting tribal members exercising them and extension of state regulations to tribal members. Federal government acquiesces in state activities.

1960s

Great Society programs like housing, community development, vocational education, legal aid, Headstart, and funding for local projects are extended to reservations and urban Indian concentrations. On reservations, the tribal councils obtain grants and administer them, which provides a source of governing power not dependent on the BIA officialdom. Local priorities are tribal priorities.

1968

American Indian Movement (AIM) is founded by Chippewas in Minneapolis, Minnesota. Initially, an urban movement to protect Indian civil rights, AIM rapidly becomes a national movement asserting civil rights. AIM members blend their efforts with tribal governments to defend treaty rights, practice traditional religions, and demand sovereignty. AIM members attempt to reform tribal governments, occupy off-reservation sites, and rally at demonstrations. As with other civil rights organizations, AIM tactics are sometimes extreme and sometimes opposed by tribal leaders, but AIM plays a role in assertions of tribal and individual Indian rights.

American Indian Civil Rights Act extends most of the Bill of Rights to Indian country. Some exceptions like separation of church and state are omitted to recognize that tribes have the right to be governed by religious leaders provided that freedom of religion is protected.

1974

Sault Ste. Marie Reservation is established by presidential executive order.

The Tribble brothers from Lac Courte Oreilles Reservation are arrested and file suit in federal court based on treaty rights. Tribal president Alex Le Beau is arrested for illegal fishing in Michigan the following year. He contends in court that he was exercising treaty rights. Chippewa reservation governments join the proceedings eventually called the Voigt settlement.

1975

Congress passes PL 93-638, the Indian Self-Determination and Education Assistance Act, which formalizes a new federal Indian policy. The new policy is self-determination in a government-to-government relationship. The act itself establishes a process for transferring administration and funding from the Bureau of Indian Affairs to tribal governments by contract. Tribal control of programs allows funding of tribal priorities, tribal policies, tribal hiring of employees, and exercise of governing authority. Tribes can make decisions that affect their citizens and quality of life on reservations. Chippewa Country reservations exercise the right to contract BIA and other agency programs.

1976
SCOTUS rules that Michigan tribes have treaty fishing rights and orders Michigan to halt enforcement of state laws.

1978
Oliphant v. Suquamish declares that tribal courts have no criminal jurisdiction over nontribal members. It is one decision in a pattern that restricts tribal government even on reservations from governing non-Indians. Self-determination is difficult when non-Indians have extraterritorial privileges.

The Indian Child Welfare Act (ICWA) recognizes tribal court control of the placement and adoption of Indian children—even off-reservation Native American children where their tribe can be identified. Decades of state and federal practice had been to place most Indian children in foster and adoptive non-Indian homes. Congress finally accepted tribal complaints that they were losing their futures as children were taken from tribal cultures. State courts and social agencies are required to comply with the law, even Minnesota and Wisconsin (despite PL 280).

The Tribally Controlled Community College Act (TCCCA) provides funding for tribally chartered tribal colleges. Turtle Mountain Community College is one of the founders of the American Indian Higher Education Consortium group founded in the early 1970s. Other Chippewa reservations establish tribal colleges, which are accredited as are other colleges.

1983
Voigt decision by U.S. Court of Appeals reverses district court finding against Tribble brothers. Court returns the case to district court where Judge Boyle is required to rule on the extent of tribal rights in hunting and fishing in ceded land. He orders Wisconsin to negotiate with tribes to design a process of sharing wildlife harvests off-reservation in the cede territory.

1984
Great Lakes Indian Fish and Wildlife Commission (GLIFWC) is created by a consortium of the Lake Superior tribes that signed the treaties of 1837, 1842, and 1854, which guarantee Chippewa rights to hunt and fish. Its mission is to interact with Wisconsin and Michigan to determine and enforce fishing and hunting regulations, to provide research on environment, and to work with other agencies to improve the environment. It adds an educational component to educate the Chippewa in culturally enhancing practices and traditions. Michigan tribes form a similar organization.

Grand Traverse Reservation is created by executive order.

1985

The Chippewa exercising treaty rights are subjected to assaults, vandalism, armed threats, and intimidation by antitreaty groups joined by White Supremacists. Judge Crabbe issues an injunction against the protest activities. Eventually, Wisconsin sends large numbers of officers to protect Chippewa spear fishermen. Protesters are fined, and even RICO cases are filed. By 1990s, only perfunctory efforts have interfered with Chippewa fishermen. States grudgingly accept the Voigt rulings and negotiate as required.

1987

The *Cabazon v. California* case establishes that tribal gaming is subject to regulations by states. Casinos are economic development opportunities available under tribal laws.

Non-Indians and Native Americans form organizations like the Midwest Treaty Network to support Chippewa treaty rights and other Native American causes.

1988

The Indian Gaming Regulatory Act responds to state demands and federal concerns by establishing the Indian Gaming Commission to make and enforce rules for Indian gaming. It specifies that tribes and states must enter into compacts or tribes cannot have casinos. Casinos must be owned by the tribal governments, and they must be on trust land. Minnesota is cooperative with tribes, and Wisconsin and Michigan are more concerned with obtaining funding and exercising state control. In 1991, Wisconsin and Chippewa tribes sign the first contracts. Most reservations in Chippewa Country have casinos today.

Lac Vieux Desert Ojibwe Reservation is established within Michigan.

1990

HONOR is established under the leadership of Sharon Metz. Honor Our Neighbors' Origins and Rights is a joint Non-Native–Native American organization that counters the propaganda of antitreaty rights organizations across the United States. HONOR is illustrative of the support many non-Indians have provided to Chippewa and Pan-Indian causes. Non-Indian allies have always been sought and appreciated.

1996

Bad River Anishinaabe Ogitchida, a tribal rights organization, blockades railroad tracks on reservation to stop transportation of sulfuric acid. The Environmental Protection Agency halts the trans-reservation shipments. Throughout the remainder of the century and into the first quarter of the 21st century, Chippewa governments and groups align with environmental groups in court filings and demonstrations. They oppose new pipelines, demand toxic waste cleanups, litigate for dam removal to protect rice fields and fishing, and demonstrate against proposed mines in Chippewa Country. Winona LaDuke (White Earth Chippewa) becomes a national figure and vice presidential candidate.

1999
U.S. v. Mille Lacs reaffirms the Minnesota tribes that signed the 1837, 1842, and 1854 treaties have retained their hunting and fishing rights in ceded lands, not just on reservations. Treaties remain as bastions protecting tribal sovereignty.

2000
Chippewa bands and supporters gather to commemorate the Tragedy of Sandy Lake and continue memorializing the tragedy annually.

2000–Present
Individual tribal governments use casino revenues to support efforts to expand reservation economies, particularly with businesses that encourage traditional economic activities and services to the reservations. Many maintain fish hatcheries, for instance, and most support grocery stores. A few are able to spin off businesses that employ tribal and other people in light industry.

2002
The wolf population in Chippewa Country grows. The Chippewa have always seen linkage between the well-being of the Chippewa and of the wolves.

2004
An excellent rice harvest benefits all.

GLIFWC and U.S. Forest Service renew and expand a 1988 Memorandum of Agreement on the management of tribal ceded land harvesting.

National Museum of the American Indian opens in Washington, DC, and Chippewa leaders attend.

Federal Eighth Circuit rules that Mille Lacs Reservation within Minnesota is 61,000 acres, not the 4,000 that the state said it was.

2005
Tribes protest being excluded from Canadian provinces–states discussion on water policy for the Great Lakes.

"Famous Dave" Anderson, owner of a chain of barbeque restaurants, resigns as assistant secretary of the interior for Indian affairs. Anderson started his business on his Lac Courte Oreilles Reservation. He feels he can help Native Americans more by being out of government.

Raymond DePerry, head of the Great Lakes Inter-Tribal Council and chairperson of Red Lake Reservation, addresses the Wisconsin state legislature. He calls for the end of Indians as mascots of non-Indian schools. Many Chippewa agree with him and organize statewide protests.

2006
Jim Zorn, one of many non-Indians who have worked for tribal sovereignty and treaty rights, is chosen to head GLIFWC.

Lac Du Flambeau Reservation applies for "treatment as state" status from the Environmental Protection Agency. Iron and Oneida Counties of Wisconsin oppose.

2007

HONOR created to counter antitreaty protests of "Save a Walleye, Spear a Squaw." Treaty rights are now observed by the states of Wisconsin, Michigan, and Minnesota, though some protests and bones of contention still exist.

Patricia DePerry, chairperson of Red Lake Reservation, delivers the "state of tribes" address to Wisconsin legislature.

2008

David Treuer, Leech Lake Reservation, notes that language renewal and preservation efforts continue throughout Chippewa Country. About 10,000 Objibwe speakers exist, but the number is being augmented through tribal schools and other intensive efforts.

2009

Wisconsin passes GLIFWC Warden Bill (Wisconsin Act 27). It extends legal safeguards for tribal wardens, access to criminal databases, and emergency frequencies. State support for cross-deputized and other GLIFWC wardens is indicative of changing state approach to treaty rights.

2010

Joint tribal-state research of 329 mahnoomin (wild rice) fields to provide basic data on the health of the fields, including restoration efforts.

2011

Tribes protest Wisconsin intent to weaken mine regulations at state hearings. Tribes demonstrate participation in state politics as well as federal and tribal politics.

2012

Multiple Chippewa language and culture summer camps abound throughout Chippewa Country. These are part of concerted, widespread efforts to acculturate Chippewa youth and to reinforce tribal knowledge and traditional practices.

2015

Federal Judge Crabbe accepts treaty tribes' proposed regulations for night hunting. Hunting begins November 1.

Basil Johnston (1929–2015), celebrated Chippewa author of 17 books and myriad writings, and purveyor of cultural knowledge, dies. He is from a reserve within Canada and is mourned throughout Chippewa Country.

2017

Dennis Banks (1937–2017), one of the Chippewa who founded the American Indian Movement, dies. He is symbolic of the continuing efforts by many Chippewa to assert civil rights and tribal rights in the postreservation era. Like many leaders, Banks was controversial.

2018

Lac Courte Oreilles chairman, Mic Isham, speaks out against Enbridge oil pipeline because of 800 leaks that damage the environment. He joins nearly all tribal chairpersons in opposition to pipelines through Chippewa Country.

The Lac Courte Oreilles Tribal Governing Board declares Ojibwemowin the "official language" of the tribe and the reservation and specifies double-vowel orthography system. The tribe and its members have been leaders in language restoration efforts.

The story of the Chippewa continues.

NOTE

A note from the author: Chippewa reservations and organizations continue to have noteworthy events. Most are specific to particular reservations. Events are noticed by the national and regional press only when a major conflict erupts. Many of the reservations have small newspapers that appear periodically, but news rarely seeps out to all of Chippewa Country. One quarterly publication, *Mazinaigan,* does offer notice of significant events mainly within the GLFWC membership areas. I have selected some noteworthy events that are mentioned in the quarterly, which eschews tribal politics but notes important Chippewa Country events and occurrences. It provides a record of the struggles for sovereignty, treaty rights, tribal environmental concerns and accomplished programs that allow readers to see some of the continuing story of the Chippewa. Its major focus is on protection of the environment in a culturally sensitive way and on making sure that treaty rights are exercised and protected. Events may be mundane or national, but they are still part of the story.

1

Chippewa Country—Anishinaabewaki

The Chippewa homeland of the 21st century is comprised of individual reservations, reserves, and communities within their historical homelands, Anishinaabewaki (the land of the Chippewa). It extends from eastern Quebec province to western Manitoba and from Georgian Bay in Lake Huron across Lake Superior and on across northern Wisconsin and northern Minnesota to the Turtle Mountains in North Dakota and beyond into Montana. This huge swath of land, encompassing around 400,000 square miles within the boundaries of Canada and the United States, is also home to other tribes and non-Native Americans.

The Chippewa are a minority within their homeland, but they have retained enough political control of a fraction of their homelands to maintain sovereign nations recognized by both Canada and the United States. Culturally speaking, the Chippewa have many traits that would be recognizable to their ancestors and at the same time have made multiple adjustments dictated by changing times.

Chippewa Country was not always as widespread. Expansion from the point of ethnogenesis in the area around Mackinac Straits in Michigan occurred over several centuries. Chippewa self-identification as a social, cultural nation developed as their geographic reach expanded from the Misty Past until the mid-19th century. Chippewa genesis as an ethnic group and their expansion begins in the Upper Great Lakes drainage basins of Lake Huron, Lake Superior, and Lake Michigan.

Chippewa Country, ca. 1800

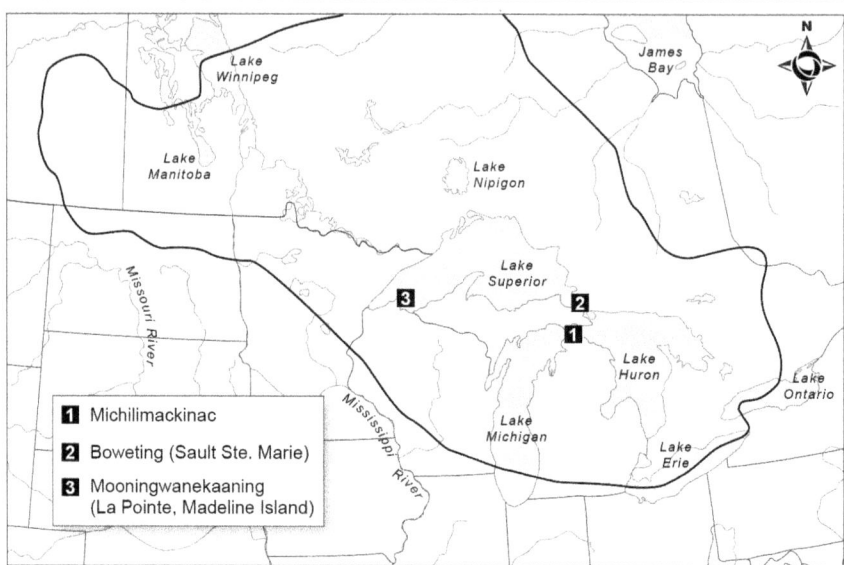

Chippewa Country: Major Chippewa Communities and Points of Interest, ca. 1800

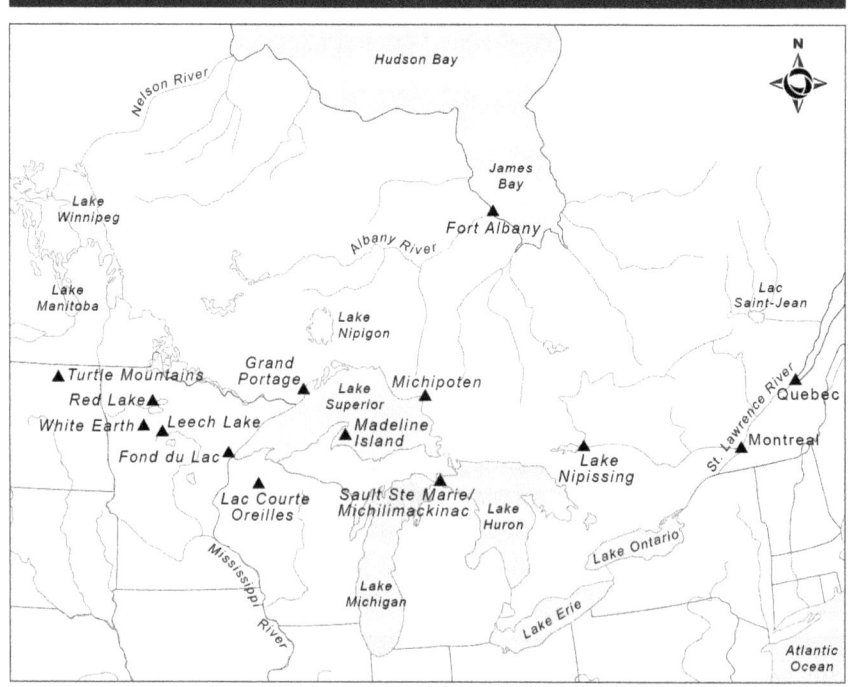

Chippewa Federal Recognition

There are 20 federally recognized Chippewa reservations. Each has its own government, citizens and identity. The Minnesota Chippewa Tribe provides an umbrella, confederated government to provide a common front, but each member band (tribe) is essentially autonomous. Little Shell Band is not federally recognized; it is the most prominent of several bands that seek independent recognition as tribes because of a history of autonomous existence. As of 2018, the Little Shell Band, Montana state recognized, was recommended by the BIA for recognition, but action has not been taken by Congress.

Bad River Band of Lake Superior Chippewa (within Wisconsin)

Bay Mills Chippewa Indian Community (within Michigan)

Chippewa-Cree Indians (within Montana) Reservation is named Rocky Boy Reservation after an Ojibwe leader, Stone Child.

Grand Traverse Bay Band of Ottawa and Chippewa Indians (within Michigan)

Keweenaw Bay Indian Community (within Michigan)

Lac Courte Oreilles Band of Lake Superior Chippewa (within Wisconsin)

Lac Du Flambeau Band of Lake Superior Chippewa (within Wisconsin)

Lac Vieux Desert Band of Lake Superior Indians (within Michigan)

Minnesota Chippewa Tribe (within Minnesota) includes six component tribes:

- Bois Forte Band (Nett Lake)
- Fond Du Lac Band
- Grand Portage Band
- Leech Lake Band
- Mille Lacs Band
- White Earth Band

Red Lake Band of Chippewa Indians (within Minnesota)

Sault Ste. Marie Tribe of Chippewa Indians (within Michigan)

Sokaogan Chippewa Community (within Wisconsin)

St. Croix Chippewa Indians (within Wisconsin)

Turtle Mountain Band of Chippewa Indians (within North Dakota). Includes Trenton Indian Community, near Montana border with North Dakota.

Note: Little Shell Tribe of Chippewa Indians is Montana state recognized and has been recommended for federal recognition. For many purposes, the Chippewa of Little Shell Tribe receive acknowledgment of legitimacy from the federal government but are not accepted as a sovereign nation.

BEFORE THERE WERE CHIPPEWA

Until about 11,000 BCE, a continental glacier prevented human occupation. Lake Agassiz and Lake Ojibwa-Barlow encompassed the present Great Lakes basins. As the lakes followed the glaciers northward, humans speaking proto-Algonquian, -Siouan, and -Iroquoian languages sifted in. By 7000 BCE, the Great Lakes, its tributaries, and thousands of lakes, ponds, swamps, wetlands, and creeks formed to create the land where bands evolved into the historic tribes.

Glacial retreat northward also gouged the terrain, created hills and rocky expanses, deposited minerals like iron ore and copper, and allowed first the growth of plants and then access to animals and finally to people. The water systems created a huge accessible area for Chippewa expansion. Canoes could be carried and there were as many as 60 portage sites that permitted goods and people to range throughout.

Chippewa Country had a hardwood forest of birch, beech, maple, and hemlock in its southern reaches, while its northern region was the northeastern pine forest of white, Norway, and jack pine. Hundreds and hundreds of herbaceous plants were harvestable. The land provided abundance in flora and fauna, which humans would learn to utilize and coexist with. Wild rice, plums, cherries, blueberries, maple sap, cranberries, strawberries, ginger, wild mint, raspberries, milkweed, and various roots became staples in human and animal diets. First came the mastodons and mammoths; then came deer, buffalo, elk, moose, caribou on the northern fringes of the country, and multiple varieties of fish. Humans and other animals harvested whitefish, sturgeon, trout, catfish, bass, and smelt. Beaver, wolves, coyotes, marten, black bears, foxes, otters, muskrats, weasels, mink, lynx, fishers, and wolverines shared the land with humans.

Chippewa Country provided well for its denizens when the weather was good, but its climate created a constant challenge. Hard freezes could begin in mid-September and continue until the end of May. Sometimes it was cold enough to freeze the Great Lakes. Snow often coated the land with around 30–40 inches annually; it stayed on the ground nearly all winter. Blizzards were frequent. Survival was a dominant concern of all living things. Chippewa stories describe the hardships of the starving times of January and February. Climate shaped the possible actions of humans and other life.

During the winters, food was difficult to secure, so food needed to be processed and stored during the seasons of abundance. This fact influenced living patterns. For instance, it required that large areas be available for securing food even for small groups of humans. Spring, summer, and early fall offered opportunities to secure and store food for winter that extended to as much as six months. Even after agriculture brought corn, beans, and squash (among other plants), extensive gathering and hunting were a necessity. A pattern of band and family group movement with the seasons developed. Most Chippewa did not farm.

The first peoples who entered Chippewa Country were Paleo-Indians who left evidence of their fluted points to indicate they were part of the widespread Clovis technology. It is likely that they lived in parts of the area from about 10,000 until around 7000 BCE. These peoples seem to have been displaced by communities called Aqua-Plano because of their leaf-shaped points until about 5000 BCE.

Archaeologists often name a population after characteristic artifacts and decorative objects, which speculation identifies as religious symbolism. The Archaic-Boreal societies left polished stone tools, particularly adzes, axes, and gouges, which must have been used on the deciduous forest fostered by the area being its warmest it had been for the previous 18,000 years. They were replaced about 500 CE, although the copper culture might have moved away around 1500 BC.

Beginning about 500 CE, movements of bands from Woodland societies arrived from the south and east. These Woodland arrivals brought domesticated crops like corns, beans, and squash to the area, although the core of Chippewa Country did not permit extensive farming in its rocky, well-watered regions. Burial mounds and pottery were another feature of Woodland cultures. Archaeologists generally divide the Woodland Era into Early Woodland (500–100 BCE), the Middle Woodland (100 BCE–800 CE), and the Late Woodland (800 CE–1600 CE).

Filtering northward steadily, populations from the east and south brought their cultural knowledge with them. They also maintained or created contacts through commerce with their places of origin. The southern large-scale societies extended their influence and their populations as part of the dynamic ebb and flow of American Indian populations throughout the millennia since their arrival in North America. The Adena-Hopewell culture, which was centered in the Ohio Valley, undoubtedly extended influence into the developing Chippewa Country during the period from about 500 BCE. Mississippian cultural influences followed and continued direct and indirect contacts until about 1600.

Chippewa oral traditions describing interaction with peoples from other societies indicate the interchanges. Chippewa traditions of conflict with urban dwellers during their own migration might well refer to a historical clash with an Adena-Hopewell city or perhaps a Mississippian polity. Neighboring tribes like the HoChunk (Winnebago) describe Mississippian encounters.

CHIPPEWA ETHNOGENESIS

The evolution of groups of hunter-gatherers into distinct societies and cultures requires an extensive period. The proto-Chippewa experienced several millennia of change, introduction of new peoples, and language and societal protocol development. Scholars cannot date when a people said, "We are Chippewa and we are not like others."

Oral genesis traditions merely point out that the Chippewa became Chippewa when they were created and were taught to be Chippewa by supernatural beings like Nanabozho. However, there were communities throughout Michigan that considered themselves Chippewa sometime in the period after the glaciers receded. Around 1600 is a good place to start because Chippewa societies and culture had been fully formed for centuries.

By 1600, the population of Chippewa Country probably exceeded 100,000 according to estimates related by Ives Goddard in the *Handbook of North American Indians* (p. 586). A population of Algonquian speakers had migrated to the Sault Ste. Marie area where rapids joined the three Great Lakes: Huron, Michigan, and Superior. Migration alluded to in the Chippewa creation narrative did occur historically in one form or another. By 1600 some of the Native Americans who lived in the areas adjoining Sault Ste. Marie called themselves Anishinaabeg. At some point before or after the arrival of French explorers and priests, they developed distinctions within their population that came to be known as Chippewa, Ottawa, and Potawatomi.

Other ethnic groups, like the Fox and Menominee and even the Siouan-speaking Winnebago and Dakota and the Iroquoian-speaking Hurons, developed in the general area. However, the Anishinaabeg anchored the area as the core of Chippewa Country. (Note: Tribal names used are those utilized in American English and institutionalized by both anthropologists and the federal government. The indigenous populations had their own names for themselves and for each other.) Traditional geographic boundaries were not rigid, and various other tribes interacted within the same sphere. The vastness of Chippewa Country allowed a flexible national territory where others were allowed or impinged.

Constructing the story of the Chippewa is helped by the many who have contributed to the story. Many Chippewa have described their own societies' culture and history in scholarly and other narrative self-reflections. In the 19th century, a few writers preserved the oral narratives of Chippewa, Ottawa, and Potawatomi history in print. Some of the more well known are William Warren, George Copway, Andrew Blackbird, and Peter Jones.

Their work offered an antidote to the Eurocentric writings of early Americans and Canadians.

Additionally, non-Chippewa have described the tribe from the viewpoints of travelers, merchants, missionaries, government officials, fellow inhabitants of Chippewa Country, and a wide range of academic disciplines. Chippewa materials have been published over the past four centuries. A rich lode of material enables a synthesis of the story of the Chippewa.

Problems do arise. Most written materials, with few exceptions, reflect the assumptions of non-Chippewa and were written often to support a particular colonialist mentality. Missionaries, for instance, saw and described Chippewa as heathens and primitives. French, British, and American officials exercised official ethnocentrism to disparage the Chippewa. Even the academic community has brought along its discipline-related baggage and tried to force the Chippewa to appear to conform to models and paradigms, particularly in anthropology. During the past half-century, the syncretic discipline of ethnohistory has introduced upstreaming and sidestreaming as techniques for describing Chippewa development over the centuries, providing a better lens for representing the Chippewa story.

Upstreaming mines oral traditions to balance the one-sided printed materials in an attempt to provide a Chippewa perspective that is more accurate than previous works. Sidestreaming draws upon studies of similar cultures and societies to portray what must have existed in Chippewa societies. Fortunately for the story, anthropologists worked to catalog Chippewa cultural practices along with oral traditions. Academics since the late 20th century have developed a perspective that acknowledges Chippewa agency in their own lives and which lends legitimacy to oral traditions.

Ironically, the most obvious danger in the techniques of ethnohistory is that it can create stereotypes just as earlier studies did—a stereotype of a static, unchanging society unaffected by events and time. "Chippewa men hunted and women gathered" can become the only description, but the reality is that women also hunted as needed, men assisted in gathering, roles changed, and although men were the spokesmen usually to the outside world, women controlled much of Chippewa decision making.

Another danger is creating a stereotyped romantic idealization of Chippewa society. The noble savage in balance and harmony is a tempting picture. All Chippewa communities were not and are not alike. It is true that they share common values and backgrounds, but each of the communities translated these values into action as it judged appropriate. Individuals did the same thing. As Sally Cole pointed out, "Culture is located in the interstices between formalist rules and individual behavior" (Landes, 1997, xi). Cultural norms are not followed to the letter by its entire people all of the time. There were reasons for the existence of sanctions in traditional Chippewa societies.

During the period from about 500 CE that began the coalescence of the Chippewa, Anishinaabeg adapted the material and spiritual cultures they had carried northward. They created technology to allow them to live in the harsh Chippewa Country. Agriculture was not a major factor in traditional Chippewa communities at first, but some corn, beans, and squash along with other crops were grown in the southern parts of their country. Ridge agriculture was an innovation that allowed plants to mature despite growing seasons of about 90 days for most of the area. The Chippewa also bought farm products from more southerly tribes in exchange for Chippewa-produced items. Contact and commerce served Chippewa interests.

Chippewa inventors mainly concentrated on taking full advantage of what was available. For fishing, they developed gill nets, fish spears, weirs, and traps for harvesting fish that varied in size from a few ounces to 50- or 60-pound sturgeons. They took advantage of the abundant willows for making mats and other materials. Women and men learned to use the plants for food and medicine and made careful studies of how to harvest them and to encourage their growth. Fire was frequently used to encourage some growth and discourage others.

Chippewa also drew on the knowledge of other tribes, like the Fox, Huron, Menominee, Winnebago, and others further south and north who were dealing with a similar environment and developing their own tribal identities. Exchange of goods, ideas, and even people characterized Chippewa communities from their inception. European goods would just be added to a familiar Chippewa process.

The Chippewa discovered the value of birchbark. Birch trees were much larger and more abundant than they are today. One tree could provide

---

BIRCHBARK CANOES AND CULTURAL USAGES

The birchbark canoe became a marker of the tribe. It enabled travel on the Great Lakes, rivers, and creeks that were a primary geographic feature. Their engineering allowed large loads to be carried in relatively light vessels. Canoes allowed trade and long-distance traveling to utilize the resources of a wide area. They also facilitated warfare. The construction of canoes illustrates the way Chippewa interacted. Men and women each had usual roles in assembling raw material and crafting the vessels. Women and men both owned canoes. According to oral tradition, Nanabozho, the Chippewa culture hero, taught the use of birchbark for canoes.

sufficient bark for a canoe. Sheets of birchbark were large enough to be used for sides of wigwams. Birchbark was renewable as its removal did not kill the tree. Food could be cooked in birchbark vessels as long as bowls were kept moist. It also provided the writing material for the Midewiwin scrolls. The basswood tree provided its inner fibers for ropes, thread, and utensils.

Chippewa wigwams and temporary camping buildings were made with birchbark. Dome-shaped wigwams were made with wooden framing covered with sheets of birchbark sewn together with basswood fibers. Some buildings were Quonset-shaped for more families and ceremonial centers. Woven mats provided insulation in winter and replaced birchbark walls in summer to allow more circulation. Wigwams were long enough to house a few nuclear families or sized for just a nuclear family depending on the seasons. Birchbark is transportable as communities moved to semipermanent sites. Temporary housing when Chippewa were in transit featured the well-known tipi shape, but it was covered with birchbark, not hides as with the plains tipis. Building wigwams was a combined gender activity. Hunting usually had men doing the search and kill and women doing the food preparation, but that was not always followed. Women also trapped and hunted and fished.

Wild rice (mahnoomin) was the food that grows on the water that marked the place where the Chippewa migration could stop, according to tradition. Wild rice, zizania aquatica, provided a nutritious, storable food that could be harvested from the sloughs and shallow lake waters that were abundant throughout Chippewa Country. Its harvest coincided with the maturation of fruits and other seeds. It was generally harvested by women in traditional times as was the case with the gathering of other plant products. It was stored in birchbark baskets along with other foods that were needed in the winters.

The Chippewa invented a means to convert maple tree sap into sugar. Each spring, thousands of maple trees were tapped and processed in a pattern and style continued today. It is told that Nanabozho favored the Chippewa with a constant supply of maple sugar sap, which dripped into many Chippewa mouths with no effort on their part. But the Chippewa grew lazy and ceased to show gratitude to Nanabozho and other Manitos. As the teachings provided, Nanabozho punished the Chippewa by making them work hard to make sugar. Maple sugar is a gift, but it is also a reminder that humans are dependent on Manitos and that hard work is necessary for a good life.

Songs were a cultural manifestation for all Chippewa activity. These songs were given by Manitos, dreamed by humans, and sometimes invented

Rice Gatherers by Seth Eastman, ca. 1867. Wild rice (mahnoomin) was a primary food source, harvested in late summer. While women traditionally carried out the harvest, everyone—men, women, and children—participated in the ceremonies, feasting, and storytelling associated with this important activity. (Collection of the U.S. House of Representatives)

through inspiration. As Alice Fletcher, a Native American anthropologist noted: "Among the Indians, music envelops like an atmosphere every religious, tribal, and social ceremony as well as every personal experience. There is not a phase of life that does not find expression in song." Chippewa tradition indicates that song is particularly pleasing to Manitos. Most of the time song was accompanied by drums and rattles. Flutes played songs, too. Singing was for praise, gratitude to the Manitos, celebration, amusement, courting, and lullabies.

THE TRADITIONAL ANNUAL CYCLE

Generations of experimenting resulted in successful adaptation to Chippewa Country. An annual cycle of movement as resources developed allowed the Chippewa to take advantage of the resources provided by Manitos to the Chippewa. The cycle had been long in place in the 1600s when French writers described it, and it was maintained until the 1850s and, although much circumscribed, it is visible in the 21st century. The Chippewa people are adaptable, not frozen into rigid behaviors.

Although later Europeans would describe the Chippewa as nomadic, this is misleading. Chippewa communities occupied a regulated environment, and each community had recognized territory acknowledged by other communities, even down to individual family lands. Movement was not haphazard; it was designed within patterns legitimized by tribal norms.

Winter

During the winter, roughly from October to March or early April, the Chippewa lived on extended family sites throughout Chippewa Country. Kinship-based groups used the same areas annually, and all knew where each family's hunting territory was.

A typical winter community consisted of a father and, perhaps, his brothers, his sons, their wives, and children. Other kin might be part of the group, too. Generally, the community was between 10 and 20 people. During these winter months hunting was difficult and other resources covered in snow and ice. Subsistence depended on cached foods like dried meat, smoked fish, wild rice and other plants, and maple sugar. Winter was also the time to trap fur-bearing animals because their fur was thickest then and they were all edible. Women provided the bulk of the required food for winters because they were the farmer-gatherers and they stored foodstuffs.

Evenings were the time to tell stories. The sacred stories could be told because the snakes were hibernating and would not be able to use the stories against the people. Stories provided children with the knowledge of values, expected behavior, and an understanding of their past. They also served to remind adults. Storytelling was a participatory activity with other adults and children augmenting, reminding, and enjoying their repetition. It reinforced respect for the knowledge of the elders and conveyed Chippewa culture. They were also told for fun or could be a form of social pressure on those not following community practices. Unlike stories read from books, stories varied from telling to telling and from storyteller to storyteller.

If a winter was particularly harsh and too long, food became scarce and hunters were unable to operate. Blizzards in Chippewa Country often immobilize people and animals for days at a time. Famine was a winter specter threatening the Chippewa. During starving times, the Chippewa feared the only completely evil being in their culture, Wendigo. Wendigos are described as monsters made of ice who ate people. They could also turn people into cannibal Wendigos, too. Many Chippewa children were warned of the dangers of venturing out when Wendigos were about. Stories of Wendigo depredation and Chippewa heroic responses were told throughout Chippewa Country.

Spring

In late March or early April, the snow began to melt and the waterways thawed. Chippewa winter communities moved to their sugarbushes. Allocation of these maple groves was based on tradition and decisions made by community councils. Women were in charge of the sugarbush sites. Maple sap began to flow and several winter groupings, perhaps clan members or other kin, joined in the groves. Men were able to hunt and fish again, and women were freed to tend to the creation of maple sugar and to replenish other stores consumed in the winter.

A vital part of the harvesting and hunting was the celebration of Manitos' gifts. Feasting, prayer, consultation, dancing, singing, and visiting marked these community endeavors. Spring was also a time to assemble military expeditions as war was a constant for Chippewa communities.

The Chippewa considered the spring to be the beginning of each year. To them, it seemed obvious that birth and renewal were marked by this season. Winter was dormant; spring was the new year.

Summer and Fall

Although summer in Chippewa Country only lasted from May through August, it was the time of greatest tribal activity. The fish begin to run toward spawning grounds and back to the Great Lakes, and the Chippewa concentrated near the narrows to await the fish. Often, several thousand Chippewa and other tribes gathered at the Sault Ste. Marie–Michilimackinac juncture of Lakes Huron and Michigan and Superior. Thousands of pounds of fish were speared, trapped, smoked, and consumed amid a constant celebration of the gifts of the Manitos. As the Chippewa expanded their realm, other sites like Madeline Island in Lake Superior became summer concentration sites.

Once the spawning runs ended, the Chippewa moved to nearby village sites. Village bands were probably members of the same clan along with their wives from other clans, but the passage of time made villages multiclan communities. The average odanah (village) was about 100–150 people, but villages were located in clusters, which had the effect of increasing the actual interacting population. Visiting was a common feature particularly during the summers.

Tribal issues were discussed and decisions made by the many ogimaag (translated as "chiefs" by Europeans but actually meaning "leaders"). Most of these villages or towns had a commons area for religious ceremonies, dances, councils, and other community activities like games. Intergroup disputes were adjudicated, courting and marriages abounded, allocation of lands to families were made, military expeditions were often initiated, and delegations and visitors were received. Farming and fishing continued along with hunting.

Rice fields generally matured by late August, and harvesting the rice provided the last large-scale socializing of the annual cycle. Extended families were awarded specific ricing areas according to tradition and decisions of tribal elders. Often a "rice leader" supervised the harvesting and decided when the crop was ready. Land allocations for hunting, raising crops, fishing, sugarbushes, trapping ranges, and rice harvesting were made by the community, both male and female decision makers.

Once set by the community, any encroachment on land allocations could be a capital offense. Rice harvests varied from year to year, which required annual adjustments in allocations of ricing areas. Harvesting was accompanied by ceremonies of gratitude to the Manitos. Feasting, dancing, singing, and public prayers were markers of these events.

As the women harvested the rice traditionally, this freed the men to launch group hunting, primarily for deer during the rutting season when deer clustered and were most active. Women and children gathered the ripe fruits and dried them for storage. Caches of processed plants could last up to two years. Fishing also intensified to maximize the available supply for winter. Meat was generally turned into pemmican and fish smoked for storage. Warfare and diplomacy were common in summer and even early fall.

In late September and early October, extended families began moving toward their winter sites. Families had the right of possession for these sites, and other Ojibwe honored their rights to use the resources for winter. These winter territories varied in size depending on the number in the extended family. Like allotments of ricing areas, consensus decisions recognized winter boundaries, too.

TRADITIONAL GOVERNANCE

The operative principle in Chippewa government was decision making by consensus. Tradition based on the received directions given by Nanabozho augmented by various Manitos' actions provided the framework for governing. Most of the functions performed by governments in the 21st century were handled at the family and kinship level during traditional times. In its idealized form, Chippewa government provided a recognized justice for all within the context of tribal values. Naturally, people did not always conform to the ideal forms, but communities exerted efforts consistently to restore balance when imbalance occurred because of human behavior. Justice for all and community welfare were goals.

Most villages had hereditary civil leaders (ogimag). These leaders provided continuity for certain families and clans to act as directors of daily patterns and decisions. They did not have coercive power and could be replaced if they did not reflect the consensus of their village. In other areas, the Chippewa usually assigned or recognized leaders depending on their qualifications. Shamans led in religious matters. Military leaders demonstrated their success in war. Decisions about land allocation were made by the women who did the gathering of produce and some farming. Elders were looked to for their wisdom in traditional behaviors. Leadership always included consensus development and persuasion. Coercion was seldom appropriate.

Marriage was between families and not marked by community-wide ceremonies. Generally, all that was needed was agreement between the individuals, family acknowledgment through gift exchanges, and the couple having joint living quarters. Families exercised considerable influence to see that marriages benefited the family. Leaders' children often married leaders' children. Usually, the husband spent some time living with the wife's family but then they moved to a location within the husband's community.

Descent was determined by the father's doodem (clan). Clan members offered whatever advice, support, and assistance were needed. Children belonged to the father's clan. Wives retained their clan membership. Clan members were considered brothers and sisters; therefore, one could not marry another clan member. The pattern created intricate networks of kinship, which were the foundation of nearly all relationships. Most clans were present in most towns and villages, therefore helping unite all Chippewa.

According to tradition, the original clans were Crane, Loon, Fish, Bear, Marten, and Deer. Other traditions suggest other original clans. Additional clans were added to allow for large groups to become Chippewa, and subclans also were added. The idea of clans was not based on rigidity but on providing identity, extended kinship, and tribal-wide support systems.

Divorce caused no problems because there was no private property to be apportioned, and children belonged to the clan family. Polygamy was acceptable but mainly only utilized for leaders whose obligations required hospitality and extensive connections. Although infant mortality and female death in childbirth rates were rather high, men seemed to have died at a higher rate. Since families were the basic economic unit of Chippewa communities, marriage was generally a necessity.

The behavior of individuals was regulated by community pressure to conform or to behave according to the teachings. In small communities like the Chippewa, gossip was usually all that was needed to correct behavior or to remind people of their duties. Heated arguments, even fights, were generally handled by family-clan members. Damages were settled through negotiated agreements between families.

Even the rare, most egregious crime of homicide was an interfamily matter. Family members of the victim had the recognized right to punish the offender or a member of his or her family, even to killing the offender as retribution. The family could also decide to adopt the offender, particularly in an accidental homicide. Often the offender's family would offer gifts to the victim's family as compensation for the loss. In particularly difficult situation, elders would offer advice and encouragement to the victim's family to accept these "covering the dead" efforts. Death was a tragedy for the community, but killing another person in revenge was a double tragedy.

Individuals were free to do what they wanted to do. For instance, no one had to participate in war even if most of the community did. No one had to join a community religion, because there was no single religion and people had their own relationship with Manitos. Behavior was highly individualized, but community pressure was applied if the community perceived that the community was endangered. Then, and only then, would others intervene.

The community chose its leaders. The generic Chippewa term for leader is "ogima" (pl. "ogimaag"). However, ogimaag came in several forms and functions in the political process. At the smallest unit of Chippewa community, the winter group, it was customary for the eldest to be the spokesperson ogima for the group and to exercise an understood authority over the other 15 or 20 people. If there were a younger man with skill, he would be the leader. These ogimaag were called gitchi-anishinaabeg (headmen or elders; the literal translation would be great Chippewas). The same title was applied to the recognized leader of several hunting groups, called bands, as they gathered for the sugarbush season. Bands combined into villages, and the accepted leader of each village was an ogima.

At some point, probably sometime in the late 17th century, the position of band ogima became hereditary but in a flexible way. Usually the eldest son succeeded the father, but not if he was incompetent for some reason or if a particularly skilled man was available. Inherited positions tended to be held within clans. For instance, the Crane Clan provided many of the ogimaag for many of the villages. Other villages drew on the Loon Clan, and it was not unusual for other clans to supply leaders. Ceremonies recognizing the succession of an ogima were elaborate demonstrations of his legitimacy.

The village, or town, was independent, sovereign, in all matters. By the 1600s, villages or towns were called bands because they were populated by several extended families belonging to several clans. Typically, a band or town had a population of about 150 up to about 300. This is where collectively, but not individually, binding decisions were made.

The Chippewa never developed a tribal-wide governance system that had the power of coercion similar to 21st-century nation-states. It was common for several villages to agree on common goals and to interact, but these were equals interacting among equals.

One might call the Chippewa tribe a confederation of villages bound together by culture but not laws. No leader of one band would think he could commit other bands to anything, nor would he make decisions without consultation with his own community. Despite an absence of a single government, Chippewa communities were able to generate unity and common actions frequently. War expeditions, for instance, often entailed coordinated assemblies of several hundred from multiple towns.

Chippewa political theory expressed a horror of one person making a decision for all. Ogimaag were expected to reflect the views of their village councils. Village councils consisted of the band leaders, headmen, and elders. Other adult members of the community were welcome to attend and to participate in discussions. Criticism and even removal greeted any ogima who exceeded the wishes of his council. Ogimaag based their authority on their constituents but reflected their networks of support from Manitos, kinship, and their generosity. They provided gifts and largesse to their people, and they convinced others to follow them.

Being an ogima required not only inherited right but also persuasiveness toward good decisions. It was clear that they were supported by Manitos because they were successful. Ogima were not supposed to be wealthy or to consider themselves above others. They were expected to be the poorest people in the community because they were generous. These were difficult expectations to meet, and all ogima did not meet them all of the time.

Other village level positions included the spokesperson for the village and general assistant to the ogima. The Ojibwemowin word is oskabewis, often translated as messenger, but they were also pipe carriers for the community's official pipe. All solemn occasions and councils began with a pipe ceremony. War leaders, mayosewininiwag in Ojibwemowin, were an important part of the village-wide government, as were the most revered of the shamans. Positions and function varied quite a bit depending on the size of the village.

Women had political roles and authority in traditional Chippewa society. Women controlled about 70 percent of food production and decided how it was to be used. The sugarbushes were allocated and controlled by women. Agricultural land assignments were doled out by women. Each village had a women's council guided by a woman leader supported by women elders. These councils made decisions in many areas without conferring with the men's council, and their support and opinions were part of any village-wide decision making.

Men did not even declare war without support from the women. Women were shamans with individual powers just as men were. Women had the right to reject suitors and to divorce. In the 19th century, women were identified as ogimag for some bands and as priests in the Midewiwin healing societies. Women decided if they would marry a person supported by the family, and women could initiate divorce.

As Nanabozho had given to them, women and men existed in a symbiotic relationship. Each was necessary for Bemaadiziwin, living the good life. Gender did determine what authority and function a Chippewa had, but even this was somewhat flexible. Women warriors existed, as did women who performed other masculine functions. Generally, men and women had parallel functions, prestige, and authority (ranging from most prestigious and powerful to least), but within gender-related realms. The relationship can be described as parallel verticality, not superior-inferior.

Relatives and Enemies: The Surrounding Nations

Numerous tribes developed in and around Chippewa Country. Some of these nations competed with the Chippewa for resources and control of lands, while others became allies or at least trading partners. International dynamics among Native American nations were similar to those in the rest of the world. Chippewa leaders explored opportunities to improve their nations and acted in enlightened self-interest in the crucible of diplomacy and trade.

The largest and most collectively unified neighbor was the Haudenosaunee, the Iroquois Confederation. Five separate tribes, inspired by Hiawatha and Deganawida, had negotiated their historical enmity to develop a means of settling disputes and reaching collective decisions in the Great Law of Peace. The five tribes are Mohawks, Cayuga, Onondaga, Oneida, and Seneca. Their country extended to the Finger Lakes region of

New York and northward to a section of Ontario. They had demonstrated an expansionist pattern and an effective military.

North of Lake Superior, Huron villages shared an effective boundary of Chippewa Country. Despite being an Iroquoian-speaking tribe, they had a separate, competitive relationship with the Iroquois. Other Iroquois-speaking tribes like the Erie, Neutral, and Tobacco were sandwiched between the larger tribes.

Dakota, a Siouan-speaking tribe, bordered the Chippewa on the west. In 1600, their towns and territory were in what would become Chippewa Country in the 18th century. The Chippewa were still concentrated in the Michilimackinac area where the three Great Lakes met. Relations with the Chippewa were generally amicable as they did not compete for resources in 1600. Farther south in Wisconsin, Winnebago Siouan-speakers had villages that dotted the area.

Miami, Fox, Sauk, Cree, and Menominee are Algonquian-speaking tribes not part of the Three Council Fires. They formed an arc generally south and southwest of the Chippewa heartland. Many of them interacted consistently in sharing territory and resources with the Chippewa particularly during the summer fishing concentration of populations near the Straits of Mackinac.

Each of the tribes recognized the others' boundaries and sovereignty. Tribes did not see these boundaries as rigid. Sharing of resources, permission to cross the boundaries, and even live within the boundaries were common occurrences. Generally, all of the nations recognized which nation had preemptive rights to determine usage. Often these rights were exercised by individual villages because villages were independent polities.

WAR

War was a common feature of intertribal relations. They were fought for resources, to avenge wrongs committed by the other, and for glory. All Indian males were expected to prove themselves against an enemy. Success in war was a launching pad for becoming a leader and having status. It was more important than hunting prowess. Success in both demonstrated to others that the individual had a special Manito relationship and, therefore, was favored. Women and their councils often weighed in and supported or denied military expeditions or war.

As each village was independent, all villages did not participate in all wars. Sometimes, one village would be warring on the Fox while other Chippewa villages were engaged in trade with other Fox communities.

Individuals did not have to follow their fellow villagers to war either. Individual choice determined what one did.

Expeditions were organized by war leaders. A leader would send tobacco to others, or he would call for a meeting at his village to discuss a campaign. Individuals and clan relatives adhered to successful leaders, and they were often able to raise significant numbers. The general pattern was for individual forays by small groups, but when the whole was threatened the village councils would send spokesmen to create combinations. Once decided, war leaders would then invite volunteers from other villages and even other tribes because joint action was needed. Chippewa communities did not have military societies as the plains tribes did, but evidence indicates that the military-aged men and war leaders were a constant influence group that extended beyond just a single community.

War was brutal. There were no noncombatants. Women and children were often killed in attacks on communities. Torture of enemies was not uncommon, and even a kind of defiant, ritualized cannibalism was practiced to demonstrate power. Prisoners were taken, and sometimes captives were even the object of military expeditions. Most prisoners were women and children, and they were often adopted or enslaved. Ransoming of prisoners was common. Adoption of captives provided a way to replenish Chippewa losses to war and disease. The practice was common throughout Indian Country.

Numerous stories describe adopted people as being major figures in Chippewa history. One of the major leaders of the Red Lake Chippewa was born a Dakota but fought heroically against the Dakota when he became an adult. Being Chippewa was not as much a question of genetics as it was acting like a Chippewa. The Chippewa in the 1600s knew the differences that distinguished different groups, but they did not consider them immutable. Outsiders were welcome if they volunteered to become good Chippewa and acted accordingly.

Although the Chippewa individualistic approach to war appears chaotic, the Chippewa were able to defend their communities and lands against formidable forces and to coordinate long-distance war. Military expeditions involving hundreds of men from multiple villages and clans were noted throughout the period after 1600.

Chippewa Country Boundaries

The boundaries of Chippewa Country were not set according to national, exclusive lines on a map as Europeans and Americans did. Land was not owned by individual Chippewa. It belonged to all within the parameters of tradition and community decisions. For instance, traditional hunting territories did belong to family groups, and its resources were for their use, but the allocations could change according to community needs. Others from the same or other bands needed permission to use the hunting territory. The same pattern generally applied to the use of sugarbushes, harvesting areas, and fishing sites.

Bands also had understood areas that they controlled that were recognized by other Chippewa bands. A protocol of requesting permission to use another band's usage area existed. Disputes over areas of use were generally the same pattern of discussion leading to solutions and were applicable to bands from other tribes. The Dakota and Chippewa often negotiated land use, as did Chippewa and Winnebago bands. Violation of recognized band areas by other tribal bands was a leading cause of war.

"National" Chippewa boundaries were perplexing to Europeans as they tried to determine which "tribe" owned what lands. They often forgot that there was no central Chippewa government. One leader could indicate that a piece of land belonged to his band, but another Chippewa leader would indicate that it belonged to his band. Permission had to be gained from the band that held the rights to use a particular portion of Chippewa Country. Violation of commonly understood boundaries was a frequent cause of intertribal war.

Chippewa bands often shared usage with other tribes like their relatives, the Ottawa, and even allowed usage to outsiders like the French, English, or Americans. The Dakota allowed Chippewa usage on the western shores of Lake Superior, although the area was "theirs." Over time, these tribal territories were fairly well understood by all Indian bands. When Chippewa communities expanded westward to challenge the Dakota, war ensued.

When Europeans began arriving in Chippewa Country, they met leaders and community that were confident in their identities as given to them by Manitos and secured by their own efforts. Chippewa Country was prepared to deal with newcomers whether they were the dangerous Iroquois or the French who wanted to acquire Chippewa resources and support.

2

Traditional Foundations of Chippewa Worldview

The foundation of traditional Chippewa society is its worldview. This worldview is understood to have been transmitted to the Chippewa by Manitos, supernatural beings who not only created humans but delivered instructions on the important values that directed Chippewa peoples toward living a good life as productive human beings. The goal of life is Bemaadiziwin, which translates into English in many ways depending on context, but most often it is parsed as "the good life," or living in balance and harmony.

Chippewa identity and worldview begins with the creation narrative in traditional time (known as the Misty Past) when the environment, living animals, and humans were made and assigned their behaviors and characteristics. From time to time, additional information is imparted, usually in dreams that allow new behaviors and perspectives to explain and process new situations. Dreams and visions direct Chippewa people and individuals on necessary paths.

CREATION AND GUIDANCE

Once there was formlessness; nothing existed but Manitos, and then the world was called into being. This is a common beginning of the Chippewa traditional understanding of the creation of the world. During the course of Chippewa cultural and religious development among the various, widely dispersed Chippewa communities and over some thousands of years, many variations in the narrative have been related, and all are true.

Traditional time, the Misty Past, is not bound by dates or sequential progression. "It happened" is enough to know. Sometimes the stories of tradition overlap one another; sometimes they are discrete events. Sometimes the passage of time modifies them. Sometimes they are internally contradictory. Contradictions do not matter because they describe supernatural truths.

There is no Chippewa religion that resembles the sects of institutionalized Christianity—rather, Chippewa religion is a combination of individual-based spiritualism and a common rehearsal of various efficacious ceremonies with specific results desired. Chippewa spiritual practice is individualistic with each person given the direction needed through the oral traditions and inspirations. Ceremonies of unity provide the interstices of Chippewa society, as they reinforce what distinguishes Chippewa from other societies.

The Chippewa world was created by supernatural beings (Manitos). Sometimes Manitos are described as other than human. Humans and other living things were dependent on Manitos. Most Manitos had specific powers, but none were omnipotent. Even Manitos had limitations, and as they were numerous, sometimes they worked toward separate or conflicting ends. One Manito could repair the damage done by another. The Chippewa world was created within a swirling interaction among Manitos, Chippewa, and other living beings. However, humans could affect Manito behavior, and if they followed the teachings, the world existed in balance and harmony, which made it possible for the Chippewa to live in a good way. Bemaadiziwin is the word that incorporates this idealized state of existence for individuals and society, which is the result of Manitou protections and support combined with individuals following the teachings of correct behavior.

Manitos exist in several manifestations. Some say that there was a single origin creating Manitou, Gitchee Manitou, who responded to Chippewa needs but was somewhat distant from their day-to-day needs. The next class of Manitos included Nanabozho, his brothers, the Thunderers, Mishebeshu, and the Four Winds. Other Manitos acted upon the Chippewa world in general to create, to punish, to bring good things, and to help the whole in particular ways. Another class of Manitos is those who are personal to individual Chippewa. Generally, these personal Manitos appeared in dreams and act as particular guardians.

There are Manitos who are guardians and leaders of each species of living things. If Chippewas did not treat animals with respect, their Manitos would step in to refuse to let Chippewas find them. Humans must respect and demonstrate care for all living creatures or Bemaadiziwin is not possible, and Chippewa people will suffer consequently. Another group is the Pukwudinniewag, the little people who were mischief-makers but often helped the Chippewa in one way or another.

It is tempting to those from a different cultural tradition to see a Manitou hierarchy. This is emphatically not true. Some, like the Thunderers, seem to have more power than others, but Manitos (also spelled Manitous) are independent and can even use their powers to neutralize or correct actions by a different Manito. Chippewa people lived in a world of constant interaction with these other-than-people beings, sometimes giving thanks, sometimes supplicating, sometimes angering, and then propitiating. Above all, humans realized they did not do anything on their own. Manitos' action and permission were necessary for human activity. Ceremonies of propitiation and gratitude are a vital part of human interaction with Manitos.

The distillation of the Chippewa genesis that I offer is a synthesis of the creation and migration story that most Chippewa will recognize even if their particular community's renditions are different. Each of the elements described are not necessarily part of the belief of all traditional Chippewa, but the essence of Chippewa belief rendered is familiar to all. The Chippewa do not have a traditional canon. They freely follow religious leadership of various shamans conducting ceremonies, select beliefs from available choices, and vary ceremonies as needed.

As the narrative is repeated by multiple narrators over generations and sometimes over the course of several evenings, tangents and asides help explain many of the ingredients necessary in Chippewa belief and understanding. Readers are reminded that Chippewa communities are dispersed over an area larger than Europe and have had hundreds of years to adapt their understanding of the creation and of spiritual belief. As most Chippewa would agree, consistency on all points is not necessary. The Chippewa origin tradition has always been a mutable perspective evolving with Chippewa society and the passage of time. There is no single, correct narrative.

CHIPPEWA GENESIS: ONE OF MANY VERSIONS

In the beginning, in the darkness, only the power of the Manitous existed as did a solitary Sky Woman. Some say that a Gitchee Manitou (Great Spiritual Power) took pity on the lonely Sky Woman and gave her a pregnancy that led to the birth of twins. Sky Woman created Chippewa, the first humans, from megis shells, and some say she created the Four Winds. Some say the twins created the Four Winds. Some say the twins died. Regardless, the Chippewa were created—they were Anishinaabe, the first man.

West Wind visited the human Winonah, and she became pregnant. He left her to return to his home in the West because he was a Manitou and had commitments. West Wind returned four separate times to impregnate Winonah. Four sons were born. Mudjeekewis (Warrior Sun) was eldest, and he became defender of the Chippewa and bringer of warrior skills. Pukawis (Son Who Breaks) brought music, dance, and esthetic values to the Chippewa. Chibiabos (Ghost Rabbit) brought love, harmony, and song. The youngest and most dominant and revered in Chippewa cultural knowledge is Nanabozho. All of the sons were Manitous despite having a human mother. Each of the sons (Manitos) brought particular skills and gifts to the Chippewa people. Winonah died after giving birth to Nanabozho, who is sometimes called The Great Hare by some, and others call him Wenabozho.

Part of the creation narrative includes Nanabozho's quest to revenge himself on the West Wind for abandoning Winonah. After many adventures, Nanabozho fought West Wind, his father, for four days, but neither could defeat the other. In reconciliation, West Wind taught Nanabozho the pipe ceremony and he, in turn, brought the ceremony to the Chippewa. Forever afterward the pipe ceremony marked solemn occasions and provided particular access to Manitos. West Wind made himself into corn and taught Nanabozho to grow it according to some traditions.

Nanabozho is the accepted culture hero of the Chippewa. In his dual nature, he is both a creator and a trickster. Most American Indian worldviews include a creator culture hero. They are supernatural beings with powers to create, and often culture heroes teach the tribal members all of cultural behaviors and values. Without the teachings and creations of

---

TRICKSTERS

Tricksters are common in American Indian cultures, as they are in cultures throughout the world. They often exemplify behaviors and attitudes that are just the opposite of what is expected of a good tribal member. Nanabozho, the Chippewa trickster, was vain, selfish, solitary, and disregarded others. He committed incest, adultery, theft, and wantonly killed animals and people. In himself, Nanabozho exemplified the dualism of all things, Manitos and humans. He was both a protector and creator as well as a wanton force. Stories of this trickster's misadventures are part of the education of Chippewa people.

Nanabozho, the Chippewa could not exist. Nanabozho, the creator, taught the Chippewa to use fire after he took it from an old man, and he gave animals their behavioral characteristics among his many other creations. He named all things and would be the maker of the second creation of the world and humans.

Like all Manitos, Nanabozho was both good and bad. He could be capricious and generous. He could be vengeful and gracious. In sum, his character was similar to humans and demonstrated the dual nature of humans, the power to be both good and evil. Nanabozho just had more powers than humans, so his deeds occurred on a grander scale with more consequences. Nanabozho also displayed human emotions and reactions like anger, sadness, joy, and loneliness.

Nanabozho was raised by Nokomis (Grandmother). As he matured he had many adventures including acquiring a brother who was a wolf. Wolves had taken pity on the poor human, adopted him, and encouraged his brother to go with him in his adventures like naming things. Animals often partner with humans in traditional times because animals have skills that humans do not. Chippewa individuals often duplicate this pattern by receiving assistance from an animal Manito, which infuses the individual with special powers like that of particular animals. Often Chippewas acquire their particular Manitos in dreams, and they are then able to appeal to their Manito for assistance and direction.

Nanabozho invented the bow and arrow but, as trickster, he began wantonly slaughtering the game even as creator he named them and other living things. Chippewa hunters followed suit by mimicking Nanabozho's disrespectful, wasteful killing. Mishebezho, the underwater Manitou and guardian of animals, was enraged at this egregious behavior. He decided that Nanabozho had to be punished as did the Chippewa. He lured his wolf brother to his death.

Nanabozho swore revenge and killed Mishebeshu through trickery. The murder of Mishebeshu led the rest of the underwater Manitous to rise in righteous anger and cause a great flood, which inundated all living things. In memory of his brother, Nanabozho instilled a mutual relationship between the Chippewa and the wolves. Chippewa accept that they must protect the wolves. As long as there are wolves, there will be Chippewa according to the word of Nanabozho.

As the flood engulfed the earth, Nanabozho clung to a floating limb, and various animals rested on it, too. After some time, Nanabozho determined that he needed soil to restore earth and living creatures. He sent the otter, but instead the dead otter floated back to the surface; Nanabozho breathed on it and brought it back to life. The same result followed when the loon and the beaver tried. Finally, the lowly muskrat offered to try despite the ridicule of the other animals.

Nanabozho chided the detractors, and the muskrat plunged into the water and remained an interminable seeming time. Finally, his body floated to the surface. Nanabozho found mud clutched in its paws. Even the smallest of creatures is vital to the world and contributes to the good of the whole. Many other stories emphasize this truth. Often small creatures and children emerge as saviors of the people.

Nanabozho looked for a surface, and a massive turtle offered itself as a base. He created Turtle Island by breathing on the mud and spreading it on the turtle's back. Once Turtle Island was created, Nanabozho re-created all living things including the Chippewa (Anishnaabeg). In some traditions, all other Indians and world populations are descended from these original people. In Ojibwemowin, Anishinaabe translates as Original Man. Nanabozho then brought healing knowledge to the Chippewa, taught them the skills needed to survive through hunting, gathering, and farming, and gave them religious ceremonies.

West Wind, his father, also taught Nanabozho the pipe ceremony, and he passed it on to the Chippewa. The pipe ceremony conveys Chippewa prayer to Manitous. Chippewa pray in gratitude and for assistance. Manitos must be thanked for exercising their powers on behalf of the pitiful Chippewas. Without intervention by Manitos, humans have no chance to live successfully. Other ceremonies have the same function and are also used to propitiate offended Manitos.

A synthesis of the many creation and prophetic narratives indicates that the values given are Respect, Generosity, Courage, Wisdom, Family, and Consensus. If observed or acted upon, these values lead to Bemaadiziwin for Chippewa society and individual Chippewa. Inevitably, disaster follows if the values and teachings are not followed.

If Nanabozho does not punish the Chippewa, then other Manitos like the Thunderbirds or Mishebeshu will. It is said that Nanabozho called the Thunderers into being to counterbalance the underwater Manitou and to protect the Chippewa. Thunderers are often called Thunderbirds.

Nanabozho divided the Chippewa into clans as a vital organizing principle establishing kinship and greatly extended social integration. In most traditions, the original dooadem (clans) are Crane, Fish, Loon, Marten, Bear, Eagle, and Deer. It is said that the Deer clan people were too gentle and became extinct. Clan membership descended from the father, making the Chippewa patrilineal. Marriages within the clan were considered incest because clan brothers and sisters were family. As time passed, the original clans morphed into additional clans, and by the 19th century, some commentators noted as many as 20 clans. Added clans were descended from the original clans, and an affinity was recognized.

The Chippewa identified themselves by clan and then by their personal name. Animal totems/symbols were really emblems indicating clan membership. As the Chippewa divided into bands and spread throughout their homeland, each band contained members of more than a single clan. This provided a vital factor in maintaining identity and a sense of kinship for any Chippewa among other Chippewa.

Any Chippewa could be assured that no matter where they went in Chippewa Country, they would find relatives and the support relatives provided like food, shelter, and other assistance. "We are all related" is a common ingredient in many Chippewa prayers and has meaning within clans, too. Clans united the autonomous bands across Chippewa Country, and intermarriages continuously supported cross-band actions and cultural identity.

A Chippewa shaman poses with regalia. Shamans were intermediaries between Manitos and humans. They interpreted dreams, healed people, and predicted the future. Americans called them "medicine men." (Minnesota Historical Society Collections)

Tradition indicates that particular clans were gifted by the Manitos with specific abilities. The Cranes were peacetime leaders and spokesmen. Bear clan members were warriors, defenders of the communities. The Fish clan provided intellectuals endowed with wisdom. Martens provided leadership in celebrations, entertainment, and community solidarity. Loons provided political leaders when there were not enough Cranes. Eagle clan members were skilled fighters, too. However, ability and particular talents from members of any clan would allow them to be leaders, and many war leaders came from clans other than the Bear.

The Chippewa lived a bounteous, delightful existence on the eastern coast of Turtle Island. Some say the origin location is now called Nova Scotia, and others relate that they were taught that the Chippewa had moved eastward immediately after Nanabozho created Turtle Island. Most traditions have the second creation as occurring on Mackinac Island, in Michigan's Mackinac Straits.

The straits area is called Michilimackinac (Great Turtle). The Plains Chippewa picture Turtle Island as in their Turtle Mountains of northern North Dakota and southern Manitoba. Perhaps after initial creation the people drifted eastward to the area of Nova Scotia, where they lived and awaited more instructions. Turtle Island was created in mystical time—as needed.

As populations grew and other peoples developed, a sickness visited the Chippewa. Especially attuned Chippewa shamans sought guidance from the Manitos. A vision instructed the Chippewa to migrate westward to survive. Manitous provided a guide to lead them. In some traditions like those of the Midewiwin, the guide is a megis shell. In the tradition this author was given, the guide was Ajijawk (far calling bird), a Sandhill Crane. The Chippewa have no difficulty accepting that both were true. It is understood the migration was not a single mass of Chippewa moving at once.

The Crane guides led the Chippewa to live for a time in four different places. Each time they remained until the Manitos urged them, through dreams, to continue westward. Some say they moved because the Chippewa failed to observe the teachings. Others account for the stopping points over generations as periods of recuperation.

Chippewa tradition identifies specific sites where the pauses in the migration occurred: Nova Scotia, Boweting or Sault St. Marie on the Saint Mary River, which connects Lake Superior and Lakes Michigan and Huron; Machilimackinac at Mackinac Straits; and Mooniingwanekaanig (Madeline Island–Chequamegon Bay) in western Lake Superior. Each remains a center of modern Chippewa population. Machilimackinac translates as Great Turtle and mackinac means turtle.

At the Sault (Rapids in French), the Anishnaabeg (the Original People) divided into the three historic tribes: Chippewa, Ottawa, and Potawatomi. Collectively, the tribes knew themselves as the Three Council Fires. The Potawatomi moved southward toward the southern end of Lake Michigan around Green Bay; the Ottawa remained concentrated around Michilimackinac although some bands did move toward Manitoulin Island and southern Ontario.

The causes of the separation into distinct tribes are not part of the migration narrative, but their continued confederation as kin is. One story has those Anishnaabeg who concentrated on commerce taking the name

Ottawa (Trader), while the Potawatomi (Keepers of the Fire) was merely descriptive of a function delegated. The larger of the divisions were simply called by their language, Ojibwe—heard as Chippewa by Europeans. Fire remains an important metaphor for national identity and is a necessary opening of many traditional ceremonies. Fire as a sacred emblem of societal existence long predates Chippewa societies historically.

Historically, tribal names were assigned by Europeans as they sought to identify the societies they interacted with. Historically, Anishinaabeg includes all of the three fires as one vast kinship network. Anishinaabeg accepted these as translations and came to use the designations themselves.

The term "Chippewa," derived from Ojibwe, came into widespread usage only after the English replaced the French in the Great Lakes. Americans continued the usage and embedded the tribal names Chippewa, Ottawa, and Potawatomi in the legal usage of treaties and government documents as Native Americans were incorporated into the U.S. political system.

At or near the same time as the separation of the Three Fires, Chippewa bands began fanning out from Boweting and Michilimackinac. Several bands traversed northward into Ontario. Some of these northern moving bands continued westward from Ontario until they reached Manitoba, where they became known as the Plains Chippewa. Other bands continued westward across Lake Michigan and to the western and northern shores of Lake Superior.

These southwestern-moving Chippewa reached the final stopping point for the inspired migration, Mooniingwanekaanig, Madeline Island. The French named it La Pointe de Chequamegon when they received permission to build a fort/trading post on the island.

Although the narrative seems to imply that all of the Chippewa moved each time, a better understanding is that the Chippewa glacier calved as it spread outward from its core. It is said that Madeline Island was the terminal point of the migration because the guiding dreams had told the Chippewa to move to the land where food grows on the water. Wild rice grows on water and is one of the staples of traditional Chippewa diet.

War and struggles assisted by Manitos were a feature of the migration narrative. The Mandua were a large society living in a city by a big lake, and they tried to block Chippewa westward progress. Mandua contemptuously assumed the raggedy Chippewa would be easy to defeat, so they sent their young boys to fight. The boys were wiped out. The next attack came from Mandua young men who issued forth from the Mandua city. They were killed in great numbers, so the Mandua seasoned warriors streamed into the fray. They were vanquished with the help of Thunderers, but Mishebezho protected some of them with a fog.

Eventually, the women, children, and male survivors were adopted into the Chippewa, and they became the Marten clan or were added to an existing clan. Various groups joined the stream of Chippewa and were absorbed, a pattern that continued historically.

The Midewiwin society offers a major variation in the basic Chippewa origin and migration narrative. The Grand Medicine Society or Midewiwin is particularly widespread among the southwestern Chippewa from Madeline Island to North Dakota. Its version has gained widespread following, particularly after World War II. Mide elders relate that there were seven stopping points: a turtle shaped island on the St. Lawrence River, Niagara Falls, along the Detroit River, Manitoulin Island, Boweting, Spirit Island near present Duluth, and Madeline Island.

Mooniingwanekaanig (Madeline Island) is cast as the epicenter of Chippewa culture, and the Midewiwin healing society has spread from Madeline Island and the adjacent mainland of Chequamegon Bay to the western Chippewa communities across northern Minnesota and even into the Turtle Mountains within North Dakota and Manitoba.

The Chippewa in the Turtle Mountains know that these mountains are part of the homeland given to them by the Manitos, as its name indicates. The Mide narrative includes multiple variations, but the basic theme of Chippewa migration to their homeland known as Chippewa Country remains constant.

Midewiwin, the Grand Medicine Society, is an apparent exception to the individualistic character of Chippewa society because it is hierarchical and each medicine lodge specifies patterns of healing ritual. Adherents belong to a lodge. Its origins are the subject of scholarly debate. One school represented by Christopher Vecsey contends that the Grand Medicine Society is a product of the mid-18th century and was greatly influenced by Christianity, particularly the Jesuits. His argument is that the Mide narrative traces its origins to Madeline Island, which was not a Chippewa site until the 18th century. It has a hierarchy of priests, the Mide. It posits a paramount God, Gitchee Manito. These characteristics were not mentioned by commentators on Chippewa society after French contact in the 17th century. This interpretation of evidence has been widely accepted by the scholarly community.

Mide adherents do not accept the conclusion that Midewiwin is a recently developed religious movement. They contend that Nanabozho brought Midewiwin to the Chippewa in the Misty Past, and it was not influenced by Christianity, although some Christian elements were added here and there as time passed. There is no disagreement that the society has priests who pay to be initiated into the many degrees of healing knowledge. It does have a specific tradition of creation that posits a single creator, Gitchee Manito. The most prominent academic who considers the society an ancient one is Basil Johnston. This school of thought indicates that at some point in the Misty Past, the Manitos inspired the establishment of Midewiwin.

Selwyn Dewdney, among others, points out that all of the elements of the Grand Medicine Society are derived from Chippewa practices that do exist before the 1700s. Analysis of the separate parts of the Grand Medicine Society indicates a consistency with traditional religion: the emphasis is on healing; part of the ceremonies include healing by shooting those seeking help through the medium of medicine bags, and sucking foreign disease-causing objects from the afflicted; the creation narrative repeated includes Nanabozho as the central supernatural being, the flood and migration always occur, and each individual Mide, a blend of priest, shaman, and healer, heals according to his personal knowledge independently of other Mide.

Dewdney hypothesizes that the Midewiwin evolved from its traditional times baseline practices into the form it grew into in postcontact Chippewa Country. Like other religions or religious patterns, the Grand Medicine Society evolved through time and place. Adaptations as new ingredients and influences occur can become part of traditional religion that has ancient roots and does not invalidate the integrity or age of the religious practice. Probably no religion follows the precise form with which it began. An interesting addition to Midewiwin format is the Big Drum Society that was

---

BIRCHBARK SCROLLS

Birchbark scrolls are another feature of the Grand Medicine Society, and they provide mnemonic devices for Midewiwin ceremonies. The Chippewa used birchbark for inscribing symbols known to all in order to convey information. Chippewa hunters could leave messages for those following them or information about communities via birchbark. The continuity of the Midewiwin narrative is maintained through the use of mnemonic picture writing on the inner bark of birch trees. The scrolls provide a means to read the story from one generation to another as well as the sacred songs and particular medicine formulas. After pointing out that the scrolls as interpreted by senior Mide often varied from one another, Selwyn Dewdney provides a plausible interpretation. Scrolls on birchbark served to communicate songs, ideas, and even more mundane messages conveyed from person to person and from community to community. Commonly understood symbols and patterns allowed complex messages.

given to the Chippewa by the Dakota in about 1867 as a healing ceremony emphasizing curing the ills and stress brought by American dominance.

The Chippewa see no contradiction in incorporating additional approaches to healing into the Midewiwin. Dewdney also suggests that Midewiwin played a crucial role in the development of a common identity for the decentralized Chippewa nation. This common identity has helped them survive despite the crises of the past 400 years. During the Indian Renaissance since the 1960s, many Chippewa have worked hard to return to the teachings and practices of prereservation, traditional times. Sometimes they are quite zealous about what they have learned as traditional practices and insist that those who are different are not even authentic Chippewa. Revivals often take on such characteristics throughout the world and can create a kind of intolerance that is, ironically, the antithesis of Chippewa cultural norms.

The academic argument about the time of origin for Midewiwin is of doubtful importance to contemporary Chippewa. Midewiwin is accepted widely as the Chippewa religion by many traditional Chippewas, and there are adherents throughout contemporary Chippewa Country. Some prefer different understandings to the Midewiwin. They follow the traditional healing practices, and they accept the creation and migration narrative that emphasizes the role of Manitos in Chippewa life. Chippewa religion like Chippewa culture in general is not a prescriptive exclusivist religion. Historically, the Chippewa have been receptive to other practices and incorporated them. Christianity, Mediwiwin, the Dakota gift of the Drum Society, and individual and community-specific practices can be observed simultaneously without conflict by any Chippewa. Some Chippewa are not practicing traditionalists or Christian, but they draw on the base of traditional narrative for understanding what it means to be Chippewa. The purpose of all approaches is to secure Bemaadiziwin. The good life is attainable in many ways.

After the migration and once settled in the homeland communities, the Chippewa translated their basic beliefs and values into the distinctive cultural traits and norms of a traditional society divided into multiple bands. Chippewa Country expanded and contracted according to the favor or disfavor of the Manitos. It continues to do so.

INGREDIENTS OF CULTURAL TRUTHS

The traditional Chippewa society drew its identity from the nexus of interacting information that constituted its genesis narrative augmented by further revelations and directives from Manitos. This information constituted the cultural truths upon which the search for Bemaadiziwin was founded and which provided specific guidance for behavior. Cultural truths cannot be falsified because they explain what to do in which circumstances, how to evaluate behaviors, how to amend the present, and how to receive necessary support from Manitos. Cultural truths do not have to be logical, and they can be mutually exclusive without endangering the truths. They exist as a belief system and are proven by faith.

The Chippewa people interacted with the other-than-humans as individuals and in communal ceremonies. Each band and even individuals had a way of praying, specific knowledge imparted by dreams or teachings and a daily requirement to interact with Manitos to preserve balance and harmony in the world. Chippewa traditional religious beliefs emanated from the foundational truths of the creation narrative and the Manitou-inspired migration to the Chippewa homeland where we still live. Right behavior principles and instructions have been given by Nanabozho and the many Manitos.

* * *

Human responsibility is to create balance and harmony in a quest for Bemaadiziwin. Humans do this by living according to the teachings and by honoring the Manitos through prayers and through ceremonies. Ceremonies and prayers could be individualized or collective. Intentional or inadvertent human behavior could bring punishment from the Manitos to individuals and even communities. Manitos could respond or ignore supplications, but humans had to make respectful efforts. Manitos could be capricious because they were like humans in many respects. In the main, Chippewa expected Manitos to be generous especially in facilitating acquisition of food.

Myriad Manitos were present in the skies, the earth, underwater, in trees and rocks, and in animals and plants. The most powerful was Nanabozho, but others were particularly important in determining Chippewa well-being. The Four Winds collectively controlled the weather and created seasons. The Thunderers wreaked havoc on wrongdoers but also balanced the underwater Manitous while governing the behavior of the sky animals. Mishebeshu, the underwater Manito, punished humans for excessive destruction of the natural world but also allowed humans to fish and protected them in their water travels.

Individual Chippewa acquired the protection of personal Manitos in the vision quest dreams that were part of Chippewa puberty rites. Both men and women received visions, particularly in the transition to adulthood. The Chippewa appealed to their personal Manitos for assistance and guidance throughout life. Indeed there were myriad Manitos for Chippewa to beseech. Human beings did little on their own—they were allowed to do things.

One of the most common ceremonies was the sweat lodge. Sweat lodges were usually conducted by shamans assisted by disciples. Sweat lodges included several others seeking to pray for well-being. The sweat lodge is one of the most widespread ceremonies in North America and is a common purification for those preparing for other ceremonies like vision quests and naming ceremonies. It is even more widespread than the pipe ceremony in Indian Country.

Chippewa individuals might be known by several names during their lives. However, the two that were most significant were the name given to a newborn by an elder and the name determined at puberty. The name was unique to the dream-revealed nature of the child. At puberty, a second name followed a vision quest. This was chosen to reflect the dream and often the personal Manito of the supplicant. Shamans played a role in supervising vision quests. Often names were changed to reflect accomplishments or to honor ancestors. For instance, two of the most famous Chippewa, Biauswah and Hole-in-the-Day, assumed their famous fathers' names.

Boys' vision quests were elaborate. They included a sweat lodge ceremony, guidance from a shaman, and fasting in isolation. Throughout the process, family offered encouragement and support. Often the fasting lasted for four nights, but once a dream vision had occurred, the fast ended.

Feasts usually followed the seeking of a vision. A shaman often assisted the boy in interpreting the meaning of the blessing he had received from a Manito, but detailed explication was not encouraged. Sometimes specific instructions and taboos were given to the boy. After a successful vision quest, the boy could call on his personal Manito for the rest of his life.

Women did not require visions because it was said that women already had the power of life. Adolescent girls, like adolescent boys, were encouraged to fast and seek Manito inspiration and protection. Women's puberty ceremonies were conducted by women at first menses. In the creation stories, women were assigned particular roles and behaviors as were men. Gender division was considered a given. This division did not imply subordination, as many women were leaders in Chippewa communities, and many were shamans.

There are traditions of women who were warriors. Essentially, the Chippewa accepted that one did what one's skills allowed as guided by Manitos. Homosexuality was seen as fulfilling one's true calling regardless of gender appearance.

Each of the animal species was watched over by a spirit keeper, a Manito. Sometimes the keepers have been called owners of a species as they controlled behaviors. For the Chippewa, the most important keepers were the ones for deer and bears. Owners determined whether or not successful hunts occurred.

Chippewa hunters who disrespected the spirit keeper or who failed to respect the animals by giving thanks to the animals for allowing themselves to be killed would find that hunting failed. It did not matter how skilled the hunter—supernatural assistance is what made success possible. It followed that successful hunters had spiritual power. Humans were dependent on Manitos and therefore spent a great deal of time imploring or expressing gratitude.

Any action required prayer and usually a gift at least of tobacco. Gifts of food to the Manitos were common, but tobacco was de rigueur. The Chippewa beseeched assistance from the Manitos with offerings and prayers, then thanked the Manitos when they were successful. Tobacco was given to Mishebeshu for safe travel and for good fishing. Throughout the year, the Chippewas held ceremonies of unity.

Feasts, dancing, and prayers of thanks followed wild rice harvesting, collective hunts, maple sugaring, wild fruit gathering, trading expeditions, and war, which were collective expressions of Chippewa culture. Feasts provided societal reinforcement, and health crises led to group and individual prayers and offerings. Other solemn occasions, like naming ceremonies, visions, dispute settlement, international relations, and burials, required the pipe ceremony, the most significant expression of prayer. Individuals and families performed the same observances on a lesser scale.

Individual Chippewa see themselves as pitiful supplicants in the face of the powerful universe embodied in the Manitos. Prayers to the Manitos begin with a statement emphasizing how pitiful humans are and how much they need help. The Chippewa language even has a pitying conjugation for its verbs. Vecsey posits that only Ojibwemowin (Chippewa language) has such a form.

Chippewa seeking assistance from important people used the begging supplication form as well. For instance, the Chippewa usually opened their speeches to European and American treaty negotiators with pleas for assistance, for pity, and for help in their hunger and poverty. Americans and Europeans consistently misinterpreted the message to the detriment of Indians and negotiations alike.

Although individuals had their own Manitos and healing knowledge, some Chippewa were particularly attuned to the spiritual world and received special powers through dreams and apprentice-like acquired knowledge. Some were taught the healing properties of plants and treatment of injuries but were successful only if they gained the assistance of Manitos through prayer.

Sucking doctors were able to draw poisons from their patients. The most powerful religious leaders were the Djessakids, who interpreted dreams and predicted the future through the shaking tent ceremony. A collective term for these specially empowered individuals is shaman. Shamans had specific powers, but Europeans and Americans often lumped them together as "medicine men." Many of the religious leaders were women.

Religious leadership is difficult to describe, as Chippewa did not have institutionalized religion with the exception of the Midewiwin healing society, but its actions were just one part of the spectrum of religious practices. Some scholars classify Chippewa religion as animist. Just about anyone could become a religious leader given the right circumstances or as a result of a specific dream. All elders were thought to have the power of wisdom, which included religious knowledge.

Often, a respected elder was called upon to name a child. He or she was expected to think on the nature of the child, pray, and perhaps dream a name for the child. As a general rule, elders were expected to have spiritual power because they had lived long lives, and this required favor from Manitos. The only example of what might be termed a priesthood is in the Midewiwin (Grand Medicine Society). Unlike the western European analogy, however, all members of the society were healers at one level or another.

Dreams can foretell events and demand action from humans. Anyone can dream and share the message of the dream with the community. The call for the great migration came in a dream that prophesied that the Chippewa could thrive in the West. Dreams gave instruction about the guides and where to stop. "Move until you reach the place where food grows on the water" was a directive conveyed in a dream.

Oral tradition abounds with stories of dreams that came to children when a crisis faced a Chippewa community. Manitos often used the weak or the young to reveal what was needed. Jessakids, specially endowed shamans, utilized the shaking tent ceremony to interpret dreams and foretell the future. Shamans sought dreams to assist them in curing individuals.

Chippewa beliefs did not see Manitos as either good or evil. Manitos, like humans, were dualistic; they had the ability to do good things and evil things. Shamans and Mide (priests of the Midewiwin) were sought out for their power and were feared for the same reason. Particularly in times of stress, accusations of witchcraft were common. Witchcraft was blamed for many bad things that happened to people. The only recourse was to seek help from a shaman. Most Chippewa employed charms and sought magical medicine to help and protect them. Sometimes witches were killed.

The only completely evil beings were the cannibalistic Wendigos. These were often pictured as humans who had been crazed by hunger and witchcraft into becoming cannibals. They were also thought to be giants made of ice. The Chippewa lived in a stark and challenging environment. In the winter, food could easily run out, and the desperation of starvation could lead to people eating their dead and eating one another.

Perhaps the fear of Wendigo was a manifestation of the evil that could come from starvation. Chippewa oral tradition has a number of stories about Wendigo and how he stalked the woods near the communities during the times of desperation. In latter times, some Chippewa have metaphorically described Americans as Wendigos eating Chippewa resources and threatening Chippewa existence.

In one narrative, a community was on the brink of starvation, and desperate hunters ranged widely each day. One hunter did not return, and then two hunters did not return, and the community prayed for an explanation. A girl dreamed that a Wendigo had claimed them as victims. Her dream also explained that a pit could catch Wendigo, and the community did as she had dreamed.

Wendigo fell in the pit, and the men rained arrows down onto the Wendigo, but he would not die and threatened retribution. The girl instructed the men to use pitch and torches to burn the Wendigo. He did catch fire, and ashes floated out of the pit. Each ash turned into a mosquito. Wendigo got his revenge by taking the blood of generations of Chippewa since then.

Chippewa beliefs included an afterlife that all experienced, if the souls of the deceased were able to make the four-day journey to the sky world. The Chippewa had two souls: the body soul and the traveling soul. The body soul resided in the heart but could move around the body and even leave for a period. It provided the ability to act, intelligence, reasoning, memory, and consciousness. It experienced emotions.

The traveling soul could leave the body for extended periods of time and existed separately from the body. During dreams, this soul was free to journey and learn before returning to the body. It could also act like a guide for the humans and even provide warnings. It worked with the other soul to harmonize the body.

On death the body soul left immediately, but the traveling soul might linger. The Chippewa tried to encourage the traveling soul to leave for the afterlife as soon as possible because it altered the balance of natural life. Funeral services were four days, with fires lit to guide the soul on its way and survivors urging the soul to leave.

On the fourth night a feast with dancing and singing marked the end of the journey. Corpses were bundled and placed in trees with the feet oriented westward. Mourning for close relatives lasted for a year and ended with feasting and dancing. In some communities there was a Feast of the

Dead periodically. Remains were brought to be buried as skeletons in a communal mass grave.

There was no sin in Chippewa ontology. All could go to the afterlife regardless of how one had behaved during life. If one did something wrong, punishment occurred in this lifetime. The only souls not allowed into heaven to recreate the appearance of their body were those who failed to surmount the obstacles on the way. Most traditions identified a precarious log bridge over a creek as the primary obstacle. Those who fell off the quivering log became toads. Younger people and children have the most difficulty traversing the route.

The location of the afterlife was either toward the West or the South, depending on which of the Chippewa communities related the story. All agreed that the afterlife was a happy place of reunion with ancestors. Most think the afterlife is a place of dancing and feasting. One tradition is that the Northern Lights are the dead dancing. Others consider the Northern Lights as beacons to guide the souls of the dead.

Punishment and Disease: Consequences of Human Behavior

The Chippewa worldview held that all illnesses were caused by Manitos punishing humans for bad behaviors or for cooperating in witchcraft. The intervention of Manitos did not include routine simple illnesses like colds or mishaps like broken bones. These were dealt with by skilled healers utilizing an array of homeopathic medicines and corrective techniques. Chippewa healers set bones, cured headaches, settled stomachs, protected against infections, and eased the tribulations of colds and flu. It is said that every plant had healing properties.

Diseases or serious illnesses were consequences of human action. When a Chippewa was seriously ill, his first question was, "What have I done to bring this on myself or my family?" The only way to treat serious disease was to propitiate the offended Manito with the help of a shaman. The victim publicly sought a cause through a self-examination process. Had he violated a taboo, particularly one that he had been uniquely given in a dream? Had he violated one of the prohibitions concerning animals? Had he been cruel? Had he tried to gain power that set him above others? Had he been greedy and selfish? Had a sorcerer-witch caused the illness?

With the guidance of a shaman, ceremonies could save the victim of disease. Several of the most well known were designed to heal. Among those who followed the Midewiwin, victims could die and return through the intervention of Mide who could suck foreign objects implanted to cause illness. Sometimes sweat lodges provided sufficient means to supplicate assistance from the Manitos. Jessakids could hold a shaking tent ceremony where Manitos visited and gave explicit instructions to humans. Offerings to Manitos were part of the healing process, and payment to shamans was expected.

Chippewa traditional society reinforced itself and maintained a common identity through frequent interactions within families, clans, and larger seasonal gatherings. Stories reinforced identity and were at the root of Chippewa culture. They introduce the young to the teachings, reinforced the knowledge of adults, and especially honored the wisdom of the elders who were usually the storytellers.

Typically, family groups told and listened to stories during the winter when all were constrained by the weather. However, instructions on how to behave were often contained within parable-type stories. Entertainment was part of storytellers' repertoire, too.

The story of the Chippewa can be seen as a composite of myriad stories.

3

Securing Chippewa Country, 1600–1736

By 1600, the Chippewa, totaling 25,000 to 35,000, were aggregated in autonomous communities in their core homeland. From the Ontario Peninsula to northern Michigan, multiple independent, culturally homogenous communities were centered on Machilimackinac—the Great Turtle Island—where Lakes Huron and Michigan joined at Mackinac Straits and around the contiguous area where Lake Superior flowed through Sault Ste. Marie on St. Mary's River.

Anishinaabewaki (Chippewa Country) continued to expand for the next 300 years. Their early 17th-century world was challenged occasionally by only a few of the neighboring tribes for the resources and trade routes that converged at their Straits of Mackinac. By 1600, their Ottawa relatives had secured Manitoulin Island in Lake Huron, and they shared Michilimackinac.

Ottawa traded up the St. Lawrence River as far as the tribal environs of the Montaignais and other Algonquian speakers. Potawatomi relatives had moved south and west toward Green Bay, northern Indiana, and Chicago, although some remained in the area. The Three Council Fires remained allied in their kinship throughout their histories, and they called themselves Anishinaabeg (the Original People).

Chippewa Country was not secure in 1600. There were competitors like the Iroquois, Huron, and Fox. All jostled for resources and security. Tribes were in contact with the French and Dutch newly arrived on the perimeters of Chippewa Country. Even as Chippewa communities solidified their identity and way of life, their story became inextricably entwined with the increasing presence of others.

THE NEW PEOPLE

During the early 1600s information about new commercial opportunities and a radically different kind of people trickled into Chippewa Country along with a few unique goods. The trickle grew steadily larger in the 17th century as the newcomers were allowed access to the Chippewa commercial network.

Soon, some made their way into Chippewa Country. What scholars later called the Columbian Exchange of goods, people, knowledge, and ideas now included Chippewa Country, along with the rest of the world. The Chippewa called the new customers Wimitigoozhig (the French, literally those who wear wood).

Chippewa oral traditions allude to early knowledge of the appearance of French ships on the St. Lawrence and their interactions with the local Algonquian populations. During the first decade of the 17th century, knowledge about French, Dutch, and English activities reached Chippewa Country, and the Chippewa went north to investigate while they digested information from their south. The new people built towns as trading centers rather than bringing goods to existing Native American trade fairs or to individual towns initially. They wanted furs and food from Indians and were eager to give them metal and other wealth in exchange. They were also violent and capricious. They did not behave, at first, like Indians, but it did not take long for them to learn Native American protocols necessary to be allowed to trade.

Probably, Europeans had traveled to American coasts since the Late Middle Ages, but there is little documentation. Basque whalers and northern Europeans visited the Newfoundland and Labrador fisheries with increasing frequency after the late 15th century. Sailor-fishermen became fur traders as a secondary and profitable sideline. Native Americans hailed many to their shores and sold them furs and bought European manufactured goods.

John Cabot was among the first explorers of North America's eastern coast in 1497 and 1498. His son may have reached Hudson Bay by 1509. Gaspar Corte probably sailed into the Gulf of St. Lawrence for Portugal. Corte captured 57 Natives, probably Algonquians, and brought them to Portugal. Estevao Gomes, serving Spain, kidnapped 58 Indians in 1525.

Native Americans had to factor attacks and captive taking into their assessment of the newcomers. Violence became common.

In 1534, Jacques Cartier made a voyage down the St. Lawrence and then made two other voyages. He claimed the entirety of the St. Lawrence watershed for France according to crusades-rooted papal law. Europeans believed that they had a Christian right to govern pagans along with a mandate to convert them to Christianity. This Doctrine of Discovery accepted that the first Christian nation to claim and secure pagan lands were entitled to rule the native populations and dispose of them as they saw fit. It was the foundation of assertions of European and American empires throughout the world.

Europeans introduced more than trade goods to North America. They also brought European power struggles with them. European nation-states were engaged in a contest for hegemony that dominated world history for several centuries. A Chippewa alliance was sought by the French, the Dutch, and later the English as Europeans contended with one another for their "new world." The Chippewa and their kin were pivotal forces in the struggle with Europeans.

Dutch efforts influenced Chippewa history for only about 40 years, but their support of Iroquois expansion created a major crisis for the Chippewa and other Native Americans. The English supplanting the Dutch did not halt Iroquois invasions of tribes from the Carolinas to Canada and Chippewa Country because the English supported Iroquois expansion. France claimed Chippewa Country, but her claims were inter-European maneuvering. The Chippewa thought the claims hyperbole, but leaders found that Anglo-French rivalries were advantageous. They could play the Europeans against one another as each importuned Native Americans to join them in trade and war.

Europeans were carriers of diseases. American Indians had no resistance to the virulent diseases that sometimes killed Europeans but devastated Native Americans. Diseases destroyed entire villages and left wastelands. Although data are sketchy, some tribal communities lost 35–90 percent of their populations as wave after wave of epidemics swept the Americas.

The diseases were many, but smallpox, cholera, and measles were particularly devastating. Smallpox was recorded at the Straits of Mackinac as early as 1670 and was followed in 1681 by another outbreak. Diseases struck Chippewa Country throughout the 18th and 19th centuries in a repeating pattern.

The tragedies of disease epidemics extended beyond just deaths. Shamans searched for the causes of the holocaust but found their curative efforts useless. Many blamed the Europeans. Some concluded that these powerful Frenchmen could bring disease through witchcraft; probably

Jesuits were culpable. Some Indians accepted baptism as a protective ceremony against disease. Some retaliated against European intruders.

Although recovery was possible, Indian communities felt disease effects long afterward. Women's fecundity was reduced, and Chippewa birthrates declined. Many of the dead had been leaders in the communities, and their knowledge and skills were lost. Survivors often had to combine with those from other bands to create new bands and villages. Family structures had to be reconfigured after so much death. Sometimes famine followed epidemics because there was no one to hunt, farm, and gather.

Europeans injected another unfamiliar element into international relations: religious proselytizing. The Chippewa found French efforts to convert them odd, as they saw religion integrated with being Chippewa and had no intention of becoming French. American Indian religions were generally tolerant of others because prayer was part of culture, and if you were from a different culture it followed that you would practice your way of prayer.

Chippewa leaders told the French something like: "What is good for you is good for you and what is good for us is what has been given to us by our Manitos." The Chippewa were happy to adapt specific ceremonies from others to improve effectiveness, but they made the ceremonies Chippewa. Some Chippewa did try baptism because they figured that the Jesuits had brought disease and maybe their ceremony would work.

The pipe ceremony that probably originated among Missouri River tribes was embedded in Chippewa Country because it offered a means to pray

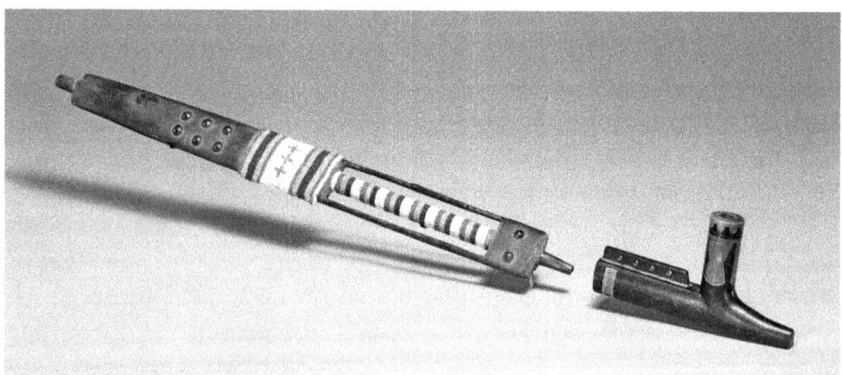

Pipe bowl and stem, Chippewa, ca. 1885. The pipe ceremony was a near-universal practice used to mark significant events and convey prayers to Manitos. Such pipes were often mistakenly called "peace pipes." (The Metropolitan Museum of Art/ Ralph T. Coe Collection, Gift of Ralph T. Coe Foundation for the Arts, 2011)

effectively and to mark solemn commitments to Manitos and in tribal interactions. The Chippewa creation narrative indicated that Nanabozho had brought the pipe ceremony to the Chippewa.

The elaborately carved pipe became a kind of symbol of peaceful intent and was honored by enemies and friends alike. The pipe was sacred throughout Indian Country. The French were taught the use of the pipe ceremony, and most of their explorers made sure to show the calumet, or ceremonial pipe, as they approached tribal communities in order to show their good intentions. Refusal to smoke the pipe was an insult. Pipe ceremonies began all solemn negotiations and discussions and marked the advent of other ceremonies.

Europeans had a different view of their place in the world and the function of their religions. To them religion was exclusive and nonbelievers were evil. The Chippewa would learn that French Catholics disagreed with each other about a single truth and that they hated other Europeans for their Protestant beliefs.

Europeans wanted Indians to become subjects following the dictates of Europeans, working as peasants, acknowledging the one true God as they termed it. France, for instance, introduced its priests who would work very hard to make "les sauvages" into French Catholics. Europeans, whether French Catholics or Spanish Catholics or one of the Protestant faiths, were convinced that they had the right to rule heathen Indians for their own good. In French North America, priests were part of the vanguard of exploration and interaction with Indians.

French missionaries in the 17th century concentrated on Huronia and the Ontario Peninsula. Thirty-two missions were established. L'Anse on Keweenaw Bay on the southern shore of Lake Superior was the first mission in Chippewa Country. Sault Ste. Marie near Bowetin was the second in 1668.

St. Ignace, nearby, was established in 1671 to seek converts among the concentrations of Ottawa and Chippewa. St. Ignace later became a center for French traders and their mixed-blood families but remained a Chippewa town. There were very few priests, and Chippewa Country was spacious, which hampered conversion. Some accepted baptism, listened to Jesuit preaching, and then continued their lives as Chippewa.

Although the English did not send missionaries, they did value trade with Indians, particularly for fur and food, and each wanted Indian military support against the other. As the English gained control of the land and conquered tribes along the eastern seaboard, they did force Indians to convert and even created religious communities, the first reservations. Protestant missionaries did not enter Chippewa Country until the 19th century.

The French brought some settlers to first Acadia (later Nova Scotia when the English took it away from the French) and then to the sites of Indian communities. Quebec was built in 1608 and Montreal in 1642. The French governor, Samuel Champlain, committed the French to alliance with Algonquians against the Iroquois. He joined Algonquians against the Iroquois in 1609 and was convinced that his guns were the deciding factor. French guns became part of their trade and supportive generosity to the Algonquians, Hurons, and eventually Chippewa.

Iroquois were not favorably disposed toward the French afterward. Conflict became endemic as French communities were added to the Algonquian and Huron targets of Iroquois warfare. By 1610 Dutch merchants reached Albany where they built Fort Orange and settled. English colonizers founded colonies on the eastern seaboard of North America from the late 16th century on. War was a frequent accompaniment to European settlements as they necessarily contested with established Indian nations for their land. On the other hand, Indians and Europeans often developed mutually supportive coexistence.

The Chippewa listened to the stories about the alien peoples. They understood that the newcomers were not like stranger Indians; they were strangers of a different kind. They spoke different languages and despised and attacked each other. Marauding English pirates expelled Frenchmen from Quebec in 1629. French ownership was restored from a European perspective in a 1632 Franco-English treaty that recognized French sovereignty

---

THE FRENCH IN CHIPPEWA COUNTRY

French emissaries penetrated Chippewa Country proper during the early 17th century. The first recorded Frenchmen were Etienne Brule in 1622, Jean Nicollet in 1634, and the Jesuits, Charles Raymbault, and Isaac Jogues in 1641. They commented on the large numbers of "saulteurs" living and working at Boweting–Sault Ste. Marie–Michilimackinac. Sault is the French word for rapids, and the Chippewa were often called saulteurs.

After an extensive exploratory visit of Pierre Radisson and Paul Medard in 1659, traders and Jesuits provided more detailed accounts of the saulteurs and their neighbors. Father Jacques Marquette established a mission at Sault Ste. Marie in 1668 but departed in 1669, an oft-repeated pattern. French maps combined words like Michilimackinac and Boweting with French names for the same areas like the St. Mary's River, Sault Ste. Marie, St. Ignace, and gallicized names for tribes like the Chippewa and Ottawa.

over Canada. By the mid-17th century, the Chippewa joined Ottawa kin in their annual treks to Montreal, and the French were accepted as a foreign power by the Chippewa and other Native Americans.

It is difficult to know what Chippewa people thought of their first contacts with Europeans. Oral traditions indicate that the Chippewa thought them strange but powerful people. Perhaps they were even Manitos or at least they had powerful Manito support? The Chippewa soon learned that they were completely human.

Clearly their wealth in goods reflected power, and their effectiveness in war was impressive. They brought their shamans with them, and the Jesuits were held in awe at first despite their repulsive commitment to celibacy. They also thought the French were odiferous and wondered if there were any French women because they saw none.

Frenchmen were considered duplicitous, awkward, and malleable, but the French had wealth and they could be useful allies. Some Chippewa were sure that the French were stupid because they were hairy, a sign of ignorance and weak minds. French actions reinforced initial, negative impressions because Frenchmen demonstrated that they could not survive without Indian help.

Chippewa Country was quite distant from the centers of initial French settlement, but other tribes were nearer and could fully exploit this new society of people who did not know how to behave as kinsmen and allies. However, the French did learn to follow Indian protocols and to work within Indian trade systems. A frequently awkward middle ground between almost binary societies was created to enable both French and Indians to collaborate in trade and war against common foes. Each of the tribes developed its own tactics in dealing with the French.

Huronia, on the Ontario Peninsula, was near Quebec and Montreal. Huron leaders saw the advantage of an alliance. Huron traders could funnel furs to other tribes in exchange for French goods even when annual fur brigades traveled to Montreal's trade fair. Huron power was enhanced by French willingness to be military allies against Iroquois. Hurons even allowed French Jesuits to enter their communities to seek converts.

Often, French officials made it clear that trade and priests were a package deal. The Franco-Huron alliance made Hurons the primary conduits for Chippewa and others' furs because the Hurons controlled the vital routes to Quebec and Montreal. It also obviated the need for French extension into Chippewa Country for a few decades.

The Chippewa and Ottawa welcomed French goods in exchange for their furs but did not have to make major adjustments in their lifestyles. French manufactured goods were simply incorporated into existing Chippewa patterns. Aside from extending their trade to take advantage of the new markets, Chippewa Country did not change. French goods were welcomed and integrated into traditional life, but they were not crucial to living a good life.

THE IROQUOIS WARS, 1641–1701

South and east of Chippewa Country, below Lake Erie, a dangerous competitive trading and military challenge emerged. Five Iroquois tribes had followed the inspiration and guidance of Deganawida and Hiawatha to form the Iroquois Confederation and League governed by the Great Law of Peace. The Iroquois tribes were the Mohawk, Cayuga, Onondaga, Seneca, and Oneida. The Tuscarora joined the league in the early 18th century. The League was dominant in upper New York long before the Dutch began making their way from New Amsterdam up the Hudson River. Dutch merchants responded to the willingness of Mohawk to host a trading town in Iroquoia by building Fort Orange (later Albany, New York).

The Iroquois first drove out the Algonquians, like the Mahicans, and established a monopoly on access to trade and localized fur trapping. Soon the area around the Finger Lakes of New York was trapped out. Iroquois wealth was fueled by control of furs, which meant they had to find new sources. The Iroquois concluded that they had to control more plentiful resources and developed a means to organize combined forces that could overwhelm other tribes. Iroquois leaders also wanted to control more territory to make themselves invulnerable.

The Dutch provided guns, ammunition, and food that allowed Iroquois men to leave their families while they expanded into other areas. The League governing structure allowed organization of large expeditions to continue conflicts that had erupted regularly before the Europeans arrived. Expanding the fur trade was just another cause of conflict, not the only one. The Iroquois felt that they had a right to dominate their neighbors. The Great Lakes and southern Canadian resources seemed accessible, and there was a long history of conflict between the Iroquois League members and the Hurons and Algonquians. Intertribal war was common in the history of nearly all tribes.

The Iroquois launched what later historians named the Beaver Wars in 1641. Initial eruptions of Iroquois devastation destroyed many of the smaller tribes near Lakes Erie and Ontario. Neutral, tobacco, Nipissing, and allumette remnants scattered westward or were adopted into an Iroquois tribe. Fur flotillas en route to Montreal were interdicted frequently. Iroquois forces spread havoc throughout large areas, and refugees streamed away from Iroquois incursions.

Iroquois yearly expeditions attacked the Susquehannocks, New England tribes, and the Shawnee along the Delaware River. The destructiveness of the Iroquois invasion created a shatter zone from Lake Erie to Illinois where a constant roiling of peoples established new communities.

The Chippewa called the Iroquois "Nadoweys," or venomous snakes. Communities like Green Bay offered safe havens for thousands of tribal peoples, including many refugee Chippewa. Populations of Chippewa and other tribes ebbed and flowed from place to place with the fortunes of war.

The entirety of the Iroquois Confederation launched campaigns against the heart of Huronia in 1648. They destroyed two villages and forced the abandonment of St. Ignace, Ontario. The next war season included around 1,000 Seneca and Mohawk. Their assaults on St. Ignace II and St. Louis convinced the Huron that their villages could not be defended.

After burning their remaining villages, Hurons fled to Quebec for French protection, forming the town of Lorette; others joined the remnants of other tribes south of Lake Erie; still others joined the Seneca and even set up their own town in Iroquoia; and others fled further south toward their former trading partners like the Chippewa and Ottawa. A large refugee community was formed on Manitoulin Island, in Ottawa Country. The refugees were soon identified as a new tribe, the Wyandots.

Widespread and continuous warfare created a churning of refugees, who were victims of the Iroquois or feared they would be. Chippewa villages near the Sault were abandoned, and they fled to Green Bay on the western shore of Lake Michigan. Refugees, including Chippewa, formed an intertribal concentration of several villages united by fear of the Iroquois, intermarriages, and various other affinities.

French officials involved in trading joined the refugee communities and made Green Bay their first large site in the Great Lakes area south of the 49th parallel. The French wholeheartedly offered assistance to their partners as they feared loss of the fur trade to the Iroquois, who did not trade with New France. The specter of English challenges to the French colonies added another reason for French efforts.

In 1655 a large Iroquois push reached the western shore of Lake Michigan near Green Bay, but they were forced to retreat. Iroquois oral history indicated they retreated because they could not find food, but the Chippewa and their allies pursued the Iroquois all the way to Sault Ste. Marie. A battle raged for days, and hundreds of Iroquois died according to Chippewa and Ottawa histories.

The tide of war in Chippewa Country turned against the Iroquois, but they did try to regain their victories. Chippewa communities resumed their lives as did many other tribes that had recoiled from Iroquois invasions. The war continued for another 46 years.

The Iroquois wanted revenge, prisoners of war to adopt to replace lost men, and the resources of the Great Lakes area. Chippewa leaders joined other tribes in coordinating defense against renewed Iroquois fury. A confederation of several tribes awaited Iroquois columns a few years later.

The 1662 Battle of Iroquois Point in June halted Iroquois efforts to conquer the Chippewa homeland. Wyandot, former Hurons, were part of the killing of several hundred Iroquois according to the accounts passed down through Chippewa generations. The battle site is located on Bay Mills Chippewa Reservation in Michigan.

The Battle of Iroquois Point has become part of the Chippewa creation narrative. In the oral tradition and its recounting, the battle expands into Manito intervention on behalf of the Chippewa with Chippewa heroism in saving Chippewa Country. The tradition begins with Chippewa scouts discovering a large Iroquois force assembling to attack. Chippewa leaders sent for Nipissing, Wyandot, and Ottawa allies and prepared to defend their homeland.

Iroquois arrogance was such that they marched to where the St. Mary's River empties into Lake Superior and decided to celebrate in anticipation of destroying the Chippewa. Two Chippewa shamans drew on their Manitos to change into an otter and a beaver so they could reconnoiter the encampment. They summoned the combined Chippewa and their allies to surround the Iroquois.

After four nights of dancing, the Iroquois awakened to a dawn attack. Hundreds of Iroquois were killed—all but two of them. The two were sent back to tell their relatives of the ferocity of the Chippewa. For generations, the bleached skulls and skeletons of the Iroquois littered the battlefield. The point is still called Naudowewigoning, the Place of Iroquois Bones.

Relieved French officials established St. Ignace in Chippewa Country between reoccupied Boweting and the Straits of Mackinac. Life went on as before. The fur trade resumed, and the French expanded efforts to claim more land to keep the English away from New France. The Chippewa Country's homeland was secure.

In 1671, Sieur Duluth Saint Lusson inaugurated the new French policy of claiming land and acquiring subjects in Chippewa Country and the Ohio Valley. Representatives from more than 14 tribes responded to a French call for a grand meeting at Sault Ste. Marie.

Amid a medieval pageant, Duluth opened the gathering with a pipe ceremony and prayers by his shamans, the Jesuits. He distributed presents and held a feast for the assembled peoples, which demonstrated that the French had learned the necessary protocol for Native American diplomacy.

Duluth raised a pole that had a plaque announcing French sovereignty and possession of "Lakes Huron and Superior and all lands and waters contiguous and adjacent, from one sea to the other." He declared that the Indians had placed themselves "under the protection of the King and subject to the laws and customs of France."

Although Chippewa clan leaders attached their clan symbols to the pole, they did not accept Duluth's hyperbolic claims even if they understood what he was proclaiming. The Chippewas and other tribes recognized alliances, but they did not accept that the French king had any rights over them.

Other French officers conducted similar tours of Indian country. They planted plaques and recorded grandiose claims of sovereignty over Native American subjects. Indians accepted no restrictions on their freedom. Chippewa Country belonged to the Chippewa, and they determined who could live there and who could not. French pomp was interesting to watch but signified only that the French wanted an alliance. Chippewa leaders did grant permission to establish forts that doubled as trading centers. Other tribes welcomed French forts as well in Illinois and throughout the Ohio Valley.

French claims to North American territory expanded during the Beaver Wars and their aftermath. Jacques Marquette and Louis Joliet reached the Arkansas River and were soon followed by René-Robert Cavelier, Sieur de la Salle, who got to the mouth of the Mississippi in 1682. The entire Mississippi watershed was claimed by France within European international laws of discovery. Colonies at Mobile Bay and New Orleans in 1718 secured the French claims.

Antoine de la Mothe Cadillac secured Michilimackinac to his satisfaction as a French possession and then moved to establish Detroit outside of Chippewa Country. He built Fort Pontchartrain as a key site, blocking potential English expansion. Cadillac tried to induce tribes to move to the Detroit area and bring their trade with them.

Here in a village built by the French, Cadillac thought, different tribes could act as a buffer against any English expansion and he could control them. Most Indians scoffed at Cadillac's attempts to order them about.

French troops supported a large allied tribal retaliatory expedition into Iroquoia. They drove the Iroquois before them and earned glory and renown for the Chippewa, Ottawa, and Wyandot particularly. The Ontario Peninsula became untenable for the Iroquois. Many other victories against the Iroquois were noted, like a 1696 defeat by a combined Chippewa and Wyandot force.

The Native American alliance assisted by the French even penetrated into New York and burned some Iroquois towns. By 1696, Mississauga, another name for Chippewa, had replaced Iroquois in the Ontario villages of the Iroquois. Even the Miami and Potawatomi felt safe enough to go home, south and east of Lake Michigan.

In 1701 the Iroquois asked for peace. After lengthy discussions among the tribes and the English who had replaced the Dutch in New York, the French played the role of peacemaker among allies by holding the Great Peace conference in 1701 in Montreal. The Iroquois agreed to allow the Chippewa and other tribes to have access to Albany markets and to abandon their towns on Ontario Peninsula. They promised neutrality in future conflicts between France and England. Prisoners were exchanged. The French enthusiastically agreed to allow the Iroquois access to Montreal and for hunting on the peninsula.

Chippewa leaders and their allies had achieved a near total victory. The victors had repulsed a major threat to their existence and regained control of their homelands. From their perspective, French assistance had been useful, but it was the Chippewa who had defeated the Snakes, secured their routes to markets, and established themselves as preeminent controllers of the lucrative fur trade center at Michilimackinac.

The French pledged to provide payments of goods and to support Chippewa against their enemies in return for accepting an enlarged French presence. The French called the goods "presents," but in reality they were paying to be allowed to be in Chippewa Country. French traders and soldiers soon joined the Chippewa and Ottawa at the straits, rebuilt their trading fort, and reinforced Chippewa control.

The international arrangements were never static. English power grew as did their world war with France. English colonial governments wanted more trade and access to the Indian country that France claimed. The Iroquois were smarting over their abject defeat, and other tribes were fearful of English colonial expansion.

English policies and trade would soon alter much of the fur trade pattern because they developed New York as a major center for colonization and trade. Fort Orange became Albany and the capital of New York colony. Unlike the Dutch, the English were interested in long-term political alliances and land, not just trade. They also injected many more colonists to challenge Indians for the land itself, and they were willing to commit military forces.

Not only the English colonies and the British government changed the international landscape. Hudson's Bay Company (HBC) was established in 1670 by James II to encircle New France, lure Indian trade to their posts, and counter French influences. Rupert's Land, most of Canada west of Ontario, was the chartered area for the Company.

Their charter allowed the HBC to govern Rupert's Land and conduct their own Indian policy. Like the French, the HBC used fortified trading posts and traders to acquire Indian furs. Fort Garry in Manitoba was the closest large post. It would soon be within an expanded Chippewa Country. To the Chippewa and other tribes like the Dakota and Cree, the HBC offered an alternative to the French for trade and commerce.

France realized many of its objectives during the Iroquois Wars. They gained some access to furs from New York, the Iroquois ceased attacking the French colonies and their Native American allies, and the threat of English poaching seemed lessened. They were allowed to join the Chippewa and other tribes within the Pays d'en Haute. French forts joined Michilimackinac at Detroit, Green Bay, and La Pointe in Chippewa Country with tribal permission. But the Chippewa and their allies gained even more.

The Iroquois Wars were another unifying force for the Chippewa. Their victories left them with a honed process for uniting while retaining village autonomy within the context of Chippewa culture. The experience of joint warfare among the Chippewa and sustained campaigns enhanced the kinship networks already in place. Leaders increased their skills in dealing with Europeans and in negotiations that led to gains for the Chippewa. Probably the Chippewa villages began to think of themselves and their relatives as a whole entity—the Chippewa nation.

The wars also provided grist for the Chippewa story: heroes, battles, defeats of an enemy, and assistance to the Chippewa by Manitos are all part of nationalism and the Chippewa story. The Great Peace offered security from Iroquois attacks forever. French garrisons and traders at key points throughout Chippewa Country confirmed the viability of Chippewa dominance. Ojibwemowin became the language of trade throughout the Great Lakes area.

The only glitch occurred when the French abandoned most of their forts in 1696 and closed the fur trade. They were responding to a glut of warehoused furs. Indians were incensed because they saw this as French perfidiousness. But the French countered with annual payments (presents) to compensate their allies for commercial loss. The Chippewa also pursued other options.

Quite a few Frenchmen ignored regulations and traded illegally with the Chippewa and other tribes. Coureurs de Bois (Runners of the Woods) married Indian women according to Chippewa law and sometimes French law. Frenchmen who married into tribes became part of kinship networks that favored their business dealings and imposed kinship obligations on the Frenchmen.

French licensed and unlicensed traders learned that marriage with women from prominent families was advantageous. In order to survive the winter, marriage was necessary in the absence of French supplies. The children of Indian-French marriages were called metis, mixed bloods, or half-breeds by the English-speaking. Indians called them relatives and expected them to behave as relatives. Metis were excellently positioned to act as cultural brokers.

Developments in Europe and in North America brought challenges to the Chippewa. England and France began what some have called the Second Hundred Years' War during the reign of Louis XIV and William and Mary.

In North America the wars were called King William's War (1689–1697), Queen Anne's War (1702–1713), King George's War (1740–1748), and the French and Indian War (1754–1760). Mostly they coincided with European wars, but sometimes they spilled over in between or after them.

French and English officials spent a great deal of money trying to induce their Indian allies to join one and not the other. As the 17th century ended and conflicts along the English colonial border increased, tribes made choices. Most enemies of the Iroquois opted to fight against England because it supported their colonists taking Indian land and driving Indians from their homelands. English products were valued, but the immigrants were violent and distinctly anti-Indian.

Unfortunately, a by-product of the warfare was an enduring hatred of Indians by English colonists, whose descendants would be Americans by the 1780s. Chippewa Country was remote from the major theaters of war until the 1750s, so they were able to concentrate on home and their own expansion. However, the Chippewa and Ottawa from eastern Chippewa Country decided to intervene in the wars from time to time.

Early in the 1700s, French merchants found out that they needed more furs because the not-so-carefully warehoused furs had rotted. The Chippewa and others were eager to resume the fur trade, the French market was demanding them, and a strong French presence was needed to counter the encroaching English. Content customers would want to help France in the bitter battles against England.

French forts that doubled as trading centers, like those at Detroit and the restored Michilimackinac and Green Bay, were augmented by additional locations at major focal points for the Chippewa villages. Fort La Pointe on Madeline Island at Chequamegon Bay and Fond du Lac were added along with Grand Portage. Six forts were built in Illinois and

Indiana serving the Illinois Confederation and the Miami. French efforts to maintain the alliances and allegiances included annual gift giving, payment of food, and protections for Indians who joined the French against the English.

CHANGES IN CHIPPEWA SOCIETY

By the 18th century, Chippewa hegemony was at its zenith. They had secured the homeland and avoided the disastrous changes visited on other nations. However, their success and the continuing warfare caused significant changes in Chippewa government, population, customs, and homeland. New elements were melded into traditional understandings. Change occurred, but it took place in a recognizable Chippewa context.

The need for more resources, particularly wild rice and furs, led to Chippewa Country being more than doubled at the expense of the Dakota Sioux of northern Wisconsin and Minnesota. Other tribes like the Sauk and Winnebago were engulfed in the wars, too. The churning of peoples and tribal lands continued. French forces were nearly always involved in these wars. They had to be because they were dependent on Chippewa, Ottawa, and other Indian allies.

The center of Chippewa Country shifted from the still important Michilimackinac, where Ottawa were assuming more leadership, to the Chequamegon Bay area of Lake Superior's western shore centered on the Ojibwe town at Mooniingwanekaanig, which the French called La Pointe, Madeline Island.

Within Chippewa Country, some villages became year-round communities and grew in size. But the basic pattern of winter dispersal to kinship communities continued for most Chippewa. Wars and trade increased the unity of the Chippewa as a tribe because they required interband efforts. Tribal members from northern Lake Superior joined with their southern relatives against the Sioux and other tribes. Many reunited in Minnesota's and Wisconsin's new Chippewa villages.

Traditional leaders, particularly war leaders, became more directive, unlike the egalitarian practices of earlier times. Larger villages, comprised of more clans and families, required more structured government. Military campaigns emphasized more planning, more centralization of decision making, and more military forces assembled. Coordination with French merchants and officers required a different kind of commitment to problem solving of trade disputes and more mediation for Chippewa leaders. Missionaries were yet another factor in the expanding villages and intratribal activities.

Chippewa men became producers of raw materials and women the primary processors in an expanded fur trade. This amended some of the usual patterns as men and women devoted more time to producing trade goods. Most of the fur trade operated on credit by the 18th century. Goods and supplies were charged at the trading posts and repaid with the harvest of furs at the end of the trapping season. However, the Chippewa and other Indians insisted that the traders behave similarly to relatives.

The Chippewa expected gifts from the rich traders because sharing demonstrated good will and generosity was much valued. The Chippewa reciprocated with services and goods to the traders. Each man continued the Chippewa tradition of individually deciding what to do with his goods; this was between the individual and the trader. The Chippewa shifted to more manufactured goods like the ubiquitous blankets, steel traps, needles, wool and cotton clothing, guns, metal knives, iron cooking pots, imported beads, dyes, paints, mirrors, brandy, and even imported food. However, leaders would intervene if the trader cheated or if the individual Chippewa got into arguments about dealings. The trade was symbiotic and complex because of the intertwining of social and business interactions that melded French and Chippewa values and practices.

Despite the new products, traditional goods remained predominant. The Chippewa were not dependent on French or English goods; they just liked them. They also were not converted to amassing capital and individual wealth. French and English merchants noted that the Chippewa and other Natives just worked to buy what they wanted, and if they did not like the merchandise they just would not buy. Once they had their "besoins" (needs) met, they stopped trapping or manufacturing. Material goods were meant to be shared, not accumulated.

Women's functions underwent major changes. They had to work harder at acquiring and storing food because men's contributions diminished. The French bought food from the women and hired men to hunt deer. Approximately 70 percent of all food was produced by women working collectively with their relatives. Women controlled the sale of food like rice, fish, maple sugar, corn, beans, and squash to the French traders and soldiers. They did not follow the credit pattern adopted for the actual trade in furs; they demanded payment on delivery. Women also trapped some of the luxury furs like mink and handled their own transactions involving their own property.

Women assumed some of the traditional men's roles in hunting as men diverted their usual work to war and increased trapping. French and mixed-blood husbands were valued for their ability to act as relatives contributing to the family, or they were expelled. Even some French officials wintered with Chippewa families. All were expected to behave as good relatives.

Some historians have misunderstood the relationship of the traders and Chippewa families because they view the relations as merely sexual and as exploitation of oppressed Chippewa women. These historians are wrong. The misperception about women's place in Chippewa society stems from European and American ethnocentrism. They saw what they expected to see.

One source of misunderstanding is that Chippewa leaders often "offered" their daughters as wives to fur traders and government officials. Europeans inferred that the women had no choice in the matter and were like chattel. This was egregiously wrong. Chippewa women had extensive rights in traditional society. Certainly, Indian male leaders and their female counterparts often encouraged liaisons with the wealthy French traders because these enhanced family prestige and gave access to wealth for the family. This practice was a continuation of traditional practices as marriage was a means of creating kinship bonds among people and providing the sinews of alliances and families.

The French and the Chippewa alike recognized that marriages "after the fashion of the country" were good for business and political interests. Some of the marriages became permanent while others were temporary. Chippewa women could divorce their husbands; they owned their household goods, and they were not forced to accept marriage arrangements their fathers and mothers recommended. Generally, Chippewa women remained with their bands if the husbands moved on. Within the extended family structures or Chippewa communities, this did not pose a problem for the women nor shame for the men.

Women were vital elements in the fur trading system. They were the interlocutors between their French husbands and their Chippewa families. The lynchpin of kinship in Chippewa society allowed complex systems of interaction among the French traders, the Chippewa clans, and even with other tribes.

As time passed women learned to manage the businesses, drew on their relatives for support, and instructed their husbands on how to be proper relatives. Several Chippewa women became widely known fur traders–merchants, and a few became spokespersons for their communities in interactions with Europeans and Americans.

In some areas, women spurred the creation of new kinship matrices uniting those married to Frenchmen across villages in order to cement trading and communities of traders. Susan Sleeper-Smith traced the development of this community of interest that transcended tribal identity and even clan membership. *Indian Women and French Men* (2001) provides a nuanced description of the network and how women used the Catholic practice of godparenting to reinforce and extend businesses that looked like extended families.

Frenchmen, Chippewas, other tribespeople like the Ottawa, mixed-blood children, French officials, Catholic priests, Coureurs de Bois, voyageurs for part of the year, and visitors clustered around the fur trading posts–forts at the major Chippewa communities. They followed new rules combining the dominant Chippewa culture with the fur trade business and French influences to create a new kind of society. The dynamic, changing society was a response to the fur trade, international French and English rivalries, and the turmoil created by change, but it remained Chippewa.

By the 18th century, large numbers of children were produced by the intermarriage of French, Chippewa, and members of other tribes. Generally, children were simply absorbed into the larger Chippewa societies, but some became important cultural brokers. The French used the term "metis" to designate these children and quickly recognized that they were part of the kinship network of Chippewa extended families and therefore would be part of the fur trade.

Fathers often sent their children to be educated in schools in Canada (or, in a few cases, Europe). Mixed-blood children were valuable interpreters, negotiators, and businessmen while fully participating in their tribal societies. Often, trading organizations were enhanced by the kinship ties of intermarriage as mixed-blood children married other mixed-blood children.

THE FOX WARS, 1690–1736

The Fox Wars illustrate the complexity of relations among tribes and the French. The wars were caused by French efforts to concentrate all of the tribes around Detroit and French ignorance of the depth of Chippewa-Ottawa commitment to controlling trade, the French, and to expelling the Fox. Some of the Chippewa and bands from other tribes did move to the area of Detroit. The French concluded that they could bring more tribes to Detroit at their discretion. Naively, French officials thought they could control tribal differences through their intervention. The Fox were invited and many moved to Detroit, but the Fox had a history of constant war with the Chippewa and Ottawa, who made up the majority of Detroit area Native Americans.

Chippewa leaders in concert with the more numerous Ottawa decided to settle their issues with the Fox and attacked them, killing perhaps more than 1,000. Chippewa leaders told the French that it was a preemptive strike against a Fox conspiracy. The French bought into the Chippewa reasoning and joined them against the Fox. French junior officers were no match for cagey Chippewa-Ottawa leaders.

There were three separate Fox Wars over more than 40 years. After the initial battle at Detroit, the Fox retreated, gathered their allies, and set up a blockade of the Fox-Wisconsin waterway. Neither the French nor the Chippewa could tolerate being unable to continue the fur trade.

Kinship terms described the respective roles of French and Natives. The French, in their role as father, responded to the Chippewa in their role as children in need of help in the alliance protocol. French officials decided to remove the Fox as a threat by exterminating the tribe. This drastic approach had been somewhat successful in French efforts in Louisiana as they and their allies destroyed the Chitimacha power and the Natchez chiefdom. They were engaged in a futile effort to defeat the Chickasaw at the same time as the Fox Wars.

Joint expeditions were launched against Fox towns, and a generalized war raged throughout the Great Lakes area and Chippewa Country. French support for the war was maintained in part because the Chippewa and Ottawa sold captured Fox to the French officials and settlers. Peace would have meant that these slaves would have had to be returned, as was the custom at the end of wars.

Chippewa oral history relates a large canoe flotilla battle resulting in many drowned Fox and a great Chippewa victory. French and Indian allies burned several Fox villages and eventually drove their remnants toward Illinois, where they amalgamated with the Sauk. Fox allies dropped out of the war and made peace with the Chippewa.

The Chippewa and French achieved their goals of securing the fur trade routes through cooperation and a willingness to use extreme force against disruption by the Fox. However, when the French began talking about attacking Potawatomi villages that had taken in Fox refugees, the Chippewa-Ottawa made the French halt the war. The Chippewas did not attack their Potawatomi relatives, and they had achieved their objectives.

The Fox Wars and the earlier Iroquois Wars allowed the development of a pattern of international relationships grounded in American Indian understandings and protocols. A common feature of American Indian cultures is describing relationships in kinship terms. One adage has it: "One is either a relative or an enemy." Alliances were described in kinship terminology and roles assigned based on kinship functions. The French had to be relatives or they could not interact with the Chippewa. Kinship expectations were the expectations of metaphorical, fictional kinship behaviors.

By 1730, the French were solidified in the Native American system as assuming the role of father to their Indian children. The role was not one of domination as Europeans assumed when the French governor was called father in deliberations and Indians referred to themselves as children. In Chippewa culture this meant the father, Onontio (the Mountain, the French Governor General), was expected to provide military and material support for his children, the various tribes. Children were not expected to obey their father's dictates, just be lovingly cared for.

The Onontio was responsible for securing peace, providing support when tribes were in need, and generally acting as an Indian father would. Obedience had nothing to do with it. Indian fathers did not punish nor did they dictate to their children—they just cared for them. French leaders were often frustrated by this conception, but they learned to work within the Native American framework.

The Chippewa and others realized that, as children, they were usually expected to provide assistance to their fathers if needed. There were reciprocal obligations for the tribes. Given inducements by French leaders, the Chippewa were willing to fight against French enemies like the English or other tribes. It helped that most of the French enemies were also Chippewa enemies.

Both French and Indians recognized that the relationship required constant negotiation of the family arrangements while both were pursuing their own agendas in trade and war. To the Indians, the French were equals, not controllers. If the French wished to maintain their Canadian colony and counter British expansion, they had to follow the lead of Native Americans.

4

Expanding Chippewa Country

CRANE LEADS WESTWARD: THE DAKOTA WARS, 1736–1860s

The western shores of Lake Superior were a contested, fluid arena for many tribes as late as the 1700s. Dakota Sioux bands had the most widely recognized claim to the area in the 1600s, but other tribes in the general area of northern Wisconsin and Minnesota often contested access to resources. Spasmodic, punctuated conflicts and periods of peaceful coexistence had always involved the Chippewa, Dakota, Menominee, Sauk, Winnebago, and Huron-Wyandots. For instance, the Chippewa and Dakota were on opposite sides during much of the Fox Wars but had made a détente by the latter part of the 17th century.

Negotiations with Dakota leaders allowed the Chippewa to move to Mooniingwanekaanig (the home of the Golden Breasted Woodpecker— Yellow Tailed Flicker, aka Madeline Island) and the adjacent shore of Chequamegon Bay in Wisconsin's part of Lake Superior. The French were allowed a trading fort on the island and named it La Pointe, the name that a village retains today. Chippewa origin traditions hold that Mooniingwanekaanig is the homeland to which they were summoned by the call of the Crane. It is where food grows upon the waters as prophesized.

This island community became the epicenter of Chippewa society and culture during the 18th and much of the 19th century. According to one tradition, it is where the Midewiwin matured if not originated. Machilimackinac and Sault Ste. Marie remained important but the focus of Chippewa society shifted.

Until the 1730s, Dakota were quite distant from the French. Possibly, their concession to the Chippewa simply recognized the continuing westward movement from Michilimackinac to the shores of Lake Superior as a fait accompli. One Chippewa tradition describes a formal treaty conference at Fond du Lac in Minnesota that transferred the island and western shore of Lake Superior to the Chippewa. The Dakotas were concentrated toward the headwaters of the Mississippi and westward toward the Red River of the North. Historically, Madeline Island had been occupied by Ottawa and Huron bands and then by Dakota.

The first French contact was probably in 1659 followed by Father Allouez who built a temporary mission at La Pointe. In 1665 Father Jacques Marquette arrived and stayed four years. Duluth visited the island in 1679. In 1693 Pierre LeSeur built a trading fort but left when the embargo started. In 1718 Paul St. Pierre rebuilt the French trading fort, and the French remained until the end of the French and Indian War.

As more Chippewa bands arrived, the island rapidly became a Chippewa community of importance with Chippewa band communities spreading to the Chequamegon Bay shores across from the island. Chippewa traders exchanged French goods with the Dakota for furs in a symbiotic relationship for both tribes.

Chippewa interests did not always coincide with French interests. As long as French traders did not try to offer goods directly to the Dakota, the Chippewa were content to simply act as intermediaries. French policies shifted westward, however, as they competed with the Hudson's Bay Company to their north and west. The French wanted to expand to the upper Mississippi River and add substance to their claims on the whole Mississippi drainage. Pierre Gaultier de la Verendrye (1685–1749) was given license to trade and seek a route to the Pacific by Onontio, Governor Frontenac. Verendrye and his sons along with business partners probed westward from Lake Nipigon.

To the chagrin and fury of the Chippewa, Verendrye opened trading forts in quick succession. Fort St. Pierre on Rainy Lake in 1731, Fort St. Charles at Lake of the Woods in 1732, and Fort Maurepas in 1734 on the Red River of the North were positioned to undermine Chippewa power by changing relationships with the Dakota, Assiniboine, and Cree. The situation was tense because both the French and the Chippewa needed cooperative interaction with each other, but their interests clashed over access to the Dakota and other tribes.

Significantly, the Cree were fighting the Dakota already and demanded that the French stop trading with the Dakota Sioux. Cree leaders did not want French arms and trade to flow to their enemies, the Dakota. They called on their French ally to join them against the Dakota. Pierre Verendrye joined in a Cree attack on some Dakota, and the French stopped trading with the Dakota.

In 1736 Baptiste Gaultier de la Verendrye, the eldest son of the French leader, left Fort St. Charles with 19 men and Father Jean-Pierre Auineau for supplies. Their bodies were found soon after and the Dakota were blamed, but there were Chippewa from La Pointe with the Dakota. Chippewa and French leaders were incensed. Chippewa leaders decided to retaliate on behalf of their French father and in support of their Cree allies. The Chippewa-Dakota hundred years' war began.

It is true that new trading posts and contacts did spark conflicts, and there had been some tension over trade with the Dakota, but Chippewa retaliation presented a conundrum. When they attacked the Dakota, they attacked a major trade partner. On the other hand, the good will of the French and Cree was a major goal of Chippewa policy. The answer to the problem was to expand Chippewa Country westward and remove most of the Dakota.

It is unlikely that a war that lasted from 1736 until the 1860s was caused by the killing of 21 Frenchmen. Quite probably, the ambitions of Chippewa leaders combined with the pressures of depleted beaver in Michigan and with growing Chippewa population simply allowed an incident to accelerate a process begun earlier. Chippewa leaders concluded they needed to expand at the expense of the Dakota. French leaders tried to broker peace, but French and metis traders moved westward with Chippewa communities.

In the midst of the Dakota Wars, France was replaced by Great Britain as a major actor on the Chippewa stage. The Chippewa and Ottawa had been involved peripherally in support of the French cause, but the major focus remained the Dakota Wars. Hudson's Bay Company and the Northwest Company soon were major partners in the fur trade.

Chippewa probes into Dakota Country led to new band villages in Wisconsin and Minnesota at Duluth, Grand Portage, Fond du Lac, Rainy Lake, Lac Courte Oreilles, and Lac du Flambeau. They confirmed the Chippewa conquest of Dakota land. Chippewa families for these new band villages came primarily from Madeline Island but were joined by influxes from throughout Chippewa Country. Canadian Chippewa were among them, and they moved westward to Winnipeg. The Dakota fought back.

One of the leaders who distinguished himself in war against the Dakota and earlier against the Fox was Biaushwa II, the survivor son who had taken his father's name. He became the major leader of Chippewa expansion to the headwaters of the Mississippi and toward the Red River Valley, the area where the Dakota tribe had originated centuries before. Campaigns reunited portions of the northwestern with the southwestern tribes as recruits arrived from Ontario and Manitoba to join the expeditions. Soon northerners came with their families to augment or establish new Chippewa communities.

By 1745, Dakota villages were abandoned, and the Chippewa moved in large numbers to Sandy Lake, Mille Lacs, Red Lake, and Leech Lake to establish permanent Chippewa villages and a hunting area in western Minnesota. French trading posts, often managed by mixed-blood Chippewa, were added around the new Chippewa towns.

The Dakota yielded their original homeland and shifted the center of their population along the Minnesota River in southern Minnesota. They continued trying to regain their homeland or at least to exact revenge for their defeat. William Warren, a Chippewa and historian, collected oral histories from Chippewa whose parents and grandparents had been part of the Dakota Wars and published them in 1851. They are characterized by stories of Chippewa bravery and noble acts against a worthy enemy. The stories convey a sense of Native American warfare as it was. There were no noncombatants, although women and children were as often taken prisoner as they were killed.

Big Marten (Kechewaubishash), the war leader for Biauswah II, led the expeditions that finally scoured the Dakota from their homelands. In one

---

HOW THE CHIPPEWA TOOK POSSESSION OF MILLE LACS

One story describes how the Chippewa took possession of Mille Lacs, a Dakota center consisting of two villages. The Dakota had murdered a Chippewa who was visiting them, and his father swore revenge. He gathered ammunition and supplies for two years before calling for recruits. Many Chippewa responded, and they destroyed one of the Mille Lacs Dakota villages, but the second contained earth lodges where the Dakota holed up and frustrated Chippewa could not breach them. Chippewa heroes climbed to the roofs and dropped bags of gunpowder through the smoke holes at the top of the lodges. Explosions caused havoc among the Dakota. The next day, the Dakota fled and the Chippewa moved into the area. As with many oral histories, this story is not corroborated by other sources. The Dakota did not live in earth lodges, but there is a tradition that Dakota had moved into abandoned earth lodges. At any rate, they did lose Mille Lacs to the Chippewa. Dakota oral history indicates that they abandoned Mille Lacs voluntarily.

instance, he led nearly 200 men against a large force of Dakota who were reinforced by even more Dakota in the midst of a battle. The Chippewa dug firing pits on the prairie and inflicted heavy casualties on the Dakota. The Dakota set a fire to force the Chippewas to fight, but the smoke grew too thick and Big Marten led a successful retreat.

In another battle, about 80 Chippewa defeated an invading Dakota force of more than 400 men after a battle raged for most of a day. Big Marten repeatedly taunted the Dakota, led charges, and was targeted by Dakota fire. He was killed near the end of the day, and the Chippewa abandoned the field in the night because they wanted to mourn their fallen hero.

Another tradition notes the intervention of birds. A Dakota band sneaked onto a St. Croix Lake island to stage an attack. However, a Chippewa boy heard chickadees calling, "Sioux boats on the shore." He told his family, and a Chippewa force killed all of the Dakota on the island. Children are still regaled with stories of Dakota ghosts and of the chickadee's warning.

Most of the legends about battles and wars hinge on individual incidents and are not described within the context of a Chippewa strategy of conquering Dakota Territory and incorporating it into Chippewa Country. Violations of hospitality, murders, children slain, and individuals seeking revenge abound in Warren's summaries. The result of the wars was that the Dakota lost northern Minnesota to the Chippewa within less than a generation. Oral traditions are reminiscent of the stories veterans often pass on to their children—not the grand strategies identified by commanders and historians. Individual bravery is emphasized, not the taking of territory.

WAR IN THE EAST, TOO: CHIPPEWA CONTEXT FOR THE ANGLO-FRENCH WARS, 1740–1763

Although significant numbers of Chippewa pursued glory and conquest against the Dakota, the southeastern Chippewa based at Michililmackinac weighed their responses to a renewal of the wars for empire, which the English called the War of Austrian Succession (1744–1748) and the Seven Years' War (1756–1763). In the Americas, the colonists called them King George's War and the French and Indian War (1754–1760).

The Chippewa pursued their own interests, despite efforts by the French to convince them to wholeheartedly support the French cause. Chippewa leaders wanted trade with both, and they played one against the other to obtain resources from each. Their close relatives, the Ottawa, took the leadership role among the Anishinaabek based around Machilimackinac. The

Chippewa generally followed the Ottawa lead, but joint operations and direction were the norm.

Many historians have studied the wars for empire and have focused on the French and English with only nodding attention to strategies and roles of American Indians in the several wars. Recent scholarship acknowledges the pivotal Native American agency in determining why battles were lost and won.

The Chippewa were willing to fight with the French against the British to maintain a balance of power in the Pays d'en Haute. They also had old scores to settle against the Iroquois and other Indians. The political alliances in the Pays were not simply involved with the war between English and French; Indians did not have to fight for either side, and they did not consider themselves bound to follow either British or French desires.

Some Chippewa fought in support of their French fathers, basically as a continuation of the Iroquois Wars of an earlier generation and in support of their interests in maintaining alliance with the French. However, fictive kinship with Onontio only went as far as Chippewas gained from it. English opportunities were viable. Chippewa leaders also wanted to support the winner in the contest between the European powers, but the paramount concern for them was to maintain their sovereignty and ensure their continuing independence.

The Iroquois supported the English along with remnants of the eastern coast tribes, but the majority of the Algonquian and Siouan speakers joined the French. French forts and trading posts and French relatives were integral components of Chippewa Country and the territories of most of the other tribes in the Ohio and Mississippi Valley. Iroquois leaders had demonstrated their willingness to trade with the French and to avoid war with the French. Self-interest was the guiding principle of all tribal leaders.

King George's War (1740–1748) was fought mainly east of the Appalachians and to a lesser extent in the lands of the Creek, Cherokee, Chickasaw, Shawnee, and in the maritime areas of Canada. The effects felt by the Chippewa were mainly in an increasing scarcity of trade with the beleaguered French. The French did not seem to be able to counter the growing power of the British in trade and war.

The Chippewa and other tribal leaders reexamined their options in the light of French failures during the war. They played a complex economic and power game as convoluted as any the British and French played. Diplomatic and trade experiments tested relationships, and various Native Americans sought advantages for themselves.

Some non-Chippewa band leaders created new villages, particularly in the Ohio Valley between the Wabash and Ohio Rivers to which they invited

British traders. The British built Oswego on Lake Ontario as the main new British trading center; many Chippewa, Ottawa, and others took advantage of Oswego to replenish goods. English traders and presents even made their way as far northwest as Michilimackinac.

Memeska, a renowned and charismatic Miami leader, created the town of Pickawillany as a multicultural trade center. He convinced other leaders to channel their trade through his town, and he made threatening feints at Chippewa Country. Several British fur traders moved to the town. The Ottawa and Chippewa leaders concluded Memeska was a threat to the dominance of Michilimacinac in commerce and political hegemony. French leaders feared loss of their land to British surrogates. War was discussed.

Ottawa leaders decided on caution and sent a delegation to see if Memeska would abandon the English alliance and challenge to the fur trade. Memeska insulted them and dared them to attack him and his allies. The Ottawa and Chippewa went home and prepared for war.

A trading and diplomatic delegation of Ottawa and Chippewa went to Oswego and warned the English that war was a possibility. They insisted they had no intention of attacking the British. Iroquois leaders did not say they would defend Pickawillany either, because they did not like other Indians diverting their trade. Without British or Iroquois support, Pickawillany was vulnerable.

Charles Langlade (1729–1801), an Ottawa war leader and fur trader, assembled a large Anishinaabeg (Chippewa-Ottawa-Potawatomi) force by drawing on his family and the extended kinship network they included. Various war leaders brought their adherents. About 270 Chippewa, Ottawa, and Potawatomi launched an attack on Pickawillany, captured some Miami women and children, and began a siege of the town.

Langlade offered to allow all to leave if they would just give him the English traders. In the midst of the discussions Memeska was captured. Langlade then boiled and ate Memeska in front of the defenders. Langlade returned to Detroit with four traders and 3,000 pounds of furs. The women and children were released.

The threat posed by Memeska was eliminated in a masterful display of statesmanship. Casualties were limited, thus preventing relatives from needing revenge for fallen relatives. The English were served notice not to interfere with the established balance of power. Other Indian leaders saw the determination of the Ottawa-led coalition. Diplomacy had allowed even the Iroquois to avoid a destructive war. The interest of the Indian tribes was in peace, not intertribal wars.

The attack on Pickawillany was the de facto beginning of the French and Indian War. Most historians consider George Washington's 1754 ambush of a French emissary and 12 Canadian militiamen and the subsequent response of a few hundred Chippewa-Ottawa and a few French troops that made him surrender at Fort Necessity as the beginning of the French and Indian War. The reality is that Pickawillany gave the French confidence in their Indian allies, while the Chippewa-Ottawa and other tribes drew the conclusion that supporting the French was a good choice.

The absence of an Iroquois or British response to Pickawillany sealed the Indian-French alliance. The French sent enough troops to build Fort Duquesne at the juncture of the Monongahela and Allegheny Rivers, which dominated the Ohio Valley. Hundreds of Indians joined them.

English traders fled back to Pennsylvania and New York. Indian attacks, sometimes accompanied by French or Canadians, began rolling back the western frontier of England in America. Expeditions reached as far as Carlisle and Lancaster in Pennsylvania. The Chippewa, mostly from Ontario and Michilimackinac, were part of the campaigns.

The British countered by sending about 3,000 British regulars to America commanded by Major General Edward Braddock. He was sent to expel the French from Fort Duquesne, which required a march through Pennsylvania.

British regulars and colonial militia labored into the woods where the outnumbered Indians and French awaited. Braddock displayed the typical British contempt for Indians and did not allow them to be recruited. He also considered colonials like George Washington, his aide, to be a nuisance.

The Indians positioned themselves on both sides of the British column while French troops set up across the path of the oncoming forces. Indian fire from the flanks wreaked havoc on the redcoats and the colonial militias. Braddock died with about 1,000 British and a few colonials in the Battle of the Monongahela. The force of 600 Indians and 200 Frenchmen lost 22 men. Most of the Native Americans were Chippewa and Ottawa from Michilimackinac combined with Huron and Potawatomi from Detroit.

After the Battle of the Monongahela, refugee colonial squatters fled over the mountains toward Philadelphia. Shawnee, Delaware, and Mingo contingents decided to join the war as allies of the Indian alliance. By March 1756, about 700 English had been killed. A large Indian confederation acting in consort or independently had decided to support the French against the English.

The Indians of the Ohio Valley felt that the English were the greater threat to their interests because Englishmen encroached on Indian lands. The English needed to learn their place in an Indian world. Indians did draw the line at wiping out the English. For instance, most refused to help destroy Fort Oswego because British goods were excellent and the English presence balanced the French. Native Americans also settled scores with their enemies regardless of what the French wanted.

The Chippewa continued the war as independent allies of the French. General Louis-Joseph Montcalm followed up the Indian victories by taking Fort Oswego with only French and Canadian troops and a few Indians. Then he turned on Fort William Henry after the Indian troops, perhaps 700 from the combined Chippewa-Ottawa-Potawatomi contingents, had scoured the land around the British fort.

The Indians attacked a relief force of whaleboats and barges commanded by Colonel John Parker. Fewer than 100 of the militia escaped. Indians boiled and ate some of the captives, to the surprise of the French. Most of the Native American contingents were ready to go home and pointed out to Montcalm that more war just tempted fate. After many meetings, they agreed to take Fort William Henry as a last step in the chastising of the British.

Montcalm had about 6,000 French and Canadian troops. In perhaps the largest assembly of allied Indians in history, about 1,800 from around 20 tribes joined the French in the siege of Fort William Henry. In European style, General Montcalm offered terms to the British, and they accepted an honorable surrender, which allowed them to leave with their arms and colors.

Montcalm informed his Indian allies of their great victory and told them to go home. The Indians were enraged because they were expected to go home with no scalps, no trophies of war, and no captives to either ransom or replace their dead. War leaders could not allow this to happen. English wounded and ill were scalped, the fort was looted, and as many as 300 British were taken prisoner.

The prisoners were marched to Montreal where the French were expected to ransom them. Governor Pierre de Rigaud, Marquis de Vandreuil, lectured the Indians about their atrocities and demanded they return the prisoners to the French. The Indian response was boiling an Englishman and making his compatriots eat him. Vaudreuil realized his faux pas and agreed to pay ransom and brandy for each prisoner.

On the advice of Charles Langlade, the Ottawa war leader, he held a series of farewells for groups of Indians. He lavished presents of tobacco, lace, vermillion, and brandy on the various war leaders. Langlade, an Ottawa who was also French, was appointed commander at Fort Michilimackinac as a French officer. Indian leaders had asserted their control of the Pays d'en

Haute on the battlefield and in bringing the British to heel. The English had retreated back over the mountains. The war was a complete victory for the Chippewa and their Native American allies.

The Indians' return home was accompanied by smallpox. It broke out first among the English garrisons and was carried back by victorious Indians and French forces. Detroit, Michilimackinac, St. Joseph's, and Green Bay were hit hard. Reports indicated heaps of dead lying in nearly abandoned villages. Given Chippewa and Ottawa beliefs about disease, the cause of Manito anger was obvious. Clearly, it was the French that had recruited Indians who became sick, so they had obligations to provide compensation.

The French were expected to cover the dead by attacking the British in a campaign and by providing goods to the Indians. Native Americans could not join the 1858 campaigns because they had lost too many and had to stay home to hunt. The French floundered in 1858 against the British as their Indian allies sat it out.

Leaders among the Chippewa and Ottawa had already expressed concerns about continuing the war, and the smallpox epidemic was the final straw. Despite French calls, few Indians joined the 1859 French efforts. British naval blockades made it impossible for the French to supply incentives enough to get the Indians to change their minds. Charles Langlade demonstrated loyalty to the French, and his kinship network did respond, but even this was not enough to attract many Ottawa and Chippewa to defend Quebec as the British forces arrived.

At the Plains of Abraham, Langlade led Canadian militia and a few hundred Native Americans into the woods flanking the British, and their volleys wreaked havoc on the British. But Montcalm decided that the set piece battle tactics he brought from Europe were better than the Native American approach, and he launched an attack against the superior British forces after letting them form into battle configuration. Although the British commander was killed, perhaps by Chippewa-Ottawa fire, Montcalm's European approach failed and Quebec was lost to the British.

Langlade was ordered by the French governor to return to Michilimackinac; he received word on the way that Montreal had surrendered. The fort at Michilimackinac was evacuated by the French, who decided to head for Louisiana to avoid surrendering. Langlade stayed, assumed command of the fort, and later surrendered it to the British. Charles Langlade, an Ottawa war leader who started the war at Pickawillany, was the last French officer to surrender. Michilimackinac was the last fort taken by the British in 1760.

> **WARFARE IN CHIPPEWA COUNTRY**
>
> Conflict in Chippewa Country was a constant. Prowess in war was a major stepping-stone to leadership in a world where different tribes vied for control of resources and access was limited. Chippewa justice required that attacks and killings by outsiders had to be revenged. None questioned their right to take land from enemies. Captives were either adopted, enslaved, or killed. Returning victors were widely acclaimed and honored. Clearly, they were favored by Manitos who had supported their efforts.
>
> Small populations and the weather acted as limitations on warfare. Loss of even a few meant hardship for the band. Casualties were few because a successful leader brought nearly all of his men home. Warfare in winter was practically impossible as there was no way to sustain large numbers of people, and was limited in other seasons by the number of men who could be spared from collecting food and protecting homes. Individuals decided whether to join their kin; there was no conscription.
>
> Chippewa expansion was made possible by strategic decisions by leaders to support war. The ability of war leaders to gather, perhaps a few hundred at most, for short campaigns designed to drive their enemies away from their homes led to serial campaigns. Battles were usually quickly over as one side overwhelmed the other, killed, captured, or drove off the enemy. Victors either went back home or brought families to occupy the new land.
>
> Given the rhythms of war, enemies like the Dakota could withdraw because they could not defend themselves and other lands were available. There was no need to destroy an enemy entirely. Peace agreements were common but often transitory.

PONTIAC'S WAR, 1762–1764

The Chippewa and other Indians understood that the French had been defeated by the British. The Chippewa and their allies had not. They had been part of the pan-Indian coalition that had beaten the British at every turn. They had destroyed Braddock's army, pushed the English interlopers who had crossed the Appalachians back behind them, and were major components of the successful campaign against Forts Oswego and William Henry. If the British wanted to come to Chippewa Country or to the rest of the Pays d'en Haut, Michilimackinac was still the key strategic center of the entire Great Lakes region.

British behavior caused some trepidation among the Chippewa and others as they moved to occupy the French trading forts. They did not follow protocol by going to Michilimackinac as protocol dictated; instead, they stopped first at Detroit. The Iroquois had convinced the British to go to Detroit where the Iroquois interest lay. Native Americans at Detroit were assured that peace and prosperity, perhaps with a return of Iroquois communities to Ontario, were coming. The fur trade was reopened. English officers also treated the Wyandot-Huron around Detroit as if they were British subjects.

Debate among the Chippewa and Ottawa ensued. Some of the war leaders were in favor of attacking the British immediately. The peace leaders managed to convince others to bide their time. The unease of Chippewa-Ottawa populations increased as they watched disrespectful behaviors continue. Other Indians were particularly concerned as they had borne the brunt of war in the Ohio Valley.

Intensive warfare and destruction had been a feature of the French and Indian War, particularly in the Ohio Valley. Unlike their Chippewa and other northern allies, Delaware, Shawnee, and others had their lands invaded and the fabric of their societies stretched to the tearing point. Times of crisis often generated an intense spiritual response, and the rise of prophets inspired to offer solutions to the embattled society.

Neolin, a Delaware prophet, received a vision providing a blueprint for expelling the British and British colonials. It was revealed to him that Native Americans needed to give up European-produced goods and return to the rites and ceremonies of their ancestors. If Indians would return to the ways given to them by their creators, harmony would be restored and the English would leave. This message resonated throughout Indian communities, including those of Chippewa Country. It was particularly well received among the Ottawa and some Chippewa living near Detroit. Pontiac, a renowned war leader, was a key leader among the Ottawa and Chippewa communities. He and many others adopted the teachings of Neolin and prepared to expel the interlopers.

British arrogance rankled the Chippewa when about 200 British soldiers were sent from Detroit to Michilimackinac in the fall of 1761. The English did so without sending presents and belts of friendship to gain permission to reoccupy the fort. Already, British fur traders had angered the Chippewa-Ottawa by refusing credit and disregarding the French traders. How to discipline the British became a major subject.

Captain Henry Balfour commanded the British force and called leaders to Fort Machilimackinac to tell them what to expect. He proceeded to lecture them about their duties to the British and threatened them with loss of the fur trade if they did not do as the British wished. Probably, the Chippewa tried to allow for ignorance. They offered remarks about their concerns for their communities now that the French had gone. Leaders expressed fears that their children would starve. In traditional diplomatic protocol, these statements were expected to lead to the British distributing presents to show their kinship with the Chippewa-Ottawa and their willingness to provide gifts to their hosts, the Chippewa.

Captain Balfour missed the prompt and instead demanded that the Chippewa should pledge their allegiance to the British Crown. The Chippewa said they would make no commitments to the British because they had just happened along for the meeting and they could make no alliance without authorization. They hoped the British would understand. Captain Balfour left a small number of men to occupy Fort Michilimackinac—without asking permission. The Chippewa seethed.

Major General Jeffery Amherst, commander-in-chief in the North American colonies, was determined to demonstrate that the British were rulers and Indians were subjects. He suspended gift giving, curtailed the sale of powder and guns, and he forbade traders to extend credit. These were disrespectful, intolerable acts. Only efforts to reach consensus among the Chippewa, Ottawa, and other tribes prevented immediate war with the British.

Intertribal discussions began with the Huron, Potawatomi, and other tribes as they tried to figure out what the best course of action would be. Native American young men from several tribes began harassing British traders, some settlers in bordering areas, and acting belligerently. In Indian-style warfare, these actions were often a prelude to war.

Pontiac opened the war in May 1862 with an attack on Detroit that killed and captured some British traders and soldiers. A supply barge convoy was attacked, and about 50 British were killed. A siege of Detroit began. Attacks followed on several of the British forts all the way down to Fort Ouiatenon on the Wabash River in Indiana. Native Americans from many tribes raided British settlements, traders, and military posts for the next two years.

All British forts west of Detroit were captured. Detroit and Fort Pitt were under siege; British settlers near Pitt were killed or driven off. Several battles like Bloody Run and Devil's Hole saw Shawnee, Mingo, Seneca, Ottawa, and Chippewa kill several hundred British soldiers and settlers. Refugees streamed back toward the Ohio River and the Appalachians.

The British thought that Pontiac was the sole leader of what they called a rebellion of their Indian subjects. The reality was that Pontiac was only one of many leaders from multiple tribes operating independently in a war that engulfed the Ohio and northern Mississippi valleys and the Great Lakes. The British needed to learn and Indians, smarting from British insults, were ready to be teachers. Chippewa Country was where Chippewa were sovereign, not the British.

> ### BAAGA'ADOWE (LACROSSE)
>
> Most woodlands tribes played a version of ball. Baggataway is one spelling of what the French Jesuit Jean de Brebeuf called La Crosse. The traditional version could include several hundred per side trying to hurl a leather ball stuffed with fur against a pole goal. Points were earned depending on where the ball struck. Sticks with nets at the end were used to carry the ball while opponents tried to dislodge the ball. Goals were usually 500 yards apart, there were no boundaries, and hands could not be used. The game was often violent. Games sometimes involved village versus village, bands from different tribes, and opposing clans. It was played by men, but there was a women's version, too.
>
> As with nearly every public event, prayers for success were common along with invoking of Manitous for help. Baaga'dowe was played at most major gatherings and celebrations. The famous game that led to capture of the English fort at Michilimacinac in 1762 was one of many played commonly around the area. There was no reason for the British to suspect subterfuge.
>
> Gatherings of Chippewa communities regularly involved commerce, visiting, and games like Baaga'dowe. Other communal activities were dancing, sharing of presents, moccasin games (a kind of shell game), races, and other contests. Gambling on outcomes was common.

In the heart of Chippewa Country, on June 2, 1762, the Chippewa played their most famous lacrosse (baggataway) game. They announced to the British commander of Fort Michilimackinac that they were going to have an intertribal match to honor the British. Women and children gathered to watch, and the British opened the fort so they could watch, too. As the game surged back and forth, the ball was flung into the fort, and the players rushed in and captured the fort. They used weapons the women had hidden.

Within a few minutes the entire garrison was killed or captured. All of the British traders were captured, and one was killed. Significantly, the resident Frenchmen were not harmed, and their goods were left alone. A Jesuit missionary, Father Jaunay tried to stop the killing, but the French population just watched.

Later, Langlade arrived with his Ottawa relatives and took the prisoners under his protection and warned the Chippewa that killing them all would be a mistake. Lieutenant Etheridge, the wounded commander of the fort, felt that Langlade saved his life.

In July, Langlade escorted the British soldiers, officers, and fur traders to Montreal. He was received warmly. General Thomas Gage, soon to replace

Expanding Chippewa Country

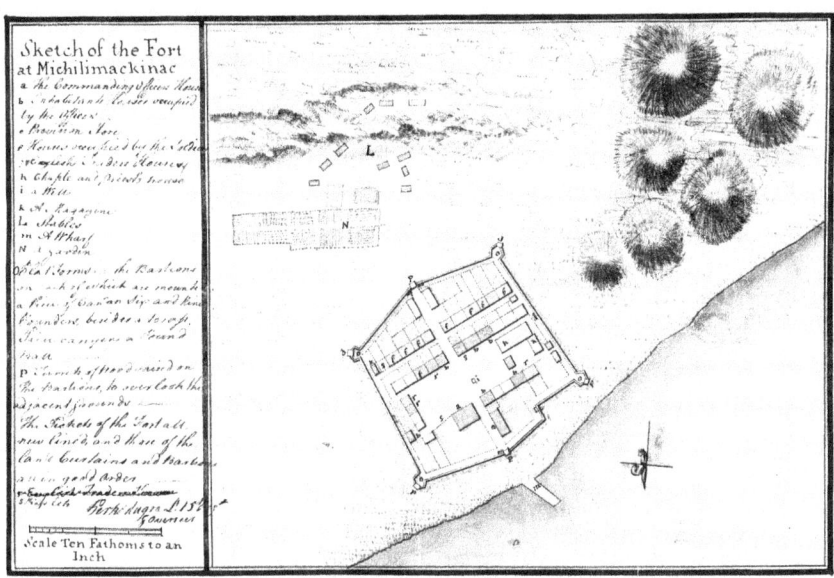

Sketch of the fort at Michilimackinac, ca. 1765. Fort Michilimackinac was built by the French in a key area of Chippewa Country, with Chippewa and Ottawa consent. In 1761, the British took control of the fort, without seeking the approval of Chippewa and Ottawa leaders. As a result of this insult, on June 2, 1763, the Chippewa captured the fort from the British through the ruse of a lacrosse game, as part of Pontiac's War. (William L. Clements Library)

the failed Amherst, met with the Ottawa and some Chippewa. Gage had the sense to listen to their lessons about how to live in Chippewa-Ottawa Country.

They offered peace to the British and indicated that they could speak for the Winnebago, Sauk, Fox, Ottawa, Chippewa, and Illinois Indians. They insisted that they had to have credit with the merchants, presents to compensate for their permission to the British to live in their country, and respectful treatment. They also pointed out that the French ancestry traders and metis were their relatives and they should continue to be traders. They would continue to live with their relatives in the winter.

Meanwhile Amherst pressed for a military punishment of these rebels. He failed repeatedly. Some Indians continued their attacks well into 1764, but the Chippewa-Ottawa suspended their actions. The British government changed, and Amherst was recalled. Prime Minister George Grenville determined to put relations with Indians on a realistic footing.

The British government had acquired Canada from the French, and it had lost a war with the Indians. The government was in debt from the French and Indian War and needed to solidify its control over their new territories. They decided to solve one of their problems by reassuring the French population of Canada that their language, religion, and property would be protected as British citizens and that Canada would be governed separately from the English seaboard colonies.

Grenville's cabinet agreed that the best way to deal with their losses in the Pontiac's War was to concede tribal independence and to prevent stirring up more war by allowing their colonial subjects to continue squatting on Indian lands west of the Appalachians. The Proclamation of 1763 insisted that the British held sovereignty over all of New France but that Indian tribes owned the land, were entitled to their own governments, and British funds would continue to provide presents to Indians as the French had done. No land could be purchased from Indians except by the British government.

Only recognized traders and British officials, definitely not settlers, would be allowed in this vast reserved area. The historian Michael McDonnell concluded that the Proclamation Act "was a declaration of Indian sovereignty, designed to appease the Indians" (McDonnell, 2015, p. 231).

In the context of North American history, the Proclamation Act in 1763 was a major irritant to the English colonists. They lost the lands they felt they had conquered from the French because the British government appeased Indians who had massacred colonists. The proclamation even denied them their right to settle in the Ohio Valley and other areas east of the Mississippi River.

Perhaps worse, the British government expected American Englishmen to pay for maintaining a permanent British army and to help the debt-ridden English government. New taxes like the Stamp Act of 1763 and the Quebec Act of 1774 exacerbated tensions between the colonists and the government of the empire. The Quebec Act served to channel the Great Lakes and Ohio Valley fur trade northward to Quebec and away from the American English. Many American Englishmen simply ignored the proclamation and continued pouring across the Appalachians. Bloodshed continued as Indians defended their lands.

Pontiac's War, although misnamed, ushered in a brief respite for eastern Chippewa Country. The British acceded to Indian dominance and followed Native American rules. The fur trade was restored in full force, and the various tribes learned how the trade was different when conducted by British companies. Of course, after the concessions forced from the British by Pontiac's War, the differences between the French and English techniques were minimized. In a relatively short span of time, the prosperity of the Chippewa and their relatives was restored.

The Great Lakes trade was in the hands of two trading companies for the most part. Smaller companies based in Montreal, Trois Rivieres, and Quebec did operate in some places just as some independent fur traders similar to the coureurs de bois of the French empire also existed. However, the well-established Hudson's Bay Company drew on their century of trade to expand into the Pays d'en Haut, the upper Mississippi, and the western reaches of the Great Lakes. Both trading companies employed the French ancestry experienced traders to interact with the many Indian tribes. The new "British" traders were mostly familiar relatives augmented by a few Englishmen.

Frenchmen and Indians had established communities at most of the posts, and they and their children grew up in the trade with their relatives. For instance, the leading traders at several posts, including Madeline Island, were members of the Cadotte family. Like Langlade of the Ottawa, the Cadottes were both Native American and French. They had business ties and kinship ties throughout the land.

Given the patrilocal tradition of most of the Chippewa, Ottawa, and most other tribes, the French-Indian families even developed their own communities and gradually evolved a new society that was integrated within traditional Indian communities. The French called these mixed descent people metis. The British and later, the Americans, called them half-breeds.

A Metis culture and society developed in the Red River Valley of the North; they are distinguished as Metis with a capital M. Centered on Winnipeg, but present at most of the Hudson's Bay Company trading forts, communities of intermingled children of the fur trade and their Chippewa, Cree, and other tribal relatives served the fur trade and their own interests. They intermingled and married one another for two centuries or more.

They developed a language, michif, that mixed French, Chippewa, Cree, and some English. Metis families were held together by kinship networks and Catholicism because the founders of the patrilineal families were French. Hudson's Bay Company Scottish employees were often integrated within the Metis societies along with their Indian and mixed-blood families.

Significant communities of metis existed throughout the Mississippi and Ohio Valleys as well as the Great Lakes region. Virtually every major town from St. Louis northward had numerous metis, French, Indian, and other migrants mixed into the communities. Their contribution was not only as traders but also as interpreters and intercultural brokers with the other peoples. The French needed interpreters, the English needed interpreters, and the Americans needed interpreters.

CHIPPEWA COUNTRY AT PEACE

All of the non-metis groups also needed workers to man the boats, winter with their relatives, staff the trading posts, and provide leadership in Chippewa communities. Langlade, the Ottawa war leader, and Cadotte, the Chippewa, were both among the leaders of Native American kinship networks, and they were fur traders working for French then English then American companies.

In Chippewa Country after 1783, the dominant company was the Northwest Company based in Montreal. It assumed control of most of the Great Lakes trading forts and expanded Grand Portage into a major entrepôt. Company owners shipped large trade canoe loads from Montreal into Chippewa Country trading forts. Voyageurs, mostly of French and metis descent, paddled and portaged the goods to central points like Michilimackinac, Madeline Island, and Grand Portage. Chippewa trappers brought their furs to the posts or traders, mostly metis, had amassed packs of furs over the winter and transported them to the forts. Traders and Chippewa sold their furs and stocked up for the winter. Many Chippewa also bought for the coming trapping season on credit for the goods they needed for winter trapping. Traders brought their stocks to whichever community they would live in for the winter.

Hundreds of Indians, traders, merchants, and families gathered for the coming of the boats at Grand Portage. It was always a festive time, and some parties achieved legendary status. Both Chippewa and the others smoothed the way with alcohol. Alcohol was an important trade item throughout Indian country and, as in other communities, its excesses led to abuse. Indian leaders tried to control it and even outlaw it completely because it relaxed standards of behavior and often led to violence and death.

Most of the trade, like most of life, was based on needs and luxuries. The Chippewa wanted pots, needles, blankets, cloth, guns, and gunpowder as well as beads, paint for their makeup, and beautiful things. For trapping, they needed traps and other gear. In most ways, these trade fairs were similar to those held in Indian country for centuries.

After a few weeks, fur-laden boats headed toward Montreal or other collection sites for the season's fur harvest. The Chippewa economy remained anchored in the cycle of winter hunting, sugarbush harvesting, fishing, and ricing expeditions that characterized traditional culture. In addition to spending more time trapping for the commercial market, the Chippewa also produced food for the trading fort communities including the garrisons.

Given the distances involved in transporting foods and the difficulty of farming for soldiers and traders, using Indian suppliers was a necessity. Chippewa leaders realized that this was a source of goods and strongly discouraged even fishing by the garrisons and company employees. Chippewa women were active suppliers of clothing and produce. Men were often hired to hunt for the traders and soldiers.

Although British companies replaced French companies, the changes did not usher in significant changes for the Chippewa. Madeline Island–La Pointe continued as a major cultural and trading center. It was where the Cadottes and their kinship network managed the fur trade pivot. The Chippewa leaders of the Midewiwin cemented Chippewa identity with annual ceremonies and refined their creation narrative. It was also a staging area for the continuing westward expansion of Chippewa Country. The conflicts of the Dakota Wars moved farther and farther west across northern Minnesota toward Pembina in North Dakota.

Fur trade channels were added for the western vanguard of Chippewa expansion. Rat Portage (Kenora) and beyond into Fort Gerry (Winnipeg) where the Hudson's Bay Company held sway benefited Chippewa commerce. Despite occasional outbreaks and even a few major campaigns by the Dakota Sioux, more trading posts were added. Chippewa communities like Red Lake and Leech Lake marked the western boundaries of Chippewa Country. Sandy Lake, north of Fond du Lac, was the home of Biauswah and his descendants and a staging area for continuing expansion. The Chippewa thrived throughout Minnesota, Wisconsin, Ontario, and Manitoba. Troubles for Indian people continued south and east of Chippewa Country.

Despite the Proclamation of 1763, American-English settlers continued to stream over the Appalachian Mountains and down the Ohio River. They violated the law with impunity and established towns like Boonesboro. The Indians of Chippewa Country watched the migration of English settlers and the inevitable battles, skirmishes, and conflict with some concern. English settlers arrived to stay and enforced their claims to land with violence. Indian nations fought back. For Indians the widespread American Revolution began as early as 1763 and would continue in various areas of the frontier until the full conflagration began in 1776.

Although geographically isolated, the Straits of Mackinac were nevertheless crossroads of trade, and Chippewa-Ottawa reconnoitering was quite extended. They knew what was transpiring in the English colonies and in Canada. Conflict between the British government and the English colonies was factored into Chippewa consensus-building conferences internally and with other tribes. Although historians tend to assume that all of the Indians were minions of the British during the Revolution, it was no more accurate than the same claim about Indians being the subservient tools of the French.

Chippewa leaders and all Indian leaders pursued their self-interest regardless of what the British wanted them to do. Over the centuries, the long-term strategy of the Chippewa, Ottawa, Potawatomi, and others was to act as the balance of power between contending European governments. When one threatened to establish overwhelming power, Native Americans either withdrew support for the dominant power or joined the side of the threatened power.

Short-term tactics were to defend their homelands against whichever European or Indian tribe seemed to want to conquer them. Indian allies rallied to support tribes that were threatened. This strategy accounts for the seeming inconstancy of the Chippewa as allies since the 17th century and for the large number of Chippewa who traveled long distances to fight. Threats to Chippewa centrality in the fur trade and to established protocols of international behavior were integrated within the overall balance of power strategy. Neither the French nor the British truly grasped Chippewa strategy and its importance to them.

A NEW CHIPPEWA PROBLEM: THE BRITISH FIGHT THEMSELVES

Arent Schuyler DePeyster became commander of Michilimackinac and exerted great effort toward convincing the Chippewas, Ottawas, and others to fight against the colonists if necessary. On the other hand, he tried to refurbish the fortifications in case the Chippewa decided to oppose Great Britain. DePeyster treated the Ottawa-Chippewa leaders with respect and convened multiple meetings with them.

Sagacious Chippewa-Ottawa leaders raised the rent and costs for allowing the British to remain. Although the British called their payments "gifts" and often used the term when describing Indian relations, it was understood that Indian leaders expected goods in return for permitting use of Michilimackinac and the British understood that "gifts" were the foundation of relations. Without them, support and permission could be withdrawn. "Gifts" were also the basis of trade exchanges with individual Indians, too. This was Chippewa Country, and they were the landlords in all senses of the word.

DePeyster was largely successful in convincing the Chippewa to be allies of the British because Chippewa leaders considered the alliance in the self-interest of the Chippewa. Even after the rebellion against the British Crown became a full-scale war and led to the invasion of Canada by American forces, the Chippewa did not abandon the British, but they did follow the progress of the war with an eye to making accommodations with the winning side. In 1775, a large contingent led by the ubiquitous Charles Langlade started for Quebec to fight against invading Americans, but the Americans withdrew before they could get there.

Other tribes also came to the relief of the British because Americans were a greater threat than the domesticated British. The British, with Indian and Canadian colonist support, secured Canada and began plans for using Canada as a launching pad for General John Burgoyne's campaign to split the incipient American country in half. British strategists believed that as many as 1,000 Indians would join the fray in 1777–1778, but many Indian leaders pivoted away because the British proved inept and blundering.

British commanders had not learned from the follies of Lord Amherst. Burgoyne issued instructions to various British commandants of forts to gather the necessary Indians. He told them that British quartermasters would distribute food and supplies directly to Indian "troops" instead of to the Native American leaders for their distribution to their followers.

Burgoyne also lectured Chippewa-Ottawa and other tribal leaders on their duties as subordinates. Most of the Indians, including the influential Langlade, just went home. Burgoyne might have had 100 lackadaisical Indian scouts when he met at Saratoga rather than the decisive Native American contingents that had defeated Braddock.

After 1778, Americans started winning more often. If there had not been continued aggression beyond the western borders of the colonies, it is likely that most of the Indian allies at least within the range of Chippewa Country would have suspended their support for the British entirely.

Withdrawal from war was especially likely when France entered the war as an ally of the Americans. Rumors abounded that the French would return and Indians were mostly hopeful. Instead the war continued well into 1784 with Indian attacks on the colonial forces being mostly successful. As with the French and Indian War, the British loss of the war was difficult to understand from the perspective of Chippewa Country.

THE NEW COUNTRY INTRUDES

The Treaty of Paris did not mention Native Americans. Britain simply transferred its sovereign claims to North America below a boundary for Canada to be determined later and east of the Mississippi. The treaty allowed British fur traders to operate in the Great Lakes, and the British left troops in place at forts as far south as Fort Miami along the Wabash River. Detroit and Michilimackinac were occupied by Americans. In 1796, Americans did occupy Fort Michilimackinac now located on Mackinac Island, but they also agreed to continue to pay for the privilege extended by the Chippewa and Ottawa.

At first, little changed for Chippewa County, but the Americans were disturbing, and there were so many of them. The fur traders remained the same French-Indian ancestry metis who were relatives; the trading posts remained the same or were expanded and worked by relatives. In 1783, the Northwest Company based in British Montreal continued the commerce under the same sorts of agreements with the Chippewa from Madeline Island–La Pointe to Michilimackinac. The Hudson's Bay Company set up competitive trading posts until the two companies merged.

Because of continuing American expansion, the Indian wars did not end. A bloody frontier war was centered in Ohio, Indiana, and western Pennsylvania, which the Americans called the Northwest War or George Washington's War. The Chippewa journeyed southward to help defeat Generals Harmar and Arthur St. Clair as an Indian coalition identified with Little Turtle, a Miami war leader, inflicted severe losses on American invaders. St. Clair lost several hundred in the largest defeat of an American army by an Indian army. Despite these victories, the Battle of Fallen Timbers in 1795 led to a large cession of territory by Indian nations. Despite the treaty forced on them, Native Americans continued to fight the continued expansionist Americans.

Given the increasing dominance of the United States, it should be no surprise that the Chippewa supported the British in the War of 1812. Some of them had been fighting Americans already, and the British were not a threat to Indian nations. Brutal warfare and continued American encroachment created stress and divisions within Indian tribes, and they turned to religion just as they had after the French and Indian War. Tenkswatawa, the Shawnee Prophet, had a vision that revealed how Native Americans could counter the Americans.

Nearly all American Indian religious beliefs included a recognition of the power of visions in offering correctives to crises. The Shawnee Prophet's dream was especially powerful, as he called for unity among all of the tribes being achieved by rejecting foreign goods and practices while returning to the values of the past. Tribal creators had shown the way, and the Prophet spread the word of unity, rejection of foreigners and their goods, and a return to pan-Indian values.

Just as Neolin's prophecies had assisted Pontiac and the war leaders of the coalition that defeated the British, the Shawnee Prophet had a counterpart.

Tecumseh, the Prophet's brother, was a renowned Shawnee war leader who added the political acumen necessary to resist the Americans. He, too, was aided by the Manitios, and he was a magnificent, compelling orator. He and his prophet brother created a large Indian town, Prophetstown, and called for Indian unity and abandonment of former tribal animosities. The Americans, led by the governor and commander of the Territory of Indiana, William Henry Harrison, provoked the Battle of Tippecanoe in 1795 and burned Prophetstown. Tecumseh had been away, so Harrison provoked a war.

Tecumseh gathered forces in the style of all tribal war leaders and moved to join the British in Canada because the War of 1812 that pitted the United States against Great Britain merged into the continuing conflict between the United States and its settlers against Native American tribes. The British made him an officer and recognized him as the dominant leader of the hundreds of Native Americans who fought alongside the British and Canadian troops.

Detroit was taken from the Americans, and a few hundred Chippewa and a small number of British troops took Fort Michilimackinac without a shot being fired. Tecumseh was killed at the Battle of the Thames in 1813 while opposing the invasion of Canada by the Americans.

Most of the southeastern Chippewa based at the Mackinac Straits had been resistant to joining the Prophet's movement. The southwestern Chippewa, centered at Madeline Island and Chequamegon Bay, had responded enthusiastically to the extent that many discarded their Mide religious bundles to demonstrate their return to the old values. Both sent men to support the British in the War of 1812.

The Americans were clearly a threat to the trade and kinship network that formed the corpus of Chippewa prosperity and dominance. However, Chippewa leaders did keep their options open and often made tentative gestures and explorations with various American leaders. If the British lost again, despite Native American help, the Chippewa did not want to be the target of revenge by the Americans the way other Indians had been.

Fortunately for the Chippewa, changeover to the American hegemony did not happen instantly. Trade continued in the hands of the same British companies, and it was conducted by the same metis or by Americans who followed the pattern of becoming kin. American traders quickly realized the place of Chippewa women in the vital kinship webbing that captured the fur trade and followed French and English patterns of marrying the powerful, influential women. The Cadottes at La Pointe and other trading posts soon had American in-laws who added to the French-British-American-metis-Chippewa.

Chippewa Country experienced what Andrew Blackbird, an Ottawa and historian, called a "golden age" from 1812 to 1836 (McConnell, 2015, p. 322). They continued to expand their economy, were able to begin a population recovery from the wars, and opened commerce in fishing, wild rice, and wild game with the burgeoning American economy and population of the Great Lakes. Even the advent of the American Fur Company in 1822 and, at first, the opening of the Erie Canal in 1825 merely increased opportunity. Most of Chippewa Country was not fertile enough to attract the hordes of Americans demanding land as they had in the southern Mississippi Valley and Ohio Valley.

The "golden age" did not last.

5

American Incorporation and Colonization

Despite the Chippewa's loss of independence to the United States and Canada, Chippewa communities and bands continued a Chippewa existence and maneuvered to remain in their homelands and to maintain a distinct identity. Chippewa leaders developed new techniques in the new environment. They never stopped trying to secure the welfare of Chippewa people and to seek the support of Manitos.

After the Napoleonic Wars in the western world and the War of 1812 in North America, a new order began with all Native American nations, Canada, the United States, and Western Europe. For Western Europe, the end of the Napoleonic Wars initiated the Pax Britannica balance of power and an end to the Anglo-French conflicts throughout the world. In Chippewa Country the result was a separation into Canadian and American spheres of control.

U.S. imperialism increased its domain from sea to shining sea and beyond. The Americans moved to subdue and corral all Native Americans enveloped by American expansion. In Canada, Great Britain steadily transferred governing powers to Canadian provincial governments operating under the protection of the British Empire and eventually to the Canadian Confederation in 1867. British-Canadian Indian policy was similar to that of the United States, without the concomitant warfare.

The most significant result of the War of 1812 for the Chippewa was that Chippewa, and other Indian nations, were now a domestic issue as far as the rest of the world was concerned. U.S. sovereignty was a barrier to other nation-states allying separately with Indian tribes as in the past. Chippewa leaders could no longer play one power against the other. The Chippewa story in Canada split from the one now within the United States. After 1815, the centuries-long Chippewa hegemony was gone. American actions even in Chippewa Country were no longer controlled by the Chippewa as they had controlled the French and the British. The rules had changed.

Initially, the victory of the United States in the Revolution appeared to be no more significant than when the British had supplanted the French. The United States was expected to be the new father to Chippewa children. Chippewa leaders must have been well content with their world even as late as the 1820s. The few Americans who made their way to Sault Ste. Marie, Madeline, and other parts of Chippewa Country arrived with hat in hand to either trade or seek permission to use the forts emptied by the British. Chippewa expansion across the northern reaches of Minnesota and even into the Turtle Mountains was progressing well, even if the Dakota launched occasional forays into newly acquired additions to Chippewa Country. The Dakota Wars just offered the opportunity for the young to acquire honors and develop leadership experience.

The story of the Dakota Wars was one of glory, bravery, and success from a Chippewa perspective. Indeed, even as the United States expanded, Chippewa Country reached its widest expanse—from Michigan to parts of Montana. Its center of gravity did shift from Sault Ste. Marie to Madeline Island and the western shore of Lake Superior, and the bulk of Chippewa population moved to northern Wisconsin and Minnesota. By midcentury, Leech Lake and Red Lake had assumed roles equal to Madeline Island as cultural centers.

Each of the Chippewa communities remained autonomous during the 1820s, despite Americans' preference for considering them a single, unified tribe. They continued the ebb and flow of their cyclical use of resources. Webs of kinship reinforced by cross-community clan membership that characterized the Chippewa nation continued to provide connections, but as communities spread further and further apart, the ties were diluted into regional networks that were not as intimately intertwined as before Chippewa expansion.

The unifying factors of war against the Dakota, of Midewiwin as a common ceremonial religion, of language, of common foundational beliefs, and of trade connections provided identity for Chippewa people, but ties

> **CANADA AND THE U.S. BORDER**
>
> During the 19th century the Indian policies of Canada and the United States reinforced regional differences and simultaneously stimulated stronger Chippewa identity as a tribe. Subdivisions that oriented Chippewa communities to regional concerns were reinforced by the establishment of a border between Canada and the United States and by the gradual admission of the states of Michigan (1819), Wisconsin (1854), and Minnesota (1859). The new dynamic of interactions presented a challenge to Chippewa leadership and the survival of independent Chippewa communities.

grew steadily more tenuous and difficult to maintain. Distance and even dialectical changes increased centripetal forces. The actions of the United States exacerbated pressures against a single Chippewa identity. Identification with bands increased as reservations were created.

Chippewa Country's regional divisions marked by clusters of similar intertwined villages and communities gained greater traction and formed quasi-barriers against unified actions. By the 1830s more than 1,500 miles, three of the Great Lakes, and numerous other waterways and forests separated the most western communities from the original homeland. Regionally based issues elicited various responses as Chippewa communities had to deal with differing intrusions and actors.

In the Canadian region, the northern Chippewa maintained communities from Quebec to Manitoba and beyond to Saskatchewan; the Sault Ste. Marie–Boweting–Machilimackinac Chippewa interacted back and forth across the U.S.–Canadian border forming a somewhat cohesive collection of communities; the western shores of Lake Superior centered on Madeline Island was the epicenter of Chippewa culture and acted as a staging area for western expansion; and the rest of the southeastern Chippewa continued to spread in northern Minnesota and on across the Red River into North Dakota. Frequently, the Chippewa from the different regions did interact particularly at the seams of the regions—Chippewa residence was fluid and followed opportunities.

NEW PATTERNS IN CHIPPEWA COUNTRY: THE AMERICAN DISPOSITION

In the governments and communities of Canadian and American decision makers, discussions about what to do with and about the Indians were a major concern after the War of 1812. The Chippewa and many other Indians remained free in their homelands. American attitudes toward Indians would determine the course governments pursued.

Burgeoning populations of both countries demanded more land and access to resources. The Americans and Canadians decided that Indian communities could remain but intended to control terms of survival. It was not acceptable that Indians would continue to control their resources and govern themselves. Certainly Indians could not interfere with national expansion and economic development by American businesses and settlers.

The Indians would have to bend to the will of the self-proclaimed rights of Anglo civilization. It was widely assumed that Indians would disappear within the bosom of the racially and culturally superior societies. If they did not assimilate, they were doomed to die out, concluded most analysts. In the meantime, Americans should guide Indians to civilization and coerce them into giving up their tribal, savage ways. By the latter 19th century, a British writer called this civilizing duty "the White Man's Burden." Popular opinion pictured Indians as primitive peoples who did not even use their lands' resources.

The Americans and Canadians cleaved to these premises about their relationships with Indian nations for a century and a half. Each country designed systems and adopted techniques of control that fit the respective political structures of each, but goals were consistent for both nations. The Indians had to surrender their lands through treaties and give up their ways of life to become sedentary farmers. The Indians had to give up their religions and become Christians. The Native Americans would be guided in their lives through a paternalistic structure of control that would usher them into Canadian and American society.

A few Indians could not be allowed to stand in the way of what both countries saw as what would be called "manifest destiny." Few questioned the right of Anglo civilization to control North America and its indigenous peoples. American racism was another factor in the equation in which Chippewa leaders had to operate during the 19th century and beyond.

Declaring that Indians and their lands were part of the United States was just a beginning. American-crafted policies and American control required action by the new government. The Americans expected to be able to live in their country whether Indians were there or not, and they demanded that the government take steps to acquire land from Indian control and to protect Americans from Indian retaliation. Often American squatters forced government action by simply moving into Indian lands and daring Indians to retaliate. In most of Indian country, Americans overwhelmed Indian nations through sheer force of numbers.

Chippewa history unfolded on several levels in the new order dominated by Canada and the United States: national Indian policies, Chippewa communities' struggles to maintain separation and cohesion, individual Chippewa attempting to make a living and retain cultural integrity, and relations with local populations that were often virulently anti-Chippewa and contemptuous of their own countries' policies and promises.

Chippewa leaders developed tactics of interaction designed to secure as much independence and control as possible. Often this included acting in consort with other American Indian tribes and in league with other Chippewa communities. Chippewa leaders worked to develop alliances with individuals and groups of Canadians or Americans to influence the actions of the federal and state policy makers.

Members of Congress, church leaders, missionaries, eastern progressive organizations, and local neighbors were drawn into assisting Chippewa communities. Alliance building, as it always had been, sometimes worked to advance Chippewa interests and sometimes it backfired. Some individuals and small bands simply lived on the peripheries in areas Americans did not want.

National policy level efforts were hampered by continuous intrusions of non-Chippewa pouring into Chippewa Country, bringing their own approaches to dealing with Indians. The rapacity of many American leaders extended to racism and willingness to act illegally in taking lands and resources from Indians. Incidents of violence became common.

Some of the new arrivals did seek to relate honorably with the Chippewa and their communities. They protested American lawlessness and exploitation of Indians, but they were not dominant in the frontier societies or even in Washington. As Indians moved aside and cooperated to support American communities, some valued the Chippewa as neighbors. The Americans in Wisconsin, Michigan, and elsewhere even signed petitions to allow Indians to remain in their homelands during the mid-19th century after coexisting with them for a few years.

American immigrants introduced new means of making a living. Chippewas had to adapt their economic cycles to an economy owned by Americans and Canadians and to the people that the lumber, mining, and fishing industry introduced. Chippewa communities had to adjust to increasing pressure on their traditional ways of life, religion, education, and even diets. After the mid-19th century, the Chippewa worked within new rules and laws and governing styles imposed by Americans and

Canadians. American agents and missionaries joined the Chippewa world, and they demanded change from traditional values and lifestyles.

The Chippewa became wage earners. Women moved into domestic work in American communities. Men cut lumber and worked in the fishing industry and as farm hands. The Chippewa men and women sold wild rice, fish, and game to restaurants. Blueberries flourished in cut over land, and Native Americans sold them in birchbark baskets to tourists and immigrants alike. Many Chippewa moved to the growing American towns to eke out a living doing odd jobs along with seasonal employment.

Some encouraged their children to go to the schools that missions built for both Americans and Indians. The Indian Service started schools on reservations after the 1850s. A few were fortunate enough to be sent to private schools. Even fewer had merchant parents who could afford to send them to schools in Canada or back east in the United States.

Most Chippewa lived in poverty. Quite a few towns and cities had pockets of Chippewa families. The old cycle of Chippewa economy could not be maintained as Indians were blocked from their old lands and forced to remain more sedentary. They did keep using natural resources where possible. Ricing, maple sugar manufacturing, fishing, hunting, and gathering of berries and other edible plants continued.

Patterns of Control

America's first intrusions into Chippewa Country revolved around the fur trade and establishing an American presence like the British posts. Government agents arrived who sought to influence Chippewa behaviors and guide them into American society. Britain continued its relationships that existed before the Revolution, and the Hudson's Bay Company remained a quasi-political and economic force in the eventual provinces of Manitoba, Saskatchewan, and westward. The Northwest Company operated the fur trade along the southern Canadian border through Fort William in the Thunder Bay of Lake Superior. "Canadian" Chippewa already knew English ways.

In the United States, the Americans established government trading posts called factories that operated from 1802 to 1822. But by the 1820s the political power of John Jacob Astor's American Fur Company secured abolition of the government posts and acquired a near monopoly stretching from Lake Erie to the Red River of the North. Later, the American Fur Company added posts all the way to the West Coast of North America.

The Company hired many of the mixed-blood traders that had been merchants under the British and even earlier in French companies. Many of these traders were also Chippewa and were part of the web of kinship that formed the basis of commerce in Chippewa Country. Metis intermingled with a few Americans remained the backbone of commerce with the Indians.

The fur trade remained an important source of wealth for the Indians and Americans through the 1820s and a bit later on the plains and Rocky Mountains west of Chippewa Country. The American Fur Company played an important role in the evolution of societies in Chippewa Country. The trading posts created in the midst of Chippewa communities added to a magnetic draw forming larger communities.

Trading posts and traders lived in the midst of Chippewa communities with their relatives and the posts acting as centers of growing Chippewa and non-Indian community growth. As more American merchants entered Chippewa Country, the old protocols of gift giving, credit, and generosity were replaced with the impersonal approach of the market economy. Profit was the purpose of sales. Gradually, a few missionaries appeared.

Company personnel included the mixed-blood Chippewa scions of marriage alliances along with American additions. Increasingly, the personnel played an important role as intercultural brokers who combined being interpreters and influential persons in Chippewa communities with acting as agents of empire for the American nation.

The same pattern occurred in Canada. In the Red River Valley the Metis drew together a French–Celtic–English–Native American synthesis. They developed the Red River cart trade from Winnipeg, Manitoba, to St. Paul, Minnesota during the first half of the 20th century. Many from this group were also the fabled voyageurs and engaged the fur trade on both sides of the border.

Yet, perhaps for the first time in their history, the Chippewa and their communities were unable to determine their own fate. Even the Canadians, still governed from London and part of the Empire, were a behemoth compared to the Chippewa. Native Americans knew the power of the United States. They had seen armies more numerous than all of the Chippewa combined.

The most generous estimate of the number of Chippewa was about 35,000, and they were scattered throughout Chippewa Country as a minority within Canada's 1,500,000 and the United States' 4,000,000 in the 1820s and 1830s. Each of the nation states developed machinery for governing Indians and objectives in Indian policy. The Native American leaders had to save what independence they could salvage while not provoking American and Canadian impulses to simply destroy them.

The Chippewa story after 1815 requires inclusion of the Indian policies of the United States and Canada to understand what happened. The

Chippewa and other Native Americans were circumscribed by decisions made elsewhere that determined their responses to the challenges of living a good life as Native Americans.

INCORPORATING THE CHIPPEWA: POLICIES AND THE MACHINERY OF GOVERNING

American policies were designed to further American economic interests and American control of resources. The Americans also stressed their desire to carry out a Christian duty to civilize Indians and rescue them from savagery. Drawing on their experiences with the Native American nations of the trans-Appalachian Ohio and Mississippi Valleys, the United States utilized treaties to force Indians into accepting the American idea of territorial boundaries for each tribe, acknowledging American sovereignty in theory and practice, and selling Indian title to their lands so Americans could get on with the business of expansion.

Various Chippewa leaders signed 46 treaties and agreements with the United States between 1785 and 1902. Some treaties involved several tribes, and others were exclusively with leaders of particular bands or regional groupings of Chippewa bands. No single treaty was ever signed with all Chippewa nations within the United States. British and Canadian officials also concluded treaties with Chippewa bands.

In addition to treaties, the United States moved to establish the intellectual and institutional sinews of

This bust of Flat Mouth, an important Leech Lake leader, was sculpted by Francis Vicenti in 1856 and is displayed in the U.S. capitol building. Flat Mouth was a key negotiator with the United States, signing every major 19th-century treaty. (U.S. Senate)

control over Native Americans within a political system created and frequently altered by the United States. Indian involvement in the structures was at the discretion of the United States; generally, Indians were not included in planning and decision making. They were expected to follow the dictates of the United States.

American military forces were scattered in Chippewa and Dakota Country, and each state or territory maintained a militia. Agents could call on these forces and often threatened the Chippewa with them. Treaty negotiations usually included the presence of American troops. Although the ultimate source of U.S. jurisdiction over Indians is based on its military strength, its "irresistible power" as Supreme Court Justice John Marshall opined, Americans rationalized other justifications.

The U.S. Constitution's Commerce Clause indicates that "Congress shall have the Power . . . to regulate Commerce with foreign Nations, and among the several States, and with the Indian Tribes" (Article 1, section 8, clause 3). Additionally, the Treaty Clause gives the president and the Senate the power to make treaties—including treaties with Indian tribes. According to American constitutional law, these two clauses provide all of the authority necessary for the federal government to have complete control over Indians and Indian tribes. These interpretations remain the justification for federal control today.

Justifications also include the Doctrine of Discovery, which is a tenet of international law that recognizes the right of the Christian discoverer of a land and the conqueror of its people to govern the discovered or conquered lands and populations. Americans argued that the United States assumed the discovery rights of Great Britain after the Revolution and was the de facto conqueror of the Indian nations, and therefore the United States has the right to govern them.

Moral duty is another justification. By becoming a nation, the United States assumed a trustee role for the weaker Indian nations. This trusteeship is described in many of the 700 or so treaties with Indian tribes. Protection of them and their property entails making laws to regulate Indians and their lands according to the U.S. Supreme Court and the laws of Congress.

Chippewa leaders did not necessarily agree with the United States' reasoning. Many Chippewa frequently reminded Americans that they had not been conquered and that their nationhood had been given to them by their creators, not the Americans. They also strove to maintain identity as tribes and the right to exercise governing powers throughout the 19th century and beyond. The Chippewa and other tribes had to acquiesce to American power, but few embraced the American justifications or ceased opposing American control.

Indian policy was enacted by all three branches of the federal government. Congress provided legislation that described some of the relationship with American Indians and their governments. Congress approved the budget and treaties. The executive branch negotiated treaties, developed policies, and administered Indian policies. Initially, the supervision of Indian relations was included within the War Department, and Congress authorized an Indian Department in the 1820s. In 1849 the Indian Service was transferred to the Department of the Interior; it became the Bureau of Indian Affairs in the 20th century.

Agents were appointed and dispatched to carry out the wishes of the government and to convey these wishes to Native Americans. The first agency for Chippewa Country was at Sault Ste. Marie. This agent was responsible for Indians throughout the upper Midwest. Their role expanded as American power and contact expanded and agencies or subagencies sprouted at Madeline Island and then west into Minnesota.

Federal courts described the relationship between Indians and their governments with the United States through the process of judicial review. Chief Justice John Marshall wrote the majority opinions that are the foundation of American Indian law. The Marshall decisions are *Johnson v. McIntosh* (1823), *Cherokee Nation v. Georgia* (1831), and *Worcester v. Georgia* (1832).

Ironically, two of these seminal cases did not involve Indians as litigants, and the third was rejected as not being filed properly. Yet all other Indian court decisions have flowed from these decisions that apply to all Indian nations and their relationship with the United States. More than one legal scholar has noted that it is necessary to have a strong sense of irony when practicing Indian law.

Johnson and Graham's Lessee v. McIntosh offered Marshall the opportunity to describe land ownership within the borders of the United States. The court opined that the United States was the sole owner because they were the successors of the country that had discovered the United States. In effect, the United States confiscated all of Indian lands through the Doctrine of Discovery, which Marshall indicated was part of international law. However, he said, Indian tribes had a right to occupy and use the land until the United States decided it needed the land for some other use. Indian possessory interest is also called Indian right of occupancy and Indian title.

As Indians do not own the land, they cannot sell it to individuals or to other countries. Only Congress can authorize sale of the land or other use of Indian land. As the owner of the land, the federal government can decide. However, Marshall indicated that the United States had to secure Indian title from the tribes in order to displace them. The United States had to either take the land by legislation or secure it through purchase of the Indian title. This decision explains why treaties included paying Indians for their title even if the United States was the owner of the land.

Marshall elaborated on the relationship between Indians–Indian nations and the United States in *Cherokee Nation v. Georgia*. The tribe had sued in federal court as a foreign nation to exclude Georgia law from within their borders. A divided court with Marshall writing for the majority answered the question of what the appropriate relationship was. He opined that the Cherokee Nation was not a foreign government because it was subject to the United States (so the case was not heard). Marshall reasoned that the Cherokee Nation and all Indian nations were "domestic, dependent nations."

This relationship was like that of a trustee to a ward, which required the United States to protect its wards and to act in their interests. The trust relationship remains one of the principles of Indian law and a justification for continuing regulation of Indian tribes and individual Indians. The United States holds Indian lands and its resources in trust.

According to Marshall's opinion, states had no jurisdiction to interfere with these sovereign governments. State jurisdiction could not extend to Indian lands and Indian people residing in the lands even when the lands are within the boundaries of a state. Marshall indicated that only the United States could make laws applying to tribes and individual Indians in order to carry out its trust responsibility.

Even as the federal courts acted to define the relationship of Indians, states, and federal government, Congress exercised its responsibility to provide regulatory laws that included all within the United States. Commerce

---

WORCESTER V. GEORGIA

The Supreme Court case *Worcester v. Georgia* (1832) described Indian governments as having inherent sovereign power to govern themselves. Sovereignty was derived from their own people long before the United States came into existence. The United States recognized this sovereignty by entering into treaties with tribes. Tribes could continue governing their own people and territories, with the United States occasionally assisting them with laws for their own good. John Marshall's other two decisions, *Johnson v. McIntosh* and *Cherokee Nation v. Georgia*, join with the *Worcester* decision to lay the basis of federal Indian law and the relationship of Indians and their governments to the federal government within the United States.

within the United States and with Indian nations was an area of some confusion after the Revolution.

A series of intercourse acts beginning in 1790, Congress created trade factories and licensing for trade with Indians, decreed that only the United States could purchase lands from tribes or enter into agreements with them and legislated against continuing encroachment on Indian lands. States and individuals were excluded from legally contracting with tribes.

The intercourse acts tried to control the many squatters who poured into the Ohio Valley and beyond by establishing Indian national borders and increasing penalties for squatters. Frontiersmen and corporations generally ignored congressional efforts. Enforcement was not within the resources of the United States and was in many ways antithetical to the expansionist policies of the Northwest Ordinance and the demands of American people.

The factory system established trading posts where the only legal commerce could occur with the idea that Indians would not be cheated and that this would stabilize relations. The intercourse acts were often violated because the weak federal government could not enforce them and American merchants were determined to evade the law. In 1822 Congress capitulated to business interests and abolished the government factories.

One result of what Francis Prucha, a premier scholar of federal Indian policy, called an "invasion" of Indian country was a great deal of violence as Indians fought to preserve the lands guaranteed to them in treaties with the United States. Indian resistance led to reprisals and demands for federal action by the encroaching settlers or corporations. American governments could not abide Indian violence against Americans even if Americans were behaving criminally.

In the 1790s American forces invaded Indian country in the Ohio Valley in response to Indian resistance to illegal immigrants. First General Josiah Harmar was trounced, and then General Arthur St. Clair lost several hundred of his forces. Militias were no match for confederations of Indians. The confederation was led by Little Turtle, a Miami war leader, but included multiple tribal forces with leaders of their own. Americans refused to accept defeat and raised more troops.

Some Chippewa joined the Native American resistance coalition. By 1795, General Anthony Wayne had assembled an army of regulars and militia to counter the coalition. He won the Battle of Fallen Timbers despite losing more men than the coalition forces.

Realistically, the Indian allies decided that they could not continue to fight ever-increasing American forces, which destroyed towns and decimated Indian armies no matter how many more men Americans lost. General Wayne dictated the Treaty of Greenville, which ceded much of the Ohio Valley to the United States and established the Ohio and Wabash Rivers as borders separating Indian nations from settlers.

Americans continued the pattern of violating guaranteed borders that led to Indians responding to defend their borders. American outrage at Indian resistance led to demands that the Indians be punished. The United States responded to their citizens by military actions and treaties of purchase. By the 1820s Chippewa leaders understood the pattern they had seen farther south. They concluded that military resistance was not possible.

Instead, Chippewa leaders called on Americans to honor promises of protection or at least to pay for the lands and resources being taken at the behest of American corporations and settlers. Cases of settler violence, illegal taking of resources, and other violations were appealed by Chippewa leaders to the new American agents throughout the 19th century.

American decision makers debated the best course of action to take with the lands that they were steadily adding to the United States. The Louisiana Purchase more than doubled the size of the United States. It was followed by General Andrew Jackson's attack on Florida leading to the sale by Spain in 1819. The Mexican breakaway country, Texas, joined the United States in 1846. The Mexican War brought even more tribes and lands.

U.S. policy first turned to removing Indians from their homelands to newly acquired territory. The West was so vast that it offered America the solution of simply moving all of the tribes east of the Mississippi River to a designated Indian Territory. This permanent solution would leave tribes out of the way of the Americans and open the rich resources of the Mississippi Valley to the expanding cotton industry and farms of the Midwest.

Although President Andrew Jackson asked Congress for the Indian Territory Act and the Indian Removal Act in 1830, several earlier presidents and American leaders had called for removal westward for Indians long before. Removal to out-of-the-way places became Indian policy for a few decades.

American rationale was that removal allowed Indians time to become civilized while removed from the deleterious influences of the American population. The best that Americans could do for them was to civilize them. To this end, Congress appropriated funds in 1819 to provide education through missionary-run schools. The Civilization Act was the first of many appropriations designed to civilize Indians by teaching them the American skills of farming and Christianity. They were expected to blend into the American population after giving up their Indian title to land. Few Americans could conceive of an enduring separate existence for Indian nations.

Removal of Indians from one area to another was pursued all during the 19th century in various areas of the country. Indian Territory was the end of the Trail of Tears for the Cherokee and about 40 other tribes between 1830 and 1890. Some of the tribes removed were from east of the Mississippi, and some were plains tribes like the Comanche, Southern Cheyenne, and Kiowa. All Indians noted that removal was enforced by American forces if tribal members chose not to remove to Indian country. Indian leaders weighed their options for delaying removal.

Removal as a policy affected Chippewa Country. Some Ottawa and Potawatomi were removed as they lived in areas first desired by expanding Americans and American economic interests. The bulk of the Chippewa Nation was not forced to remove to Indian Territory. They were fortunate not to occupy areas that were desired for settlement or farming when the removal impetus was at its greatest.

However, the removal idea did lead to one of the great tragedies of the Chippewa Nation, the Sandy Lake debacle of 1850. The impulse to concentrate all Chippewa into a single area reared its head again in the 1870s with the creation of White Earth Reservation.

American expansion rapidly made removal policy obsolete. The flood of settlement left islands of Indian tribes, and Indian Territory did not have enough room. The Gold Rush of 1849 accompanied by settlers rushing along the Oregon Trail and subsequent silver discoveries brought thousands of Americans west of the Mississippi in less than a generation. Around 1850, American decision makers began the policy of sequestration, which was applied to all of the tribes.

Reservations were the new answer to the Indian question. Consolidating Indian nations into small relatively out-of-the way parcels designated by the United States offered opportunities to keep Indians from obstructing American expansion by wandering around. On reservations, assimilationist tactics would convert Indians from savages to Americans living on private property while practicing one of the forms of Christianity favored by the federal government, and accepting the replacement of their traditional governments. Surrounded by American communities, Indians would succumb to the superior civilization and merge into the American minority populations.

One idea was that reservations could be broken into individual allotments for tribal members. Early treaties with the tribes of Chippewa Country in Michigan had designated this approach by allowing individual Indians to take their "share" of treaty payments and buy their land back as individual owners. This technique left Chippewa communities interspersed among American settlers in much of Michigan, and many were declared Michigan citizens.

The first American agent to the Chippewa was based in Sault Ste. Marie and was responsible for relations with not only the Chippewa but the other tribes of the Great Lakes and Upper Midwest. Agents were to bring together tribes for treaty negotiations, to support the civilizing forces like missionaries, to try to secure peace between tribes, and to try to prevent friction between Americans and Indians. As the century progressed, they were expected to force assimilation by outlawing Indian religions.

After 1850 when civilizing Indians became the focus of American efforts on reservations, the Indian Service turned to ever-more-active ordering of Indians' lives. Most reservations had agents and a few subagents in residence. Agents controlled the distribution of resources even if they were payments due Indians. They used their power over annuities and rations to force compliance with their orders. Measures to control Indians did not occur all at once but rather as opportunities changed and historical events altered possibilities. The core goal remained to force Indians to give up their ways of life and substitute what the Americans thought Indians should do.

Throughout the course of the 19th and extending into the 20th century, Native Americans were required to relinquish their title to the United States, which then sold or gave the land to Americans under various homesteading laws and land sales. Acquiring Indian title progressed throughout the 19th century even as American policies of removal and reservations were evolving.

Treaties began with the Michigan Chippewa because this is where Americans demanded land and access to Chippewa Country first. There was no need to acquire land until there was demand, so the pattern was sporadic and locally based responses to local pressures amid the overall policies of removal and reservations.

Although there were 49 treaties and agreements signed with various Chippewa entities, they generally adhered to a pattern similar to those with other tribes. The general outline of the treaties was to include stipulations of American sovereignty and goodwill toward Indians and declarations that there would continue to be peace and the Chippewa would have peace with the Dakota and other tribes.

Treaties described the lands that were being sold to the United States utilizing well-known geographic markers. Some treaties, like the one at Prairie du Chien in 1825, established boundaries separating tribes so the United States could determine which tribes had title to lands desired by the United States. Chippewa people had to learn about boundaries in American law.

Other clauses in treaties stipulated the amount of money, goods, and services that the Chippewa would receive for giving up their lands. Schools, technical assistance for converting to American farm practices, and annuities were part of the payments in nearly all of the treaties. Chippewa leaders insisted that they retain rights to hunt, fish, and gather in the ceded territories, and the United States agreed. Nearly all of the treaties and agreements contained these guaranteed treaty rights.

Chippewa leaders negotiated from weakness but determinedly. They could be told, as the Turtle Mountain and Red Lake Chippewa were in 1862, that the United States could bring 100,000 soldiers to take the land if the Chippewa were too difficult. Despite the reality of power, Chippewa leaders were knowledgeable of treaty processes and terms of earlier treaties. They negotiated within a framework of agreed upon goals and often managed to include terms Americans would regret later.

Often Chippewa leaders began deliberations by reminding the American commissioners of past wrongs and treaty violations. They usually asked that Americans protect them from fraud, alcohol sales, squatters, and thieves of Indian resources as part of treaty provisions. Usually, the Chippewa leaders brought advisers like missionaries, traders, and western-educated Chippewa. They often lobbied for particular terms and goals with congressmen, business leaders, national church organizations, and other pressure groups. Chippewa leaders were not naïve, and they were willing to threaten, too.

A constant concern for Chippewa people was avoiding removal to Indian Territory. Early treaties allowed the Chippewa to remain in their lands not ceded until the United States decided to take them. In effect the Chippewa managed to keep enclaves within their lands, but throughout the first half of the 19th century, the specter of removal was a constant factor.

Even after the removal policy had given way to the policy of reservations within their homelands, Chippewa still had to negotiate where they would be allowed to stay. Promised reservations did not materialize for nearly 40 years for the Turtle Mountain Chippewa, and efforts to induce or coerce Chippewa bands to move to a new reservation, White Earth, continued into the 20th century.

Several reservations ceased to exist as bands had to move to White Earth. Some Michigan-enclosed Chippewa were not even reservations but rather were allotted individually owned lands within the larger American communities. Two bands within Wisconsin received reservations only in the 1930s.

Treaties and their implementation posed problems for the Chippewa. U.S. commissioners negotiated the lowest price they could for the lands they were acquiring, which meant that Chippewa Country was sold for far less than what the land later sold for. Resources like timber were compensated for, but not at market value. Most of the treaties indicated that the type of compensation would be determined by the United States at a later time, and expected money was often converted to goods of dubious use to the Chippewa.

Payments were habitually late and often distributed capriciously. Some treaties allowed money to be set aside to pay debts to traders with little effort to determine if the debts were legitimate. The United States often took funds guaranteed by treaty to pay mission schools for educating Chippewa children or for operating expenses of the Indian Service offices.

Agents often withheld the annuities to punish individual Indians for not conforming to Indian Service rules, not sending their children to school, practicing Chippewa religion, or sharing with their relatives. Congress and the executive branch supported the use of annuities as a club.

Treaties were couched in the legalese common to government documents, which posed yet another problem. Chippewa leaders consistently contended that the commissioners would say one thing in discussion, and then the language of the treaties themselves would say something else. For instance, Chippewa leaders contended that they had only given up the right to mine copper in an 1842 treaty, but the United States translated this into a land cession. The Chippewa leaders also noted that Congress often changed the terms agreed upon, and they were then to take it—they could not leave it and start over.

Treaty rights were sometimes not protected by the federal government. The rights to hunt, fish, and gather in ceded land were generally ignored in favor of state regulations and control. Reservation boundaries were not enforced against encroaching non-Indians as the treaties required. State officials were able to interfere with treaty rights with impunity in the ceded territories and often imprisoned Chippewa for exercising treaty rights described in the treaties.

By the beginning of the 20th century, treaties and agreements had ceded nearly all of Chippewa Country to the United States. The major treaties are noted and summarized in the Chronology section of this book. In return for their land and resources, the Chippewa were allowed to reserve land in Chippewa Country, and they were left with embattled cultures, no tribal governments, and poverty. Most Chippewa did not think America was a beneficial trustee.

As the century progressed, markers of American control grew in number and inclusiveness: the creation of Indian Service schools to replace or supplement missionary schools, the disregard of traditional leaders by forcing Indians to deal with the agents individually, creating agent-controlled Indian Service police and courts to enforce American regulations and laws, criminalizing the practice of Indian religions, criminalizing the use of traditional Native American healers, and the forced allotment of reservations, continuing sale of land within reservations to non-Indians, continuing underfunding of services to Indians, resource exploitation leases to non-Indians at rates below market value, restriction of Indian treaty rights to hunt and gather, and forcing American domestic laws on Indian families. Perhaps this is when the often-heard adage "it is hard to be Indian" originated.

The United States incorporated the tribes into the American legal and political system by replacing tribal governments and enacting legislation that left Chippewa individuals with no recourse but to deal with the agents of American colonialism. Courts of Indian Offenses were instituted on reservations to enforce federal regulations and laws. Reservation agents supervised the courts, although they often appointed Indians to act as judges, and Indians were hired as Indian Service police.

Crimes that were punishable included practicing Indian religious ceremonies and following the leadership of traditional leaders. In 1885, the Major Crimes Act removed all felonies committed on reservations by Indians against Indians to federal courts where non-Indian juries provided justice. Indians were to be taught to respect law and order according to advocates of the Major Crimes Act.

In 1887, Congress passed the Dawes Severalty Act, which is more commonly known as the Allotment Act. Advocates like members of the Friends of the Indians, made up of congressmen and Progressives, were certain that Indians needed the benefit of private property if they were ever to be civilized. Faith in private property and life as yeomen farmers have been part of the American mythology dating back to the Founding Fathers like Thomas Jefferson. This article of faith was applied to Indian lands in the Act.

Allotment entailed assigning parcels of tribal land to individual tribal members. Initially, the Act provided 160-acre allotments to heads of households and 80 acres to women. After all tribal members received allotments, the remaining land would be declared surplus and sold to non-Indians with the revenue being used by the Indian Service to teach Indian males to be farmers.

After 25 years, judged to be sufficient to learn to farm like Americans, Indian owners would be deeded their land in fee simple. The now-civilized Indians would become U.S. citizens, pay taxes, and be subject to state/

territorial law. Subsequent amendments to the law responded to demands by non-Indians to accelerate the process of deeding the land to allow Indians to sell their lands sooner to non-Indians. Agents were allowed to declare that an Indian was now competent and he could then sell his land.

The most obvious result of allotment was the alienation of Indian lands from approximately 140 million acres in 1887 to approximately 40 million acres in 1934 when allotment was ended and deeds were no longer forced on Indian owners. The most destructive aspect of allotment was the introduction of non-Indian landowners throughout reservations.

Reservations came to resemble checkerboards with alternating Indian and non-Indian ownership. Another consequence was that Indians who managed to hold on to their lands saw their lands leased to non-Indians under terms set by the Bureau of Indian Affairs. Those Indians who did receive deeds to their land often lost it in tax sales conducted by the states or were bilked.

Each of the Chippewa reservations experienced being brought into the American fold at different times and in various degrees. American expansion and demand for Chippewa Country resources ebbed and flowed with the tides of historical events and American development. Although some Chippewa communities were relegated to the margins of Michigan, others became the center of Chippewa culture and continued expansion westward, and others were not subjected to reservations until the early 20th century.

White Earth Reservation in 1867 and Turtle Mountain Reservation in 1882 were the last Chippewa reservations added, even as others in Minnesota were consolidated and disappeared. All but one, Red Lake Reservation within Minnesota, would be allotted, and even Red Lake had to surrender land to the United States in a series of agreements.

The Plains Wars in the post–Civil War brought the Plains tribes into the American fold in a spectacular fashion, but Chippewa Country had already been subdivided into islands of Chippewa reservations surrounded by much more numerous Americans. All was not settled as American policy makers would take steps to undermine Chippewa culture and government and to exploit resources in land taken within the 19th century, but aside from some localized resistance, Chippewa communities had to operate within the reservation system created by the United States.

One indication of the changes wrought is that Chippewa men fought in the Civil War as part of Michigan, Wisconsin, and Minnesota regiments and not as independent Indian allies. Another indication is that by the end of the century, many Chippewa had become either Protestant or Catholic, American school educated, and even state citizens in Michigan.

Daily life for Chippewa people continued to revolve around the basic needs that all families and people face. Many clung to the age-old pattern of movement from one source of food to another—the traditional cycle. In fact, most Chippewa remained wedded to the hunting, fishing, gathering pattern to some extent even as they moved into a quasi-wage labor pattern in the extraction industries that appeared in Chippewa Country. Lumbering, commercial fishing, and even farming became part of Chippewa male life.

Women continued to raise children, enculturate them, and work within some of the American introduced economy, often as domestic help. Generally, Chippewa occupied niches alongside but separate from the ever-growing American world. Some even assimilated to the extent that they became white. Chippewa leaders continued to struggle to maintain their communities politically and culturally.

NOTABLE FIGURE

Eshkebugescoshe, a.k.a. Flat Mouth (c. 1774–1860)

Flat Mouth was a distinguished war leader of the Leech Lake Pillager Band against the Dakota. He segued into the dominant Upper Mississippi Chippewa leader for negotiations with the United States. He signed the 1837 Pine Treaty, gaining payments even for the Mississippi Chippewa when all of the land ceded was in the Lake Superior area. In 1855 Flat Mouth signed the Treaty of Washington, giving up 10 million acres for one dollar per acre. Leech Lake became permanent and enlarged by adding two other bands.

In 1870 Flat Mouth met with Dakota leaders to make a formal agreement ending their century-long war. Father Genin acted as broker between the two tribes. In combination with the Dakota gift of the healing big drum ceremony, the tribal agreement predicted a common future as friends.

In Ojibwemowin, his name translates to "Bird with the Green Bill," which French speakers somehow translated into Gueule Platte (Flat Mouth). In 1855, Flat Mouth posed for a bust by Francis Vincenti, still on display at the U.S. capital building. Flat Mouth was succeeded by his daughter as primary leader of Leech Lake.

6

The Nadir of Chippewa Country

Once the United States began absorbing Chippewa Country into the mainstream of the United States, Chippewa communities and clusters of communities were forced to interact with the United States independently more often than not and on American terms. However, the desire of the United States to acquire Chippewa title legitimately if possible, and then to govern Indians without expensive wars, operated in favor of a continuing Chippewa story. Altruistic American values helped. By the end of the 19th century, more than 20 separate Chippewa reservations and communities still existed in a drastically reduced Chippewa Country.

Selected occurrences, achievements, tragedies, and victories can provide meaningful examples in understanding the Chippewa story. Chippewa communities from Michigan to Montana experienced separate episodes in the continuing story but within the same broad contexts. Most Chippewa communities remained vital as they had for several thousand years. After the United States gained power, each of the communities had to react and attempt to guide the activities of the "irresistible power" of the United States.

Each Chippewa community's existence was threatened by the United States, by their American neighbors, and imposed poverty. Each experienced immense loss of land with little compensation. Each was challenged to maintain language, culture, and religion. Each witnessed the elimination of their government and the imposition of a colonial rule. Each saw its remaining land devastated by natural resource exploitation. Each felt racism.

Throughout this nadir of Chippewa existence in the unfolding story, leaders and individuals struggled to survive as Chippewa people. Responses to external challenges varied from reservation to reservation, yet the fabric of the story was a whole cloth worn by all Chippewa.

Several outstanding scholars have contributed to monographic studies of specific reservations. This narrative of the story owes a debt to them. In traditional storytelling, the practice is for the narrator to acknowledge those who have given stories that are drawn on, but the narrator indicates that any mistakes are his and that a more complete version can be gained from those who came before.

THE BROAD CONTEXT OF CHIPPEWA COUNTRY: RESERVATIONS AND COMMUNITIES

The Americans used treaties to acquire Indian land. More than 40 treaties and agreements structured Chippewa bands within Michigan, Wisconsin, Minnesota, North Dakota, and Montana. Reservations replaced band villages, and federal officials ruled Chippewa communities. The Chippewa were paid with commitments to pay with money, goods, and services, and they protected some rights like hunting and fishing in the one-sided treaties. Federal laws and executive regulations replaced traditional governments.

In the Treaty of 1837 politically independent Chippewa bands occupying the shores and islands of Lake Superior were described as the Lake Superior Chippewa Tribe. The newly described tribe was centered on Madeline Island's La Pointe Village, where a subagent took up residence alongside the American Fur Company headquarters. America's choice recognized history.

Earlier, the French and English sent their representatives to Mooniingwanekaanig (later called Madeline's Island). Madeline Island's Chippewa Band formed the epicenter of Chippewa culture and was the core of Chippewa activities for all of the bands. Wisconsin reservations were formed from bands that settled in the 18th century, which mainly flowed from Madeline Island, and continued to consider themselves affiliated culturally and even politically. In the 20th century, the Lake Superior Chippewa Tribe is comprised of a kind of confederation of independent reservations.

America merged Chippewa bands in Minnesota, too. In the 1860s and beyond, the large bands that made up the Minnesota Chippewa Tribe were sometimes treated separately to facilitate American land and resource acquisition. Red Lake Reservation was first joined with the even farther West Turtle Mountain Chippewa (originally called Pembina Band) in 1863, and then a new reservation was carved out at White Earth. Other reservations like Sandy Lake were simply folded into other bands for legal purposes.

In 1934, the several reservations joined in a legal confederation, the Minnesota Chippewa Tribe. Bands/reservations mostly retained separate identity while delegating some powers to the tribe. Representation includes each reservation chairperson, and various officials are hired to serve the members through various programs. Red Lake Reservation excluded itself.

In Michigan, some of the bands, like the Keeweenaw, were included in the Lake Superior Chippewa; others were distinct, but without reservations—they were just Indian communities—a new approach designed to integrate them into the state population and free the federal government of any obligations. After 1837 the new state of Michigan was encouraged to treat the Chippewa and other Michigan Native Americans as residents of Michigan.

Michigan's constitution extended state citizenship to American Indians if they demonstrated that they had abandoned Indian identity and treaty rights. No Indian selected this option. Essentially most Indians were ignored by the federal and state governments and allowed to exist as a kind of minority group. Community identity endured, however. In the mid-20th century, Chippewa leaders brought their issues like treaty rights and the right to a community to federal courts. Some also went through the Bureau of Indian Affairs process to gain federal recognition.

Michigan bands managed to repurchase small pieces of their lands with treaty revenues and maintain community identity. Keweenaway, Bay Mills, and Lac Vieux Desert bands achieved reservation status by being included in the Lake Superior Chippewa Tribe and their astute leadership. The 1855 treaty required further cessions from the Michigan-enclosed Chippewa, and an allotment scheme made them individual property owners. Some Ottawa and Potawatomi bands were swept away in the removal policy process and sent to Indian Territory.

THE SANDY LAKE TRAGEDY, 1850: PART OF THE STORY

After Wisconsin statehood, the new Minnesota Territory's governor, Alexander Ramsey, demanded Chippewa removal to protect white settlers from alleged Indian depredations. No Chippewa depredation had occurred. The Chippewa had been complaining to federal agents about American squatters, stolen resources like timber, and brutal harassment by non-Indians. In reality, Ramsey and a cabal wanted to tap revenues generated by Chippewa treaty annuities.

In 1850 Whig president Zachary Taylor ordered the Chippewa to prepare for removal. Treaties of 1837 and 1842 provided that the Chippewa would have to remove when the president needed the land for settlement by Americans. There were few eager settlers awaiting Chippewa removal from their small land holdings. However, there were pine forests and copper deposits and the income from treaty payments. Territorial governor Ramsey was a Whig appointee.

Whig appointees Interior Secretary Thomas Ewing, Commissioner of Indian Affairs Orlando Brown, and LaPointe subagent John Watrous ordered the Lake Superior and Minnesota Chippewa treaty bands to journey to the Sandy Lake Band's community in Minnesota Territory for their treaty payments. Previous payments had been at Madeline Island. Minnesota bands had received their share of the annuities at other sites.

The bands were ordered to arrive at Sandy Lake by October 25 where food, accommodations, and their annuities would be waiting for them. Subagent John Watrous left Madeline Island for St. Louis. Chippewa bands set out on several hundred miles of arduous canoe and portage travel.

Many of the Lake Superior Chippewa traveled with their families, as Watrous had instructed, because he figured they would just give up and stay if their families went along. By October 25, as many as 4,000 Chippewa had arrived at Sandy Lake from Lake Superior, and about 1,500 more came from Minnesota Territory environs.

Nineteen bands assembled. They found no provisions, no accommodations, and no federal agents. A few merchants had gathered and sold some food to the Chippewa on credit. Poor hunting and a bad wild rice crop exacerbated the crisis. Food supplied by government contractors when it did arrive was insufficient in quantity and rotten. During six weeks of waiting, about 170 Chippewa died of dysentery and starvation.

On December 3, as the winter set in, Subagent Watrous arrived and made a partial annuity distribution. The delay was designed to force the Chippewa to stay as winter set in. Canoes did not work on frozen rivers and lakes, and the partial annuities were insufficient. The Chippewa insisted on going home; there was no food even if they had wanted to stay.

The return trip claimed 230 more Lake Superior Chippewa and at least as many from the western Minnesota reservations. The Sandy Lake Tragedy claimed about one-third of the adult men and women of the Lake Superior Band. Desperate, enraged Chippewa explored responses.

In 1851, Chippewa leaders sent a petition to Commissioner of Indian Affairs Luke Lea detailing the culpability of Subagent Watrous and Governor Ramsey. They strongly requested return of annuity distribution to

La Pointe and lifting the removal order. President Fillmore responded to public pressure and suspended removal. By 1854, annuities were again distributed at La Pointe on Madeline Island.

Watrous was formally charged with lying, seduction of Chippewa women, and trying to bribe Chippewa leaders by the L'Anse Chippewa Band. Governor Ramsey heard the accusations and concluded that Watrous had done nothing wrong. He actually blamed the Chippewa for the tragedy at Sandy Lake. He said they should have been prepared for delays and not tried to go home. Chippewa leaders gathered at Madeline Island were faced with the anger of their people, and many called for war against the United States. Tradition indicates that war was a near thing.

The most influential leader of the Lake Superior Chippewa was Bizhiki, known in English as Buffalo. Bizhiki and other peace leaders seized on an idea presented by his son-in-law, Benjamin Armstrong. A delegation would go to Washington, DC, to talk with the president and present a petition calling for a new treaty that would remove the threat of removal, restore annuity distribution at La Pointe, and secure annuities that were yet unpaid. Armstrong would interpret.

Buffalo and five other Chippewa including Oshoga, a Crane Clan leader, traveled around Lake Superior to Sault Ste. Marie, then to Detroit, then to Buffalo, and by train to Albany and finally to Washington. Along the way, hundreds of American businessmen and civic leaders signed their petition. They said that the Chippewa were valuable, peaceful neighbors and should be allowed to stay.

Two different Indian agents tried to stop this unauthorized visit, but local

Portrait of Buffalo (1759–1855), principal leader of the Lake Superior Band of Chippewa. He journeyed to Washington to argue against removal and in support of retaining the Chippewa homeland. He signed several treaties, including the 1854 treaty which guaranteed reservations for the Chippewa. (Wisconsin Historical Society, WHS-3957)

Americans brooked no such interference. When the group arrived in Washington, the Commissioner of Indian Affairs told them to go home because they had no authorization from the Indian Service. Press and public opinion supported the Chippewa. President Fillmore may have met with Bizhiki. The removal order was withdrawn, and Fillmore agreed to a new treaty to create permanent reservations.

In 1854 the government convened Lake Superior bands on Madeline Island, La Pointe, to negotiate the promised treaty. Impassioned spokesmen insisted they be allowed to remain and have permanently guaranteed reservations. Some influential Wisconsin citizens were supportive. As usual, the commissioners wanted land in return for meeting Chippewa goals. Ironically, Chippewa leaders agreed to surrender much of Madeline Island. Treaty annuities were distributed.

The Treaty of La Pointe in 1854 recognized reservations for the Lake Superior Chippewa: L'Anse, Ontonagon, Lac Vieux Desert, La Pointe, Lac Courte Oreilles, Lac du Flambeau, Grand Portage, Fond du Lac, and Bois Forte.

Bizhiki received his own land at Red Cliff across the bay from La Pointe. Many of the Catholic and traditional Chippewa from LaPointe joined him, and the land became Red Cliff Reservation. Bad River, already an extended settlement of La Pointe Chippewa, replaced La Pointe as the recognized reservation. The new governor of Minnesota fired Subagent Watrous.

The Lake Superior Chippewa breathed a sigh of relief. The reservations created remain today's reservations in Chippewa Country—the Lake Superior Chippewa. Bizhiki had signed many treaties, but this one saved his people's homeland. He was buried on Madeline Island in 1855, and the Chippewa hold ceremonies of commemoration annually. The Chippewa and supporters meet at Sandy Lake annually to run a route to Bad River and Madeline Island. The tragedy of the Sandy Lake death march is not forgotten.

MOONIINGWANEKAANIG–STE. MICHEL–MADELAINE–MADELINE–LA POINTE ISLAND: PART OF THE STORY

The plot to remove Lake Superior Chippewa to Minnesota was one of many events in a continuing part of the Chippewa story. A shift in the center of gravity for Chippewa Country to Madeline Island–Chequamegon Bay is another part of the story. Beginning in the late 16th century, the Chippewa visited the western shore of Lake Superior and gradually replaced the Dakota and Ottawa with permanent Chippewa villages.

In oral tradition, the Chippewa moved to the islands and shores of western Lake Superior as part of the inspired realization of the vision to move westward until they reached the land where food grew on the water, perhaps as early as the 15th century. The historical record places increasing numbers of Chippewa bands in the area from the 1650s and incorporation into Chippewa Country by the beginning of the 18th century.

The Frenchmen first contacted a mixed tribal community in the 1660s. Four factors complicate the early history of the Islands and the shores of Chequamegon Bay: the Chippewa and the Ottawa called themselves Anishinaabe, which made precise identification of the frequently intermingled groups problematical; the French only came to the area infrequently until the 18th century; the continuing Iroquois Wars contributed to population ebbs and flows; Chippewa and even the French moved from place to place depending on seasons. Populations on the island were in constant flux.

After the end of the Iroquois Wars, Chippewa migration to the Lake Superior shores increased, and they named the largest island of a chain of islands sprinkled at the head of Chequamegon Bay, Mooniingwanekaanig—Home of the Golden-Breasted Woodpecker. The island is 4 miles long and 2 miles wide, and its western side provides shelter for boats. French merchants arrived in 1659, 1671, and 1693 and spent some time but did not stay.

In 1718 the French built a military post. A temporary Catholic mission was established in 1665. Trade remained centered at Sault Ste. Marie, but the French did map the area. They decided to name the island Ste. Michel. They also named Lake Superior and other areas because French names were easier. The island site of their early missions and forts was called La Pointe. The French fort maintained an official presence on the island and encouraged the ever-increasing number of French and mixed-blood Chippewa traders to channel furs from the western reaches of Chippewa Country through La Pointe for transshipment.

After the defeated French left in 1762, English fur traders, both independent and employees of the Northwest Company, called the island Michel's Island after Michel Cadotte, the dominant trader who moved to the island from Sault Ste. Marie. Cadotte married the daughter of White Crane, leader of the Crane Clan and principal leader of the La Pointe Chippewa band. She adopted the Christian name Madeleine when she married Michel at Sault Ste. Marie in a Catholic ceremony.

Madeleine's clan continued to provide band leaders. Her role in the trade at the post and throughout other communities was so prominent that Michel's Island was renamed Madeleine Island. The spelling was changed to Madeline when Americans supplanted the British.

Chippewa numbers and foreign presence grew as long as business was good. Madeline Island was the center of interactions with foreigners after the French and Indian War. Establishment of Grand Portage in 1768 as a new entrepôt for transshipment and distribution by the Northwest Company merely complemented La Pointe, Madeline Island.

Michel Cadotte was hired by the Northwest Company as manager on the island. The British recognized the political preeminence of the Chippewa of Madeline Island. After the Americans supplanted the British, the American Fur Company headquartered on the island in the 1820s. Protestant missionaries arrived at the behest of the fur company and served the American population.

The Chippewa community, increasingly known to Americans as the La Pointe Band, continued to enrich itself from business with the Americans as they had from British and French needs for Chippewa goods. The fur trade remained until the 1830s, but the Chippewa provided food and support services that allowed foreigners to live in Chippewa County long after.

Chippewa women were the primary suppliers of food to merchants, soldiers, and officials alike. Madeleine Cadotte was not the only important female in the economy. After arrival of the missionaries, they too were dependent on purchases from Chippewa suppliers. Chippewa women even made the clothes for the foreigners—all of this was for a price.

Mooniingwanekaanig, no matter what the others called it, was the epicenter of Chippewa culture and evolved into the main location of a growing Midewiwin religious expression or perhaps was the place where the lodge began. Chippewa bands from the west, north, and east regularly gathered to join Mide ceremonies, socialize, sell their furs, buy supplies, and plan expansion efforts westward,

After the Americans arrived, Madeline Island was the focal point for treaty negotiations with Chippewa bands. Leaders like Bizhiki (Buffalo) were necessarily present at all negotiations and discussions with merchants and officials alike. Often other Chippewa band leaders deferred to La Pointe leaders as first among equals.

Sons of Madeleine and Michel Cadotte expanded their trade contacts by setting up posts with their relatives at Red Lake on the western border of Minnesota and Fond du Lac within Minnesota on the St. Louis River. Families that originated in the mixed-blood trade community of Madeline Island–La Pointe became traders in most of western Chippewa Country including North Dakota's Turtle Mountains. The Americans joined the merchant mix with the arrival of Lyman and Truman Warren to work with the American Fur Company although the Company had employed Michel Cadotte as director.

The Warrens married daughters of Madeleine and Michel Cadotte. They bought Cadotte's trading interests in 1823. They and other Americans set up a community separate from the Chippewa town and from many of the French descent fur traders and the mixed-blood traders.

A common settlement pattern was adjacent, interacting mostly Native communities, a mixed-blood merchant community that mingled Franco-Scot-Anglo and Chippewa populations, and an official American community with American wives and children like the enclave created by the Protestant mission, the agent, and various officials. Vestiges of this pattern remain on most Chippewa reservations.

The American presence quickly changed the island from being almost completely Chippewa. By the 1830s the non-Native community of La Pointe had a school, churches, a three-story hotel named after Madeline Cadotte, a court house, the American Fur Company headquarters for the region, a dock, and several white families. By 1850, the island census noted 485 residents. About 150 were Chippewa. Forty of the residents were Cadottes. Houses, warehouses, wigwams, and churches clustered in various locations.

The New England-born Warrens encouraged a Protestant mission led by Thomas Hall in 1835. The Protestants built a church and school. The school was more successful than conversion efforts. Only seven Chippewa became Protestants.

Simultaneously, Father Frederic Baraga reestablished a Catholic mission. By 1838 he had baptized so many Chippewa that he had to enlarge the church. Most Chippewa considered Catholicism as bringing another set of ceremonies to the assistance of Chippewa people.

The French descent traders were already Catholic. Baraga also monitored the Protestant school to make sure that they did not teach religion in the school and threatened to tell all of the Catholics that they could not attend if the Protestants violated the prohibition. Hall and the Wheelers who followed complained about Catholic influence. American agents could do nothing about it.

In 1845 the Wheelers moved their mission and school to a new mainline town, Odanah, on the Bad River where a Chippewa community farmed a little and harvested rice. It was really an extension of Madeline Island and part of the annual round of hunting, trapping, fishing, and harvesting. As American numbers increased on Madeline Island, many Chippewa families moved to Odanah. The Protestant La Pointe Mission was closed in

1854, but the Catholic church of Father Baraga remained along with a Presbyterian church for the Americans.

After the Treaty of 1837 La Pointe was the site of annuity distribution. The Pine Tree Treaty (as it was called) had provided for annual payments in cash and goods chosen by federal officials in Washington and then shipped to Madeline Island. Sometimes the federal pickers made unusual choices, as in 1840 when the boat-riding Chippewa received horse saddles. The Chippewa from the signatory bands had to be present when the annuities were distributed.

Annuity days brought government officials, the subagent, multiple merchants, and thousands of Chippewa from the Lake Superior Chippewa to Madeline Island, now generically called La Pointe. Distribution days were a circus-like atmosphere for most with socializing, traders collecting money from the Chippewa to pay for bills they said the Chippewa had, dancing, games like baggataway (the progenitor of lacrosse), and political discussions. A great deal of liquor was present.

The scheme of removal foisted on the Chippewa by Ramsey and Watrous, and supported by Minnesota Territory merchants like Henry Rice, disrupted the annuity days for a few years in addition to killing large numbers of Chippewa. By 1854, Buffalo's mission to meet with President Fillmore had saved the Lake Superior Chippewa on the shores of Lake Superior from removal.

Details were finalized in the 1854 Treaty of La Pointe. Victory for the Chippewa came at a high price. The treaty surrendered even more territory to the United States, including all of Madeline Island but 100 acres. Permanent reservations were recognized, and the Chippewa were promised that they would never be removed. Reservation permanence was fleeting for the Chippewa within Minnesota, and Chippewa ownership on their own reservations was steadily reduced, but no one knew that in 1854.

The Chippewa signatories of the 1854 treaty probably achieved as much as they could in the face of demands for sale of their lands and their relative helplessness against the encroaching Americans. One of the most significant achievements was the establishment of several reservations with relatively clear boundaries, although two of the bands did not get reservations for decades.

At least the Chippewa would not have to leave their homelands, no matter how hedged in they were. A second concession wrung from the Americans by Chippewa leaders aided by Buffalo's son-in-law and several Cadottes was a treaty right to hunt, fish, and gather resources in the territory they had ceded. When combined with the same American concession in 1837, this treaty right covered roughly the northern third of Wisconsin, a portion of Minnesota, and significant portions of Michigan. The right also included commercial fishing rights on Lake Superior.

Defending the treaty rights became a major cause for Chippewa leaders into the 21st century. Commercial and sports fishermen utilized the power of the states to impede the exercising of treaty rights by Chippewa reservation citizens. Often the Chippewa were arrested or assaulted for exercising rights that neither the federal nor state governments were interested in protecting. Asserting treaty rights is another facet of the story of the Chippewa.

The Chippewa within Wisconsin and eastern Minnesota gradually created an economic niche for themselves within the larger American society. This meant continuing the conversion to a wage economy in part, continuing the round of hunting, fishing, and gathering as possible, continuing to sell Chippewa-produced goods to the Americans, and even some fur trapping. Chippewa men joined the lumber camps, and many became famous locally for their exploits in the frequent lumberjack competitions.

Chippewa women continued to maintain families and to work within the larger setting. Often this meant as domestics, but it also meant as sellers of their traditional harvests in wild rice, blueberries, and maple sugar to the Americans. The Chippewa might not have their Madeline Island, but they maintained a rich cultural life that kept customs and ceremonies vibrant. Adaptations and acculturation do not mean extinction.

Today Red Cliff and Bad River Reservations retain a small piece of the island and conduct ceremonies there. Non-Indians have summer homes, dock their boats at the marina, and are connected to the mainland by a ferry. A museum commemorates the fur trade and the Chippewa.

A Chippewa graveyard remains on Mooniingwanekaanig.

RED LAKE RESERVATION: PART OF THE STORY

After the 1854 Treaty of La Pointe, roughly the northwestern quarter of the future Minnesota remained a relatively exclusive Chippewa Country, although it was steadily penetrated by American agents, traders, and settlers. Minnesota Territorial Governor Alexander Ramsey and many of the territory's American population clamored for a reduction of Indian land and their removal to someplace else.

The blocs of Chippewa land, dotted throughout by multiple Chippewa bands and sub-bands, was not as desirable for settlement as that of the Native Americans across the southern tier of Minnesota. The acquisition of Chippewa Country was delayed, and leaders learned more about dealing with American challenges. The Dakota experience was an abject lesson.

In southern Minnesota the Dakota had capitulated to drastic shrinkage of their lands as had the Winnebago. They watched waves of German immigrants creating towns like New Ulm and Mankato. They also saw militia and regulars leaving to fight in the American Civil War. Some Chippewa and Dakota even joined the American forces. Continued squeezing of the Dakota into smaller and smaller areas made their continued existence untenable.

After a series of incidents, war began in 1862 between the Dakota and the Minnesotans. A brief, vicious war ended with as many as 800 Minnesotans dead and quite a swath of land devastated. Around 2,000 Dakota were killed, and the rest, whether they were involved in the war or not, were held in concentration camps until sent to Crow Creek, Dakota Territory. The Dakota were forbidden to live in Minnesota, although a few Dakota loyalists to Minnesota were allowed to remain. The noninvolved Winnebago were shipped off to a reservation in Nebraska.

The Dakota Wars caused widespread fear among Americans that Chippewa bands would join. Baganegiizhig (Hole in the Day), a Chippewa leader, used threats as leverage to gain concessions from the Americans and to establish himself in the eyes of the Americans as something like chief of all of the Chippewas.

At one point he even held Commissioner of Indian Affairs William Dole as a quasi-prisoner at Fort Ripley. He then called off the warriors, "saving" the commissioner and other federal officials. Bands from Otter Tail and Leech Lake did take some prisoners and burn government buildings.

Pembina band leaders collected tolls from steamboats on the Red River of the North by taking goods and then releasing the boats. Tensions kept the area in some turmoil even as the Dakota Wars provided a demonstration of what an aroused American military and population were willing to do to retaliate. The number of troops, the calls from Minnesotans for extermination of the Indians, and the number of Dakota hanged in Mankato were known to Chippewa leaders.

Moozoomoo (Moose Dung), the long-time primary leader of the collection of bands called the Red Lake Band by the United States, was one of those who refused Dakota War belts. He and leaders of the Pembina Band west of Red Lake saw an opportunity to secure their lands and to obtain payment through treaty with the United States. Earlier negotiations had been suspended because of the Dakota Wars.

Governor Ramsey, the federal government, and the Red Lake and Pembina Chippewa bands discussed the Red River Valley portion of Chippewa Country. These bands had been the forefront of Chippewa western expansion into the Red River Valley and the northern Dakota plains since the

18th century. They were primarily offshoots of bands that had migrated into Ontario and Manitoba. However, many southern Chippewa constantly filtered into the Red Lake area and on westward to Pembina and the Turtle Mountains.

In 1863 Moose Dung was accompanied to Old Crossing on the Red Lake River by Indian agent Ashley Morrill. They met Governor Ramsey, his military escort, and other commissioners who brought wagon loads of victuals and presents for their Chippewa hosts.

Moose Dung's contingent included 579 Chippewa and 22 half-breeds. The Pembina Band delegation included 579 Chippewa and 663 half-breeds. The United States insisted on treating the mixed bloods as a separate category even if the Chippewa included them as Chippewa. Confusion stems from the group of interpreters who were not from the host bands like the Beaulieus and the Roys, also Chippewa half-breeds. Who was Chippewa and who was not remained a problem for the Americans. The Americans generally did not want mixed bloods involved in negotiations because many were school-educated, spoke two or three languages, and defended tribal positions to the consternation of American negotiators.

The Old Crossing Treaty of 1863 created Red Lake Reservation and a promise of a reservation for the Pembina Band, later called the Turtle Mountain Band. It also provided a payment of $510,000 to the bands. Chippewa debts of $150,000 were subtracted from the Chippewa's payment. Payment of debts incurred by individual Chippewa was a common feature of treaty payments despite Chippewa leaders' objections. No audit of the merchants' claims ever occurred until the 20th century. Half-breeds were given scrip to allow them to claim ownership of plots of land acquired by the United States.

The Chippewa "sold" 11 million acres, virtually all of the Red River Valley north of the Cheyenne River. The right to hunt and fish was not mentioned, although later Chippewa testimony indicated that they had no intention to surrender those rights. Bishop Henry Whipple, a supporter of land sales and the American civilization process, called the treaty a "fraud," and Chippewa leaders agreed.

Moose Dung had to content himself with having saved some land, Red Lake Reservation. In 1889 Red Lake leaders sold another 2,900,000 acres and part of Red Lake itself to be excluded from the allotment process.

Red Lake remained a closed reservation held in common by all Red Lakers at a steep price. Their 1889 agreement prevented the area from being inundated by non-Indians like the other Chippewa reservations experienced. No one owns land on the reservation, and non-Indians who live on it work for the tribe or for various programs, but they are renters. Red Lake remains a center of Chippewa traditionalism. Closed reservations are unusual in all of Indian Country.

LAW AND ORDER AMERICAN STYLE: AN APPARENT TANGENT

During the Gilded Age of post–Civil War America, exploitation of natural resources ran rampant; great strides in industrial production were accompanied by disregard for the environment, for workers, and for consumers. Excesses epitomized by the robber barons generated Progressivism. Reformers wanted to curb environmental degradation, regulate industrial pollution, protect natural resources, and convert the enthusiasm of the anti-slavery movement into a nation-wide drive for education, Americanism-assimilation efforts in the massive immigrant population, civil service legislation, and myriad other goals.

Progressives launched an assault on Indian independence as domestic dependent nations. They wanted to serve Indians by making them assimilate. Their paternalistic "gift" to the Indian was a campaign of Christianity, private land ownership, and individualization of each Indian. They wanted to eradicate Indian cultures and separatism. At the same time as developers and American officials were taking Chippewa land and conniving at rampant exploitation of resources, the forces of Progressivism engineered processes to further their campaign.

Some saw subjecting Indians to American law as a civilizing benefit. The Board of Indian Commissioners as early as 1871 declared that Indians needed to be brought into conformity with "the majesty of civilized law" to protect them against "the lawless among themselves." Until the 1870s Indian communities followed their centuries-old methods of community controls, and these were left in place during the gradual absorption of Indians into the American Indian reservation system. American agents and government policies had undermined traditional leadership and community stability while promoting poverty. Enthusiasts formed a powerful lobby for forcing American Indians to be protected by American law.

The campaign to force Indians into the American legal system peaked after Sinte Gleska, a dominant leader among the Rosebud Sioux, was killed by Crow Dog in 1883 on the reservation within South Dakota. The Rosebud agent had him arrested and tried in territorial court. He was sentenced to death. The families concerned in the murder followed their legal system, and compensation was agreed upon while the American legal system ground on. Crow Dog's lawyer asked for an ex parte ruling on jurisdiction and the U.S. Supreme Court found that the United States had no jurisdiction and ordered his release. Reformers were aghast at the lawlessness of Indian savagery. Ironically, Indian savages wanted to restore the community and reintegrate Crow Dog; the "civilized" Americans wanted retribution and capital punishment.

Congress passed the Major Crimes Act in 1885, which extended federal criminal jurisdiction over acts committed on reservations by Indians against Indians. Indians would be tried by a non-Indian jury in a non-Indian community to show them how justice worked. Tribal law was not allowed any more.

The Supreme Court upheld the Major Crimes Act in an 1886 decision, *U.S. v Kagama*. Essentially, all felonies committed on reservations were now within the jurisdiction of federal courts. The Indians were thrown into the American system, a system diametrically opposite to the restorative justice approach of most Indian societies.

Courts of Indian Offenses were created by Commissioner of Indian Affairs Hiram Price in 1883 to complement the Major Crimes Act. These courts handled misdemeanors and violations of the laws against Indian religion. The agents hired tribal members as judges providing they adopted American cultural practices. The agents could overrule the Courts of Indian Offenses.

As with other tribes, the Chippewa continued to pray anyway. Ceremonies were held in secret, and the traditional culture continued below the surface whatever the laws were. Dancing is an example of Chippewa tenacity. The tourist industry wanted to see Indian dances, so they danced. The agents wanted cooperation from the Chippewa, and the price for cooperation was to allow them to dance. Eventually, more organization led to the modern powwow. They served also to maintain the traditional dances that were ceremonial and social.

WHITE EARTH RESERVATION: A CHIPPEWA INDIAN TERRITORY? PART OF THE STORY

After the debacle of the Sandy Lake Tragedy and the Red River Valley acquisition by the United States, Minnesotans returned to the idea of consolidation of Chippewa Country into a single reservation. The White Earth story is most completely related in *The White Earth Tragedy* (Meyer), but many others have added to it.

Governor Ramsey, in league with the lumbering and development advocates, joined with congressmen, federal officials, and missionaries in a new removal campaign. Their idea was to create a reservation near the headwaters of the Mississippi and west of Sandy Lake. Chippewa bands of Mille

Lacs, Crow Wing, Leech Lake, Pembina, Gull Lake, and others would exchange their reservations for White Earth. Their former land and resources would be open for development and settlement.

In 1864, government agents began thinly veiled threats couched in terms of negotiation with several Chippewa bands. All were opposed to removal and reminded officials of American promises. Pressure was applied by settlers using threats, disruptions, trespassing on Chippewa reservations, and occasional violence against Chippewas. State and county officials often actively supported pressures.

Missionaries like Bishop Whipple encouraged the idea because the civilization of the Chippewa was only possible if they became Christian farmers in a consolidated area that would protect them from the bad influences of white men. Reformers knew that Chippewa communities were suffering from alcohol abuse, venereal disease introduced by the Americans, tuberculosis, and other ills associated with their poverty. Progressives hoped that money from sales of land and the civilizing influence of federal Indian service teachers would ameliorate the Chippewa's dire circumstances.

Chippewa leaders were forced to sign yet another treaty in 1867 that established a new reservation, called White Earth, and surrendered lands guaranteed under earlier treaties. All were to remove to White Earth as designated.

Tribal citizens of Mille Lacs were arrested, their homes burned, and their fishing and hunting obstructed. Indian service agents refused to distribute annuities already earned except at White Earth. Eventually, about 1,000 Mille Lacs Chippewa moved to White Earth, but many obdurately refused to move. Their obstinacy was rewarded when the government gave up trying and recognized the continuation of Mille Lacs Reservation.

Hole in the Day from Gull Lake was the most vociferous of the Chippewa leaders who opposed White Earth, despite receiving a house and a personal allotment in the treaty. Some of the mixed bloods who were part of the commercially savvy Chippewa were supportive of White Earth Reservation, particularly as they saw opportunity to continue their businesses and work with American lumbering developers, too.

Hole in the Day threatened to kill any half-breeds who moved to White Earth, and he gathered a number of young men willing to support him. He vigorously argued with Indian agents at every opportunity and even turned to non-Indians for support. Hole in the Day was assassinated by the Chippewa hired by one or more of the mixed bloods.

Despite pressures, legal and extralegal, by 1893 only 300 families lived on allotments on the new home of the Chippewa. Promised houses, schools, rations, farming equipment, and other amenities were not available for many years. Hardscrabble efforts to live on hunting, fishing, and gathering marked the community for years. Even traditional economy was disrupted by federal dams that destroyed rice lakes and cranberry bogs. Non-Indian communities interfered with hunting and gathering in ceded territories, too.

A few Chippewa, mainly mixed bloods, managed relatively well because they brought resources with them and they had acculturated for several generations. Quite a few of the mixed bloods had their roots in the merchant fur trade on Madeline Island and had moved westward to Crow Wing in the wake of Chippewa expansion and then to western White Earth. Many of the family names remain prominent on the reservation. Beaulieu, Beaupre, Bellanger, Dufort, Fairbanks, McDonald, Morrison, Warren, Montreuil, and McGillis are common all across Chippewa communities from Madeline Island to the Turtle Mountains.

More traditional Chippewa settled on the eastern portions of the reservation in their existing bands. The Mille Lacs, Otter Tail Pillagers, Leech Lakers, Gull Lake Episcopals, and other recognized bands created minireservations distinct from others. None saw themselves as a single community. This contributed to conflict on the reservation and to the destruction of the reservation by external forces.

Even the mixed bloods who arrived in fairly large numbers were absorbed generally into ersatz clans: the Anglo-Chippewa were Eagle Clan, and the Franco-Chippewa were Maple Leaf Clan. More traditional Chippewa strengthened their exercise of Mide ceremonial life, while the mixed bloods supported schools and greater acculturation. These multiple divisions among the community of White Earth remain noticeable.

A series of laws allowed the alienation of land and resources at a breathtaking pace. Individual timber leases were approved by the Indian Service, but lumber interests remained unsatisfied because of some restrictions and a required level of fees. In 1889 12 official Chippewa reservations still existed in Minnesota.

The Nelson Act called for all to relocate to White Earth; their lands were to be sold for $1.25 an acre with proceeds to help pay for the relocation. Pine lands were set up in 40-acre lots to be sold at auction. Three non-Indians were appointed as the Chippewa Commission to supervise sales and decide how to spend the Chippewa fund money.

A surprise clause in the Nelson Act allowed the Chippewa to take individual allotments where they lived instead of moving to White Earth. Many availed themselves of this loophole and remained at home where some of their descendants are living on the few reservations remaining. Congress did not abolish the reservations. Red Lake Reservation leaders traded land for retaining their reservation in 1889.

> **TAKING THE LAND AND RESOURCES: WHITE EARTH**
>
> Congressmen collaborated with the timber industry and land speculators to accelerate their acquisition of White Earth Reservation, the permanent reservation for the Chippewa created in 1867 by treaty. In 1889, "An Act for the Relief and Civilization of the Chippewa Indians in the state of Minnesota" known for its sponsor, Knute Nelson of Minnesota, was a first step in stripping White Earth of timber and Chippewa ownership.
>
> The Nelson Act extended the Allotment Act of 1887 to Chippewa reservations. Each Chippewa family was allotted 80 acres of non-pine lands from the reservation. After allotment, the remaining "surplus" lands were open to purchase by non-Indians. After 25 years, the Chippewa would receive individual deeds. Minnesota decided that the Nelson Act extended state hunting and fishing jurisdiction to the reservations and voided treaty rights. The Chippewa saw little money as it was controlled by the Commission. They got no relief.
>
> In 1904, Congressman Steenerson of Minnesota sponsored legislation that allowed Indian agents to award 80 more acres of timberland to individual allotments. A rider named for Congressman Clapp allowed the Chippewa to sell timber rights on their trust land. By 1908, 95 percent of the virgin white and red pine on the formerly heavily forested reservation had been clear-cut.
>
> Members of the Federation of Women's Clubs of Minnesota were appalled. Their lobbying led to the creation of what became the Chippewa National Forest. It was too late for White Earth. Today, only 56,117 acres of the 837,120 acres of the reservation are Chippewa owned and controlled. Other Chippewa reservations within Minnesota suffered similar fates.

Congress, urged by local representatives and big business, amended the allotment for the Minnesota Chippewa Tribe to allow sale of inherited Indian land to non-Indians. Senator Moses Clapp sponsored a rider to the Steenerson Act in 1904 that let Chippewa sell timber on their allotments without supervision by Indian agents and gave 80 more acres of timberland to each allottee.

The Clapp Act of 1906 removed all restrictions governing sale, encumbrances, or taxation of allotments held by adult mixed bloods or held by full bloods deemed competent by the Chippewa agent. The merchants, speculators, and even bar owners near White Earth developed a cottage industry in cheating Indians of their lands. Agent Simon Michelet was later judged corrupt as land disappeared from Indian ownership.

The destruction of White Earth was noted by the press, and a congressional investigation followed. Warren Moorhead of the Indian Board of

Commissioners arranged a special investigator who discovered extensive fraud. He received an armed escort to allow him to leave the reservation safely. He delivered 117 affadavits describing more than $1,000,000 in frauds. In 1909 the Indian Service sent another investigator and began filing civil suits. More than 1,000 suits were filed in a single year alleging frauds amounting to over 142,000 acres in illegal land takings ($2,000,000), and $11,775,000 in illegal lumber profits.

Although some Chippewa received some compensation and a few culprits were jailed, the land and lumber were gone from Chippewa control. The reservation touted as a single home for Minnesota Chippewa was first a site of poverty for Chippewa; then their wood was taken as their land was bought by others. Today only 7 percent of the entire White Earth Reservation is owned by Chippewa. White Earth is the opposite of the closed Red Lake Reservation.

Although the despoiling of the White Earth Chippewa was particularly egregious, similar destruction of Chippewa resources occurred throughout the remaining Chippewa Country. Even if the agents were honest and lumber companies followed the intent of the law, Chippewa resources were lost generally at below market prices, and any management of natural resources was accidental. Many Chippewa did work in the lumber industry, and a few did well, but the bulk were mired in poverty and without access to resources.

The Dawes Severalty or Allotment Act of 1887 destroyed band communal ownership intentionally. Subsequent amendments and permutations accelerated the process of turning Indians into private landowners. Provisions for selling surplus land from the reservations and for granting deeds to individuals resulted in the Indian estate being reduced from 140,000,000 acres held collectively as reservation public domain in 1887 to about 40,000,000 acres split between individual Indians and the tribe by 1934.

Chippewa reservations were checkerboarded with land owned by non-Indians and other land held by Indians. Some reservations had more non-Indian residents than Indian, and the majority of land belonged to non-Indians. Guaranteed permanent reservations were a cruel joke.

Most Americans insisted that possession of private property and Christianity would make Indians into Americans benefiting from the blessings of civilization. The Indians were not asked whether they agreed. The effects were to mire the Chippewa and other Indians in a lasting poverty, mostly without natural resources or capital. Poverty created societal dysfunctions, and the collective idea of Chippewa culture was threatened.

FORCED ASSIMILATION THROUGH EDUCATION: PART OF THE STORY

The collective consensus of American policy toward Indians throughout the 19th and most of the 20th century was graphically summarized by the founder of the Carlisle Indian School. The Americans had "to kill the Indian to save the man." By 1887, 200 federally supervised Indian schools existed. They enrolled 14,000 Native Americans from many tribes. Twenty-five boarding schools were the centerpieces of the reformist efforts to civilize, convert, and assimilate all American Indians. Schools focused on about an eighth-grade education and vocational training.

The intent of the boarding schools was to isolate children from the bad influences of their families and communities, teach them to march, teach them vocational skills, and erase their savage beliefs. Indian Service schools on reservations (known as day schools) had the same goals but were not as draconian in their techniques as the boarding schools.

Chippewa children, like many other Indian children, had been exposed to American education through the missionary schools established by Catholics and Protestants alike. For most of the 19th century, parochial schools were subsidized by federal allocations. In most cases these private schools proselytizing enthusiasms were mitigated by the need to recruit students. Some parochial schools were as brutal as the Indian Service boarding schools and portrayed Indian religions as uncivilized superstition.

Several missionaries compiled tribal language dictionaries, Bibles, and educational materials. Their premise remained that Indians had to be educated to be integrated in Christian America. Indian parents and leaders often requested schools because they saw them as providing survival tools necessary in America, even if Native American communities were entitled to a measured separatism.

Chippewa children were sent to Mt. Pleasant in Michigan, Hayward and Tomah in Wisconsin, Pipestone and Sisseton-Wahpeton in Minnesota, Flandreau in South Dakota, Devil's Lake in North Dakota, and the flagship boarding schools of Carlisle in Pennsylvania and Haskell in Kansas. An 1898 act permitted Indian agents to remove children from homes to send them to boarding schools. Quite a few of the parochial schools (like St. Mary's on Bad River Reservation) remained on reservations. The parents were often coerced into cooperation by threats of removing all of the children from a family if one child was not sent. Uncooperative parents could lose their annuities and rations.

Many parents acquiesced in sending children to the schools to keep them from starving as they might have on reservations. Other parents realized the need for the schools, and where the environment was not too harsh, children were sent to school as the parents agreed that education was necessary. Boarding schools were useful as well to house the numerous orphans and children from broken homes that abounded in the reservations.

Discipline was harsh, church services ubiquitous, and academic learning ignored in favor of vocational education. Indian children worked at least half-days taking care of the cleaning, cooking, farming, husbandry, and domestic work necessary to run the schools on minimal budgets. The twin diseases of tuberculosis and trachoma were rampant in the crowded schools, as the number of graves on school grounds attested. Children ran away frequently.

Fortunately for the story of the Chippewa, the schools were not as effective as they intended. Damage to Chippewa individuals was often horrendous, but several factors lessened the impact. Congress never provided enough funds for the boarding schools to enroll all children. Staff members' humanitarianism mitigated the efforts to stamp out the use of Indian languages and to convince students to become good Americans. Indian children learned to resist effectively. However, several generations experienced assimilationist schools.

The racism of the U.S. population prevented Indians from integrating into American communities. Assimilation was a dream in the eyes of those not in Indian country. Most returned to their reservations to relearn how to be Chippewa. Even willing Chippewa children could not become Americans when Americans rejected them as equals. Jim Crow customs were blatantly sustained in American communities. "No Indians Allowed" signs persisted through the 1960s. School practices also changed as the Indian Service became professional and teaching methods more attuned, beginning even in the 1930s.

One of the lasting legacies of the boarding school experience for many Chippewa is that of the vicious cruelty they experienced in many of the schools. "Spare the rod and spoil the child" was a common belief in American culture, but not in Native American cultures. School punishment for acting like an Indian was often draconian. Children suffered homesickness, and many ran away from the schools. Children also were separated from their cultural learning in their own language. Too many died at school where tuberculosis was rampant; overcrowded schools and poor medical care combined to spread disease.

Another part of this chapter in the story is that Chippewa learned skills needed to become leaders in the 20th century. Peter Graves was educated away from the reservation and returned to establish the first Chippewa tribal government of the modern era. He also relearned Ojibwemowin and was a stalwart defender of traditional culture when he returned.

Poverty on the reservation made boarding schools a sanctuary for some where food and clothing were available. The Chippewa were able to build on vocational training from the schools when they returned home. Others made friends from other reservations and joined the pan-Indian movements of the 20th century.

Often tribal leaders knew those of other reservations from school contacts. A large number of Chippewa wound up at Carlisle and others at Haskell, where they received more education than was available at reservation day schools. In the period after the 1930s quite a few talked nostalgically about boarding schools. Today some boarding schools have alumni associations.

Schools provided by the Bureau of Indian Affairs or by missionary schools were not as effective as public schools for non-Indians. When the Bureau moved to pay states to allow Indian students to attend public schools, results were mixed. The Indians were often treated as second class because of their poverty and their race. Many teachers and administrators were convinced that Indians could not learn.

NOTABLE FIGURE

Buffalo, Gitchi Bizhikee (Great Buffalo); also Gitchi Waeshke (Great First Born) (c. 1750–1855)

Buffalo was a pivotal Ojibwe leader of the Loon Clan. He was hereditary Ogima (leader) of the LaPointe Band of Lake Superior Chippewa. Heredity does not guarantee continuing leadership, but Buffalo was a noted orator, distinguished warrior and war leader, and Chippewa statesman in diplomacy with the United States. He was a signator on the 1795 Treaty of Greenville.

He is most noted for being the key figure in negotiations that allowed the Chippewa to remain in their Great Lakes homeland. In 1850 he and his son-in-law Benjamin Armstrong protested vociferously in letters and personal contacts to the removal order signed by President Zachary Taylor. Taylor envisioned a Chippewa westward movement to the site of the Sandy Lake Band in Minnesota. The Chippewa from La Pointe, Madeline Island, along with other Chippewa bands, were ordered to collect their treaty payments at Sandy Lake in October. Eventually, many of the Chippewa who obeyed died because of rotten food, poor hunting, absence of government support as promised, and the harsh winter. More than 150 died at Sandy Lake, and about 350 more died as they returned to their homes. Many enraged Chippewa wanted a war against the United States and Minnesota. Buffalo led a different way.

Buffalo convinced several other leaders to go with him to Washington to talk to the president so he would understand what the bad government officials were doing. Despite the opposition of agents at the Bureau of Indian Affairs, Buffalo garnered support from the non-Indian communities. He left by canoe in 1852, caught a steamboat, then traveled by train. Many Americans signed petitions of support as he went. Government officials refused to support the visit or even meet to discuss issues, but a chance meeting with Representative George Briggs of New York led to a meeting with the new president, Millard Fillmore.

Fillmore agreed to suspend the removal order and promised a treaty that would guarantee their homeland. Buffalo returned to Madeleine Island, and the Treaty of 1854 gave him and the Chippewa people what they wanted: permanent reservations in their homelands. The United States agreed to renew treaty annuity distribution at Madeleine Island.

Buffalo had five wives during his lengthy life. He is buried on Madeleine Island, and his descendants are many. As with many Chippewa, Buffalo was a Mide priest and a Roman Catholic (baptized in his last year). Most of his band are now on Red Cliff Reservation across Chequamegon Bay from Madeleine Island. Others of his band comprise the Bad River Reservation band, which is sometimes called the La Pointe Band. Ceremonies are held annually in Buffalo's honor.

7

More Pieces of the Story of the Chippewa

As the century turned, the Chippewa faced continuing challenges to their survival as a people and even as individuals. The first third of the 20th century featured continuing struggles to adjust to the massive losses of resources and existence as wards of the federal government. Domestic dependent nations described by Chief Justice John Marshall in 1831 were mere vestiges of the past.

Individual Chippewa lived by a combination of wage labor, craft making, and sale of rice, sugar, domestic employment in the burgeoning tourist industry, and even by subsistence hunting and fishing. Treaty payments had ceased. Chippewa men worked in the lumber industry and achieved reputations as stellar workers. Others joined the commercial fishing fleets, and still others started working for the Bureau of Indian Affairs (BIA). Documentation by BIA officials demonstrates the hand-to-mouth existence of the tribal citizens. Others scattered to the non-Indian cities and towns, where they formed minority communities on the margins of the dominant society.

Chippewa political life consisted of leaders who cajoled, argued, collaborated, and manipulated the Indian agents who controlled even how much food individuals received. One factor that offered negotiating space for Chippewa leaders is the Indian agents' need for a relatively cooperative reservation populace. They had quotas to meet and supervisors who did not want scandals or controversy. The agents found that they had to make compromises in the face of Chippewa opposition.

A truism for colonial powers throughout the world remained: the colonized have to at least cooperate or the whole system falls apart. Office of Indian Affairs police were Native Americans, judges in the Courts of Indian Offenses were Indians, students in the schools were Natives, and lower levels of colonial rule were populated by Indians.

Illness followed the Chippewa to reservations. BIA records trace epidemics of glaucoma and tuberculosis that afflicted Chippewa communities. Diseases became part of their crowded communities, where extended families lived in one- or two-room tar and paper shacks. Healthy food was not part of the rations and commodities supplied by the government in partial payments for Indian land.

During the late 19th century, the Chippewa learned to make what has become the universal Native American staple, fry bread. It was made with flour fried in lard and sweetened with maple sugar or syrup. Some just called it "Indian bread." Fry bread is good but not as the mainstay of a diet. Malnutrition was common in Chippewa Country.

Multiple story lines are threaded through the 20th century. Three from the turn of the century are illustrative of threads that continue through the century: John Beargrease, a Grand Portage Chippewa; Giiskitawa (Joe White), an ogima of Lac Courte Oreilles–Rice Lake Band; and Bugonaygeshig of the Leech Lake Pillagers.

Individual Chippewa efforts combined to keep families and groups afloat. Daniel Lancaster has provided a scholarly biography, *John Beargrease: Legend of Minnesota's North Shore*. Beargrease (1858–1910) and his family left Grand Portage Reservation to eke out an existence between the non-Chippewa towns of Two Harbors and Grand Marais. They supported an extended family by combining treaty payments, short-term jobs, and some traditional hunting and fishing. He acted as the leader of the Chippewa community and was well considered by the non-Indian communities. In 1879, Beargrease obtained a mail delivery contract that required him to deliver mail through snow, sleet, ice, and heat throughout the year.

During his 20-year mail service, he became famous for his courageous rescue of non-Indians from the grasp of Lake Superior and for a time was the most celebrated Indian on the North Shore. Under his leadership, the Chippewa community held together and maintained ties to their home reservation. Today, the Beargrease Dogsled Race of 400 miles along the North Shore memorializes his courage and efforts to deliver the mail by dogsled. His descendants are numerous. John Beargrease died of tuberculosis in 1910. He was still a Chippewa following the cultural practices of his ancestors.

Giiskitawag, a Chippewa leader known as Joe White, labored for 17 years after he succeeded to leadership of his Rice Lake Band of Lac Courte Oreilles Reservation Chippewa in 1879. His story has been passed on by the scholarship of Erik Redix in *The Murder of Joe White: Ojibwe Leadership and Colonialism in Wisconsin* (2014). White led the band in resistance to being forced to leave a highly productive rice field area to move to the less hospitable Lac Courte Oreilles Reservation. They set up a village near the new town of Rice Lake.

He adamantly opposed encroachment on his town by non-Indians. Rice Lake town leaders called on the Office of Indian Affairs to force him to move. Legally, he and his band were free to live where they wanted. He insisted on his reading of American commitments to hunting and fishing rights even in land ceded off reservation.

White demanded and received rations for his band from the BIA agent on Lac Courte Oreilles Reservation. Band members continued hunting and gathering. His goal was to maintain his band in their homeland as the United States met its treaty obligations and perhaps live in harmony with the non-Chippewa community of Rice Lake and Barron County. He and his few band members did not want to be forced away from their homes.

Wisconsin refused to recognize treaty-guaranteed hunting and fishing rights and insisted that Chippewa like Joe White and his band who did not live on a reservation had to comply with Wisconsin game laws. White and others were often arrested, their guns and catch confiscated, and they were jailed or fined. The federal government did not interfere with the state officials.

In 1894, an arrest warrant for hunting out of season was issued for Joe White. Josiah Hicks, game warden, tried to serve it. When Joe White argued, the warden cuffed him and beat him, so he started to run off. Josiah Hicks shot the retreating White in the back and killed him. The game warden was tried and acquitted by a non-Chippewa jury.

Succeeding band leaders gave up and moved to their reservation. Another piece of Chippewa rights was gone. Late in the century, the Chippewa from Lac Courte Oreilles gained treaty rights through the Voigt case. The federal courts required Wisconsin to honor the treaty rights just as Giishkitawag, Joe White, had done.

Chippewa leaders resisted the clear-cutting lumber industry, which did so much to destroy Chippewa resources while manipulating federal and state law to exploit Chippewa allotment holders. Many Chippewa owners did not even receive the payments due, while others saw lumber thieves simply move in and take their timber.

Bugonaygeshig, translated as Hole in the Day, was one of the more vociferous opponents of the lumber industry. He belonged to the Pillager Band of Leech Lake Reservation and at Sugar Point. He was often arrested or called to court as a witness. This entailed a journey of a few hundred miles, usually to Duluth, Minnesota.

State and federal officials developed a practice of bringing or summoning Chippewa to appear many miles from their home reservations. After these appearances, Chippewa like Hole in the Day were simply told to go home. It was one of the indignities foisted upon those considered troublemakers.

In 1898, Bugonaygeshig received a summons to testify miles away from home and ignored it. When the sheriff and reservation agent arrived, armed Chippewa sent them packing when they arrested another Chippewa who was part of the argument. The Third U.S. Infantry from Ft. Snelling was summoned to put down this Indian uprising as hysterical officials called it. When 20 soldiers arrived, they fired on surrounding Indians. Later, 44 more soldiers arrived by boat along with BIA police and several federal marshals—and numerous reporters. When they landed, Chippewa resistance led to a skirmish.

The Battle of Sugar Point left 7 killed, 14 wounded, and 1 Indian Service policeman killed by friendly fire. Bugonaygeshig never appeared, and the forces withdrew. After this last battle between Indians and the U.S. army, the Commissioner of Indian Affairs William Jones launched an investigation into the policy of punishing Indians by "cutting them adrift" to find their way home from court. In June 1899 President McKinley pardoned the Chippewa participants in this last battle. Private Oscar Burkhead received the Medal of Honor for his heroism against the Chippewa.

Yet another investigation led to lumber company officials being indicted, agents being relieved and sometimes indicted, and a greater supervision and regulation of the lumber industry. White Earth Chippewa eventually received some restitution, and some of the fraudulently taken lands were recovered. Of course, the timber was gone, the rice fields damaged, and game driven away already.

Bugonaygeshig became a local hero. He often marched in parades in the surrounding communities like Walker and Bemidji, Minnesota. He died in 1916 at the age of 80.

RED LAKE RESERVATION

Each band of Chippewa struggled to maintain its distinctive identity. Red Lake leaders were more successful than most. Other Chippewa bands resisted being consolidated onto single reservations like White Earth, but many had to give in under pressure from surrounding Minnesotans and federal officials. Red Lake Chippewa did not.

Historically, the Red Lake area was taken from the Dakota. Several major confrontations like Battle Lake occurred in the Red Lake environs. As the westward edge of Chippewa expansion, Red Lakers moved onto the plains of the Red River of the North and the Dakotas. They added buffalo hunting, horses, and trade with the Hudson's Bay Company to their economy.

Chippewa bands continuously moved to join them, and their population grew despite near constant warfare. Permanent band-centered towns like Ponemah, Redby, Little Rock, and Red Lake were, in effect, band villages. As various crises arose, leaders emerged to become heroes of the nation.

Professor Anton Treuer's *Warrior Nation* provides a comprehensive history of the Red Lake Band through a focus on the actions of a succession of Red Lake leaders. Narrating history through personal stories have long been a common cultural means of conveying history.

Treuer's history of Red Lake nation is an excellent example of this style of historiography. Others who utilized this approach are the pioneering Brenda Child, Erik Redix, Chantal Norrgard, and Scott Lyons. Chippewa history is enriched by these and other scholars using the personal story technique.

One benefit of the biographical lens is that Chippewa people learn more about their individual heroes and, perhaps, villains. Earlier histories portrayed just "things happening" without Chippewa agency and without identifying the individuals involved. Chippewa people need to know names and events to reinforce their sense of identity and understanding of how things came to be.

Red Lakers were a Chippewa frontier society that brought together diverse pioneers of Chippewa expansion. Waabibines, White Thunderbird, is an example of Red Lake hybridity. He was born Dakota but was adopted along with a Dakota clan name, the Kingfisher. The new clan facilitated the creation of the Red Lake mix of clans. None of the traditional Chippewa clans like the Crane and Loon were dominant at Red Lake.

Moozoomoo, Moose Dung, coordinated defense of Red Lake's existence and was its most prominent leader in the second half of the 19th century. He and other leaders traded millions of acres of land in return for a reservation that retained the core of their homeland around upper and lower Red Lake. In 1863, the Old Crossing Treaty surrendered almost the entire Red River of the North valley, some of the best farming land in Chippewa Country.

The Pembina Band also signed the treaty but were only promised a reservation. They had to wait for a generation to have Turtle Mountain Reservation established by executive order. Red Lake would have to lose more land, but the band did survive intact thanks to the acumen of leaders like Moose Dung.

Resistance to the Nelson Act. which was designed to speed lumbering and access to Chippewa land by Americans, was led by Medweganoonind, He Who Was Spoken To. In 1889, He Who Was Spoken To met with Henry Rice of Minnesota and the United States to trade more land for the right to exist. The many leaders at the conference adamantly insisted on retaining both parts of Red Lake the core of their land. Red Lake was the source of much of their food and economy. In the previous decades, the lumber industry had begun harvesting Red Lake and other reservation timber, legally and illegally. Chippewa people did get some jobs in the industry, and the Bureau of Indian Affairs leases brought some money to the tribal funds they held in trust.

After an 1889 agreement, the United States allowed lumber industry access to the reservation by railroads, non-Indian navigation of the Red Lakes. Land within the reservation was alienated to churches, the lumber industry, and schools. As the United States traced out the borders of Red Lake Reservation, they took the upper third of the lake. Red Lake was not allotted, a key victory for Red Lakers.

He Who Was Spoken To and the nation united in collective grief and continued resisting. Their complaints were ignored. Professor Treuer concludes that contending with the United States provided the impetus for uniting various towns and sub-bands of Red Lake Reservation into a coherent nation. He Who Was Spoken To should be considered as its inspiration and catalyst.

Red Lake Reservation remains as the only closed reservation of the 20 Chippewa reservations within the United States. All land is held in common within its boundaries, and its use is controlled by Chippewa enactments based on tradition. This was a triumph for Red Lakers against significant odds. Checkerboarding and inundation by non-Indian populations did not happen on Red Lake. Chippewa leaders kept the land reserved.

Other challenges threatened Chippewa control of their own. U.S. policy makers wanted to eradicate traditional Chippewa culture and supplant it with American values and practices. In addition to taking the land and resources, the U.S. assault turned to religion and American-style schools to force the changes they wanted.

Red Lake community resistance to these prongs of American policy was led by Noodinoons, Little Wind, a spiritual leader of the Midewiwin Grand Society. He was born in Ponema, the most traditional of the Red Lake towns today and one that maintained its distance from the other Red Lake communities. U.S. officials shortened his name to Nodin, an anglicized version of wind; he responded to requests for his last name with a translation from Ojibwemowin, wind. Amusingly, for all in the know, he became Wind Wind.

As Americans sought to impose assimilation on Red Lake, Nodin became the focal point of traditional culture and Chippewa community control. Christianity and compulsory education were a two-pronged assault aided by the Office of Indian Affairs, Congress, and even so-called Friends of the Indian. On Red Lake, Catholic missionaries arrived first and were joined by successive Protestants. Red Lakers watched with amusement as the Catholics led by Bishop Henry Whipple (Episcopal) and Father Ignaz Tomasin (Catholic) vied for Chippewa souls and insisted the other was wrong.

The educational prong of the assimilationists was complicated further by politicians who wanted the missions to teach Indians to do manual labor in service to white Minnesotans. Governor Alexander Ramsey (1849–1853) ordered all mission schools closed until they agreed to teach only manual arts with books as "a secondary consideration" in the words of Indian agent D. B. Harrington. Ramsey then was state governor from 1860 to 1863 and then U.S. senator from 1863 to 1875. He was supportive of exploitation of Indian resources and often was an obstacle to quality improvement in Indian education. Along with other state and local elected officials, Ramsey favored a kind of assimilation. Ramsey was the enemy personified.

Catholics dominated efforts to convert even before Red Lake became a reservation. Chippewa contacts with French and then mixed-blood (metis) populations assured Catholic dominance. By the 20th century, communities of Red Lake, Redby, and Little Rock contained many who considered themselves Catholic. Their cause was aided when the Catholic Drexel sisters brought their order to establish St. Mary's mission and founded a school in 1888. Red Lake's traditional chiefs granted them land in 1889. By 1900 the school had both federal funding and about 80 students. When federal funding was withdrawn, the General Council of the Red Lake Chippewa used their funds to keep the school operating.

Episcopalians, next to the Catholics, were most influential. He Who Was Spoken To, the political and traditional leader at Redby, agreed to convert, which helped keep a significant Episcopal presence. Presbyterians, initially led by Frederick Ayers, opened a school and church, and others followed. Nodin Wind watched the developments and joined others from Ponemah in their consistent opposition to Christian missionaries and their schools. Ponemah leaders also refused to participate in the land session negotiations in 1863, 1889, 1903, and 1904.

As the Office of Indian Affairs pressed to suppress traditional Chippewa religion, Nodin Wind emerged as the spokesman for traditional religion.

Federal rules also outlawed medicine men and penalized those who practiced traditional religion. Even into the 1920s, Office of Indian Affairs circulars condemned all Indian gatherings like powwows.

Indian religion was not legalized again until 1933 despite the First Amendment and Chippewa being made American citizens after 1924. Midewiwin lodges and Big Drum societies functioned surreptitiously. Dancing and ceremonies continued anyway.

Many Chippewa complied with the prohibitions that did erode participation. Probably most converts to the several Christian sects did so with characteristic pragmatism. One could be both Christian and traditional in Chippewa culture. It was not possible to divorce oneself from one's family, which guaranteed the practices of generations would continue.

The Office of Indian Affairs was convinced that they had to control Indian education if assimilation was going to work. In addition to building boarding schools after 1876, they built day schools on reservations. In 1899, Congress authorized $20,000 to build four schools in Minnesota. Two were to be on Red Lake Reservation. In Redby the school was erected quickly, but in Ponemah, or Cross Lake, they faced a solid wall of opposition led by Nodin Wind.

Government plans were to build the school on a sacred burial ground. Leaders of Ponemah indicated they would burn it. In 1900, Indian agent William Mercer was advised to negotiate to avoid bloodshed. He deputized some Red Lakers and headed to Ponemah, where he was met by armed, angry Chippewa. Eventually, Mercer agreed to control of the school and its personnel by Ponemah residents. In effect, Ponemah had a Chippwea school board.

Nodin Wind's actions and subsequent joining in the General Council of the Red Lake Nation cemented the place of Ponemah as part of Red Lake. It also was the heart of traditional culture. The educational assault on Chippewa culture continued in other government and mission schools. Any Chippewa who attended high school had to merge into the anti-Indian schools. Many did because it was required by law and because education was the way to economic stability. Skills acquired could be used for resistance to assimilation or just to make a living.

Wind's defense of Red Lake's traditional culture was buttressed by many other determined leaders. Peter Graves (1872–1957) emerged as the dominant political figure of two generations and has been described as a political genius by Anton Treuer. He has been credited with ushering the reservation into a political posture that allowed Red Lake to counter efforts by Minnesota and the United States eventually. He was christened Peter Graves in 1872 using a name chosen for his mother so she would have a legal status, but his traditional name was Nezhikegwaneb (Lone Feather). Nicknames are popular in Indian Country, and Graves's was Zhaaganash (Englishman).

Although he began school in the first class on the reservation in 1877, Graves was sent to schools in Illinois and Pennsylvania. He worked in a variety of jobs and even played professional baseball before returning to the reservation in 1889. The traditional chiefs soon availed themselves of his bilingual skills as did federal agents. He was an interpreter, joined the police, rose to chief of police, and then became postmaster. Professor Treuer indicates that he was an astute negotiator because he was well respected by the Office of Indian Affairs and Red Lakers.

Two women of the Big Bear family weave baskets on Red Lake Reservation in 1920. Chippewa women played a pivotal role in preserving traditional culture. (Minnesota Historical Society Collections)

His first political achievement was to convince the traditional chiefs to not support the Leech Lake Chippewa in their conflict with the United States that had led to the Battle of Sugar Point. Then he turned to securing control of the timber harvest and the timber mill. He managed to secure removal of most non-Indian workers from the reservation. Eventually, Red Lake ownership of the timber mill led to expanded, controlled harvest and most profits going to Red Lakers.

Minnesota created a major problem for Red Lake under the guise of World War I necessity. The state Commission on Public Safety created a monopoly on commercial fishing that required that all fish be sold through state fisheries. One of the fisheries was established with the support of the Office of Indian Affairs at Redby on the reservation. Minnesota set prices, forbade any sales to private businesses, and managed the joint tribal-state fund. Minnesota subtracted costs for operations before returning some funds to the federal government to include in Red Lake accounts.

After the war, Minnesota continued the practice and kept the bulk of the profits. Red Lake fishermen received about 40 percent of market price. Minnesota marketed the fish throughout the United States and even abroad. As late as 1927, Minnesota's Commission indicated that the fish reserves were inexhaustible in the huge Red Lake and the Office of Indian Affairs agreed.

Under the leadership of Peter Graves, Red Lake employed lawyers to break the monopoly and secure fair prices. By 1929, Red Lake had created the Red Lake Fisheries Association and moved to joint management of the fishery with Minnesota. Many decades later, commercial fishing had depleted the Red Lake supply. After much emotional finger-pointing, Red Lake and Minnesota agreed to suspend fishing until the population rebounded.

In a continuing conflict over control, Minnesota used the funds from fisheries to buy the town of Waskish and build processing buildings. Waskish was located on the edge of the upper lake, which remains a disputed area because an 1899 survey took it from the reservation and gave it to Minnesota. Waskish allowed the state to continue tapping into the commercial fish supply of the Red Lakes. After losing in the courts, Minnesota transferred Waskish to the federal government in 1943 to hold in trust for Red Lake Reservation. The tribe has not regained ownership of Red Lake.

The political struggles for control of the reservation economy and culture highlighted the need for a unified reservation government that would be able to interact with the outside world and address reservation-wide needs. The Office of Indian Affairs preferred to work with individuals and determine reservation priorities.

Graves convinced others that it would take a recognized national government to deal with continuing challenges from the United States and Minnesota. Peter Graves, Paul Beaulieu, Otto Thunder, and Joseph Graves wrote the first Chippewa reservation constitution after lengthy discussions and contributions from leaders throughout the reservation. The hereditary chiefs approved the constitution.

The General Council of the Red Lake Band of Chippewa Indians retained the leadership of seven hereditary chiefs representing seven communities. Each chief selected council members who could pass legislation. The council chose nonvoting tribal officers. Peter Graves was first treasurer and then secretary-treasurer. He held his position until 1957 and dominated Red Lake politics in the constant struggle to keep Red Lake independent of the Minnesota Chippewa Tribe and to avoid the constant threats of allotment and even removal. Red Lake was saved from being given over to the jurisdiction of the state in the 1950s. All of the other Chippewa reservations became subject to state jurisdiction in 1953.

> **AMERICANS, CULTURAL ICONS, AND SURVIVAL**
>
> Most Americans think of feathers, dancing, and traditional clothing when they picture the Chippewa and other Indians. After the Chippewa ceased to be seen as a threat, Americans encouraged the Chippewa to act like Indians despite the official assimilation policy. Americans throughout Chippewa Country invited them to come and dance at holidays, state publications featured colorful traditional scenes, and Boy Scouts were taught traditional Indian lore. Many romantics lauded the wisdom of Indian elders.
>
> Even Indian Service schools romanticized Indians. *Hiawatha* became a staple in Haskell Indian School's publicity events. It featured Indian actors and traditional garb. Indians became mascots for schools, and products featured Indian maidens. Indian crafts were in demand. Indians were good, popular business.
>
> Although often patronizing, Americans reinforced Chippewa efforts by providing a permissive environment. The Chippewa took advantage to continue dances, crafts, and the stories that went with them. Chippewa leaders often received non-Indian assistance. Public support undermined official policy of suppressing tribal cultures.
>
> Powwows are the public, open, and accessible example of Chippewa traditional culture. The Chippewa attend, participate, and relish being Indian. Americans flock to powwows. They remain the most graphic evidence of continuing Indian persistence.
>
> Ceremonial life was integral to the picture. Although criminalized until 1932, sweat lodges, public prayers, pipe ceremonies, naming ceremonies, and healing dances like the jingle dress dance were not only tolerated but encouraged by the American public. Chippewa sources informed scholars. Objective histories publicized the treatment of Indians. Many Americans developed sympathy for Indian causes. Publicity brought Indians to public attention.
>
> The Indian Reorganization Act and return of tribal governments and publicly espoused traditional religion occurred in an atmosphere of support. Even proposed termination fell on infertile ground in the face of American inclinations to support tribal cultures.

TURTLE MOUNTAIN RESERVATION

While Red Lake and other reservations struggled to maintain community integrity and sovereignty, the Pembina Band that signed the Old Crossing Treaty in 1863 did not yet have their promised reservation. They claimed that between 8 and 10 million acres west of the Red River of the North was theirs. The United States procrastinated in designating a reservation, perhaps because of disputes about tribal rolls and what should be done to pay the band. Neither Canadians nor Americans wanted to accept responsibility for the Chippewa who freely moved back and forth across the 49th parallel boundary.

The Pembina Band awaiting a reservation had a lengthy history separate from other bands. Chippewa Country had been extended to the Turtle Mountains in Canada and the United States by the 1750s. A Northwest Trading Company post was established in 1797 at Pembina, and it was followed by other trading posts up and down the Red River Valley. The Chippewa came from all of the eastern bands, including Red Lake and some from as far away as Madeline Island. Others came from the northern Chippewa and Metis clustered around Ft. Garry at the head of the river in Manitoba.

Chippewa populations had been intermarrying with European fur traders for more than a century by the time the Chippewa reached the valley. The descendants of these continuing unions became members of Chippewa families throughout the country, and some were numerous enough to create mixed communities from Sault Ste. Marie through Madeline Island and on into Red Lake.

In the Red River Valley, the communities clustered along the valley and established a new society. Metis culture was a blend of French, Scots, Chippewa, Cree, and even other tribal cultures. They clumped together in communities where Catholic priests, land ownership, and commerce were features. However, Metis constantly intermarried with Indians, thereby retaining Native American identity to accompany their Metis identities.

Metis means mixed in French and is similar to the Spanish mestizo. In English, people of Indian and non-Indian ancestry were first called halfbreeds or mongrels. The pejorative terms gave way by the 20th century to mixed blood. Blended ancestry people were a part of the interaction between Europeans and Indians from first contact, and they have often posed a problem for European descent populations trying to figure out where these people belonged in society. Were they Indians or were they white?

Indians did not have much difficulty because they had long accepted genetic mixing. Family members were part of the community regardless of parentage. Chippewa history is replete with prominent mixed bloods. Generally, mixed bloods either merged back into the white community or they married one another or full bloods and identified as tribal citizens. Often they were separate but part of the communities.

Fur trading posts had provided a center of population and continued mixing since the 17th century, which allowed a distinct identity to develop. Metis with a capital M is the designation for the separate cultural group, while metis with a lowercase m just means mixed bloods typical throughout Indian country. Metis even developed a separate language, Michif. They lived in Metis communities centered usually around Catholic churches and modified Catholic values and practices. Metis organized the Red River hunts, fought the Lakota and Dakota Sioux, and formed the cart convoys from Winnipeg to Minneapolis–St. Paul. The cart caravans also originated in towns established at Pembina and St. Joseph, North Dakota.

The Chippewa and Metis blended groups first interacted in the fur trade and then in the Red River hunts for buffalo. Metis- and Chippewa-manufactured pemmican was a mainstay of the fur trade diet. Their Red River carts carved pathways from Winnipeg to Minneapolis–St. Paul until the 1860s.

Metis communities at Pembina and St. Joseph in North Dakota had a population of 1,089 by the 1850 census of Minnesota Territory with perhaps 4,000 more Metis in smaller communities on both sides of the international border. The Metis and Chippewa were both insistent on keeping their cultures, their lands, and their independence. Both were willing to fight for these freedoms. Those living in the United States, both Chippewa and Metis, were called the Pembina Band of Chippewa despite American misgivings about where the Metis fit in the scheme of things.

At the deliberations that led to the Old Crossing Treaty, American officials determined that the Pembina Band was represented by 663 Metis and 352 full-blood Chippewa. The Americans complained that the Metis dominated and misled the Chippewa. At the treaty, the Metis asserted their ownership of the Red River Valley, but the United States ignored this and acquired the valley from the Chippewa. Metis ownership was recognized to the extent that they were to be issued "half-breed scrip" to allow them to take homesteads in the ceded territory. The Pembina Chippewa were promised a reservation like the Red Lakers received, payment for the valley, and subsequent negotiations to buy the rest of eastern North Dakota.

The Pembina Band returned to the western Red River Valley above Grand Forks, North Dakota, and to the Turtle Mountains to await developments. Steamboats continued to ply the river up to Winnipeg, and railroads arrived at the river's edge by 1873. American settlers began arriving. The Metis and Chippewa moved down from Canada after the first Louis Riel-led rebellion and subsequent land loss in Manitoba. They also moved westward to Montana and to Saskatchewan. In 1877, the United States convinced about 200 Metis to move to the decade-old White Earth Reservation where they contributed to the difficulties of this ersatz reservation. In the aftermath of Louis Riel's rebellion, many Metis moved south to join relatives and be a part of the Pembina Band.

Chippewa resistance to white settler activities in land they still owned led to Little Shell's posted declaration: "It is here forbidden to any white men to encroach on this Indian land by settling on it before a treaty being made with the American government." Despite the declaration, Canadian immigrants founded St. John, and American squatters founded Dunseith. Frightened settlers called for help, and troops from Fort Totten arrived to protect the settlers, not the Chippewa. In October, the secretary of the interior opened the land to homesteading. To avoid violence, President Chester Arthur met one of the 1863 promises: he issued an executive order creating the Turtle Mountain Chippewa Reservation.

Arthur's order reserved 22 townships for the reservation. Under pressure, he reduced it to two townships in 1884, primarily because too many Metis wanted land. The United States counted 183 full-blood Chippewa, 731 American Metis, and 400 Canadian Metis. After 1884 they were expected to make a living on two townships that were mostly nonarable. In the winter of 1886–1887, 151 Chippewa starved to death.

Reservation boundaries met one of the Chippewa needs. Unsettled relations continued. Hungry Chippewa sometimes harvested settler cattle. White settlers in Rolette County insisted that Chippewa pay taxes on their nontaxable land, and others simply pushed onto Chippewa land and even assaulted them. In 1889 armed Chippewa recovered confiscated cattle from a sheriff, and the North Dakota National Guard was sent to restore order.

Little Shell, the dominant Chippewa leader of the Turtle Mountain traditional council, continued to threaten force to protect Chippewa rights. They demanded rations from Indian agents during a prolonged depression and severe weather. Tribal-selected lawyers John Bottineau and John Burke entered the lists, trying to get the government to provide the promised funds for land in dispute. In 1889, North Dakota became a state.

In 1890 a commission failed to clarify the situation, and the difficulties festered. Disgusted and hungry full bloods moved off the reservation and squatted. Ironically, the off-reservation town of Dunseith is now the center of traditional Chippewa culture for Turtle Mountain Chippewa.

In 1892 the United States decided to negotiate. The McCumber Commission included Senator Porter McCumber. Little Shell demanded a voice in the Commission and set conditions that the United States ignored, so Little Shell led his band to Montana. In his absence, Agent John Waugh and Subagent E. W. Brenner appointed a Turtle Mountain Council comprised of selected Chippewa and Metis.

Attorney John Bottineau was excluded from the reservation, and hearings were held in buildings too small to allow Chippewa representatives to attend. Eventually, the McCumber Commission recommended a settlement, and the puppet council signed it. Little Shell refused to sign, moved to Montana permanently, and died in 1901. Divisions within the Turtle Mountain Chippewa were exacerbated.

Congress did not ratify the McCumber Agreement for another dozen years. Tribal enrollment continued to plague the Office of Indian Affairs and bitterly divided the tribe. Some wanted to exclude Metis, some wanted the entire agreement thrown out, and some just wanted food and assistance that agents continued to promise. In 1904 Senator McCumber, a member of the Senate Committee on Indian Affairs, pushed legislation through that essentially replicated the McCumber Agreement.

The United States acquired between 8 and 10 million acres for $1 million. This is about 10 cents per acre and lives in Chippewa memory as the "ten cent treaty." Turtle Mountain's population was 2,714 enrolled. Agent Charles Davis claimed that OIA officials were intimidated into adding Canadians and others who did not qualify. The fraudulent travesty of the Ten Cent Treaty was recognized by the Indian Claims Commission in 1979 when they awarded Turtle Mountain Chippewa $52,527,338 as compensation for the land taking by the United States.

While the amount of settlement was being decided in Washington, the two-township reservation was allotted in 275 quarter sections for 326 families. There was not enough land for everyone. Off-reservation allotments from the public domain went to 650 males, 15 families on Graham's Island on the Devil's Lake Reservation, 390 families at Trenton, North Dakota on the Montana border, and 149 families in Montana.

Little Shell's band refused to be complicit and took no land. Many Metis in Montana were left out of the land allocations. The United States insisted they were Canadians even to the extent of using the military to round up and deport many of them to Canada.

During the confusion and chaos of settling the question and doing allotments, the OIA expanded services to Turtle Mountain. Catholic schools were expanded, and OIA schools were created. Many Chippewa were sent to the OIA boarding school on the Dakota Devil's Lake Reservation. As with other reservations, Chippewa continued adjusting to being submerged in the larger white society, seeing land sold as allotments were converted to fee simple lands, and struggles continued. Turtle Mountain Chippewa pursued the same goals as other Chippewa reservation communities. They maintained Chippewa and Metis cultural practices and religion while defending sovereignty.

ROCKY BOY AND LITTLE SHELL BAND

Chippewa and Metis communities had intermingled throughout the 19th century on the plains of Montana and even Alberta. The dominant tribes were the Cree in the North with which the Chippewa maintained a close alliance, the Assiniboine, Crow, Cheyenne, Gros Ventres, and Lakota.

A band led by Ashiniwin (Stone Child) maintained its identity as a Chippewa even while the United States attempted to merge, move, and assimilate the tribes of the high plains.

Stone Child and most of his band were originally from Red Lake where Stone Child had signed the 1899 agreements. Rocky Boy was the mistranslation of Ashiniwin, and a reservation that combined Cree and Chippewa was established in 1916 and called Rocky Boy's. It was intended for landless Chippewa from the east but includes a blend of Chippewa, Metis, and Cree. It is located in the Bears Paw Mountains but has isolated plots of trust land scattered hither and yon because of allotment efforts.

Little Shell's band located near non-Indian communities and survived in a near traditional round of subsistence, while Little Shell tried to get a reservation just for his band. Despite his fulminations and strong role in the Turtle Mountain story, the United States simply moved on and ignored him as they created the Turtle Mountain Reservation.

Descendants have maintained an identity with accepted band leadership and acceptance as a band by Montana. They continue petitioning for federal recognition even in the 21st century. They have come close on several occasions, but opposition from various sources leaves them as one of the last Chippewa bands awaiting recognition.

There are Chippewa communities from Michigan to Montana that have not been included as separate federally recognized bands. Several were merged into other bands by federal fiat despite their objections, and they continue to struggle for recognition of separate identities. Others like the several Metis communities in Montana join the non-reservation, non-federally recognized with tenuous relationships to the Bureau of Indian Affairs.

After Rocky Boy Reservation, the drastically reduced current Chippewa County achieved its modern, Balkanized existence. There are 20 sovereign Chippewa "tribes" today. Each has its own government.

THE INDIAN REORGANIZATION ACT

From the time that the United States became a country, its Indian policy pursued the elimination of Indian tribes and Indian people while contradictorily maintaining tribal separateness. American attitudes and policies impacted Chippewa Country. The Americans insisted that it was impossible for Indians to be sovereign at the same time that they were within the United States. Reality had dictated a measured separatism supported by law and tribes continuing to exist as "domestic dependent nations." After the creation of the United States, the story of the Chippewa is one of contending with the United States for sovereignty and for retaining resources that would sustain them as separate communities.

The United States unleashed pressures on the Chippewa and all Native Americans to conform to the superior civilization as they saw it. After reservations were established beginning in the 1830s for some and by the 1850s for others, government-sponsored efforts to eradicate Native American religions were accompanied by a direct rule administered by Indian agents of the Office of Indian Affairs and even by military officers. Tribal governments were no longer acceptable, and tribal leaders were undermined by efforts to make Indians deal directly with the agents.

After 1883, Courts of Indian Offenses dispensed laws enforced by OIA police. Meanwhile, Indian resources were blundered, and Indian health deteriorated. Most Indian people were dependent on government rations, and they languished in poverty. This was true not only in Chippewa Country but also throughout the United States. Each federal census documented a continuing decline in the Native American population until in 1910 only about 250,000 Indians lived in the United States. Still Indians did not assimilate, few became Christians, and tribal cultures remained stubbornly vibrant. Some did become western educated and learned to operate within the order imposed by the United States.

Corruption and failures of Indian assimilationist policies did not go unnoticed as American reformist groups created the Progressivism and Social Gospel crusades that tried to redress the problems of runaway development careening through the United States at the expense of workers, farmers, Indians, and the environment. Robber barons and what they represented needed to be reined in with regulations and laws, and many of these had exploited Indian resources.

There were always a few Americans who agreed with Indians that they should be allowed to remain Indian and to govern themselves. These turned to exposing the results of the failures in the trust responsibility incurred by the United States on behalf of Indians. Two of the more famous were Standing Bear and Bright Eyes. The old war leaders like Red Cloud and Sitting Bull were widely hailed by audiences that listened to their woeful tales.

American muckrakers took up the cause. Helen Hunt Jackson published *A Century of Dishonor: A Sketch of the United States Government's Dealings with Some of the Indian Tribes* in 1881. She followed this with the tragic romance, *Ramona*, in 1884. Others like Gertrude Bonnin, Zitkala Za, a university-educated Sioux, worked within national women's organizations to champion Indian separateness and cultural validity.

Even the reformers who gathered for the Lake Mohonk Conference railed against the destructiveness and tragic consequences of Indian policy and federal control. They pushed for allotment and got it in 1887, and they hoped to replace Indian cultures with American, but they did document failures. The Indian Rights Association was long a voice for reform, a watchdog against financial chicanery, and a critic of the Office of Indian Affairs despite advocating assimilation.

The National Indian Defense Association led the campaign that most Indian leaders supported. They demanded recognition of the validity of Indian cultures, the right to practice Indian religion, and a reversal of the general assault on Indian cultures. They also wanted corruption stopped and prosecuted with compensation going to the Indians exploited.

World War I blunted the reform efforts in defense of Indian cultural practices. The war did create an atmosphere for the many Native American volunteers to be rewarded with the right to become American citizens without losing their tribal status. During the Coolidge administration several steps toward reform occurred. In 1924, reformers in the larger society got Congress to extend citizenship to all American Indians living on reservations. The statute stipulated that the newly created citizens retained their rights and status as American Indians. There was no formal response from the Indians, as they did not have formal governments at the time.

The government also took note of the numerous scandals, indictments, and commission reports that emphasized problems in Indian country. Lewis Meriam was hired to conduct a complete examination of the results of federal governance of Indians. He gathered a team to do the work and visited numerous reservations for information. As officials of the government, they were able to access government records.

The Problem of Indian Administration, or the Meriam Report, came out in 1928. It was a systematic cataloging of the deplorable results of American control of Indians. It delved into a health system that killed Indians by neglect and where tuberculosis and trachoma were endemic. It revealed the depths of poverty that plagued reservations and blamed government failure for it. The report described the deplorable sanitation and education at boarding schools. The incompetence, ineffectiveness, and indifference of OIA personnel were described throughout the report. Its recommendations included more money for schooling, preventative health care, economic stimuli, and a continuation of efforts to assimilate Indians. Meriam and his colleagues laid the absence of assimilation at the feet of bad administration and lack of funding but did not challenge the idea of assimilation.

A new commissioner of Indian affairs under President Herbert Hoover took office with all of the reformers' supplied ammunition to hand. He soon came up with a 14-point set of goals but was only able to begin the health and education reforms planned. Boarding schools were going to be replaced and health care improved right away, and other reforms were to follow. Members of the Indian Defense Association led by a radical firebrand, John Collier, were quick to criticize. They attacked the premise of forced assimilation and allotment, and wanted faster action on the 14-point plan.

As so often happens in Indian country, developments in the larger society overrode plans for Indian policies. The Great Depression led to the replacement of President Hoover and those who wanted to continue assimilation policies and allotment. Franklin Roosevelt appointed John Collier as commissioner of Indian affairs. He brought reformers from the Indian Defense Association and, astonishingly Indians, into the Office of Indian Affairs.

Collier was a believer in the nobility of Indian cultures because of his experience with Pueblos. He did not think Native Americans had to give up being Indian to be Americans. In fact, he wanted to see Indians retain much of their traditional cultures. Most Indians agreed with his position even if they might doubt some of his tactics and desire different approaches.

Collier immediately used his executive power to reverse policies. He instructed agents to cease allotments and to halt sales of Indian lands. No fee patents were to be granted. In a 1934 circular, "Indian Religious Freedom and Indian Culture," he instructed employees to show respect for Indian cultural values. "No interference with Indian religious life or ceremonial expression will hereafter be tolerated. The cultural liberty of all Indians is in all respects to be considered equal to that of any non-Indian group." Indian traditional arts and crafts were to be "prized, nourished, and honored."

Opposition was immediate. Church groups opposed religious freedom for Indians, and other groups opposed the halt to allotment and the dispossession of Indian landowners. The Indian Rights Association was adamantly opposed to the changes and to legislation introduced to make them and others law. Collier was supported by the president and Secretary of the Interior Albert Falls, many Indian organizations, and the National Association on Indian Affairs and the American Indian Defense Association. Many progressives also supported reform.

After multiple amendments and dropping some provisions, the Indian Reorganization Act (IRA) became law in 1934. It was also known as the Wheeler-Howard bill while in hearings, as Senator Burton K. Wheeler of Montana and Representative Edgar Howard of Nebraska ushered the 48-page bill through to adoption. During the development of the IRA, Collier deliberately brought a number of educated Indians into working for the Indian service, and they actively participated in planning.

The IRA was revolutionary on a number of fronts. It was the first time that Congress offered Indians the right to vote on an Indian policy. Many had testified about the bill, and several Indians helped draw up its provisions. It halted allotment and extended trust protection for individual allotment holders indefinitely. All sales of Indian land were halted. It authorized preferential appointment of Indians to positions in the Office of Indian Affairs.

The Secretary of the Interior was authorized to purchase land for Indian reservations and place it in trust. It authorized an education loan fund for Indian students to attend vocational and trade schools. The secretary was authorized to issue a certificate to tribes to manage their own lands. It returned all unallotted lands to the tribes to be held in trust.

Most importantly, the IRA granted any Indian tribe the right to organize for the common good and to adopt a constitution and bylaws approved by a tribal referendum. They could incorporate to manage fiscal affairs, and a revolving loan fund could be used for economic development. At first, secretarial approval was required for implementation of constitutions. The approved tribal government could employ counsel and could negotiate with the federal government.

Tribes needed to voice their intent to implement government under the IRA by 1936. Neatly, the IRA made tribe and reservation the same entity even if more than one federally recognized tribe was on a single reservation. Oklahoma tribes were not included in the IRA coverage but instead were subject to the Oklahoma Indian Welfare Act.

Collier assembled the resources of the entire Office of Indian Affairs to convince tribes to implement this self-governance. They held massive conferences throughout Indian country, sent staff members to reservations, published sample constitutions, and provided technical assistance through a special office set up in Washington. Local tribal politics and organized opposition from outside groups played a role in the reservation-by-reservation votes. By the 1936 deadline, 181 tribes voted to form an IRA government, and 77 declined. Fourteen additional tribes were added because they had not held referendums. After constitutions were written on reservations by tribal citizens with technical assistance from OIA, each tribe held a referendum to vote on the constitutions.

By 1946, 93 tribes, bands, and Indian communities had adopted constitutions, and 73 were granted land management charters. Representative democracy with the reservation as nation was begun. Those tribes that declined IRA developed constitutions and tribal governments as well. All reservations had tribal governments by 1946.

In Chippewa Country, only Red Lake Reservation rejected the IRA among the reservation-tribes-bands. Red Lake declined because it wanted to keep its 1918 constitution that maintained traditional hereditary chiefs. Lac Courte Oreilles declined incorporation but adopted a constitution. Once they completed constitutional referenda, the "lost bands" that had been omitted from the creation of reservations in the Treaty of 1854 received newly purchased trust land from the United States and became Lake Superior Chippewa reservations, Mole Lake and St. Croix.

The federal government chooses to recognize each of the bands as a "tribe" for most purposes. The Minnesota Chippewa Tribe was formed in 1936 to be the representative body for the six reservation bands of Chippewa within the boundaries of Minnesota. Red Lake chose vociferously not to be part of the Minnesota Chippewa Tribe.

Tribal councils for each of the reservations became the political identity and focal point of the lives of individual Indians after passage of the IRA. Each reservation became the locus of identity for its citizens and the organizing concept for efforts to expand sovereignty. Today, "the tribe" is the reservation government and the centerpiece of being Chippewa in a cultural context.

The struggles in defense of sovereignty had a new foundation, the tribal council, and the foundation was the fulcrum for continuing efforts by the Chippewa to strengthen their measured separatism with the United States. The IRA gave each reservation legal standing in federal courts. Most reservations exercised their individual sovereignties to meet individual challenges, but most also had ideological support from other Chippewa reservations.

By 1940 the phenomenon of tribal, constitutional governments existed throughout Chippewa Country. In Michigan, some Chippewa tribal governments remained unrecognized by the federal government, and they would wage a continuous struggle until they were federally recognized after the 1970s. Some Chippewa communities, like the Little Shell Band, continue to struggle in a legal vacuum.

8

Self-Government and Threatened Termination, 1935–1960s

SELF-GOVERNMENT AND THREATENED TERMINATION

The scramble to secure the benefits of the Indian Reorganization Act in Chippewa Country was complicated by the Great Depression. As Roosevelt's New Deal moved to provide relief to all Americans, a novelty occurred. The Indians were allowed to benefit from New Deal social and economic relief programs. Some were even modified to fit Indian circumstances. Government agencies other than the Office of Indian Affairs extended their services to Indian country for the first time.

Although some Chippewa leaders created constitutional governments and the Office of Indian Affairs (OIA) worked to overcome its assimilationist bias to support self-government, individual Chippewa and their communities benefited from New Deal programs. John Collier got the Works Progress Administration (WPA) and the Civilian Conservation Corps (CCC) to allow Indians to participate. He argued that Indians were citizens and their poverty needed relief efforts.

Importantly, Collier was able to draw on the national funding for these programs for Native American programs tailored to Indian circumstances. Unlike the mainstream CCC, married heads of households were employed, and their families were allowed to live in Indian camps. Usually the camps were on or near reservations. WPA projects worked in Chippewa Country to build an infrastructure, repair some of the damages caused by the wanton destruction of the forestry industry, engage Indian craftspeople in maintaining traditional artifact manufacture, and even to employ people to collect and publish Chippewa oral histories.

For some Chippewa, the New Deal was the first time that they were able to earn wages. Assistance was also forthcoming for cooperative arrangements developed by the Chippewa such as the Red Lake Fisheries Association. Elders interviewed in the 1950s remembered the Depression as a time when things were better than they were in the 1920s.

Indian education improved because the Johnson-O'Malley Act (JOM) authorized the secretary of the interior to contract with states to provide access to Indian children in public schools. Funds compensated state communities in lieu of taxes. Some Chippewa were able to access better schools, but others suffered from the indifference and ignorance of the white population at best while racism afflicted others at worst. Assimilation remained the goal of the Office of Indian Affairs schools, parochial systems, and public schools. However, the policy was mitigated to a level of tolerance, and better teachers were hired.

Public schools were not required to provide for unique needs of Indian children or develop cultural reinforcing programs until the 1970s. The OIA did make efforts after 1934 to provide some native language texts, develop reading materials that showed Native American cultures, and portrayed Indians living on reservations. Most of the off-reservation boarding schools were closed, and OIA emphasis moved to on-reservation schools. The Carlisle Indian School had been closed before World War I, and most others were shuttered in the 1930s in favor of on-reservation day schools. Conditions in the school were improved.

TRIBAL COUNCIL GOVERNMENTS

Each of the Chippewa bands crafted constitutions if reservation-wide referendums supported them. Office of Indian Affairs staff provided technical assistance and offered model constitutions. Given the involvement of the federal staff, it is no surprise that constitutions were similar. A preamble indicated the hope that businesses, domestic tranquility, and measures promoting the general welfare would ensue. Constitutions described the duties of tribal government, established blood quantum criteria for being enrolled members/citizens, and authorized the tribal council to do business. Some included tribal courts, while others left the creation of tribal courts for later ordinances. Reservation government organization was limited. The Office of Indian Affairs kept an iron hand on programs and funds.

An elected tribal council representing electoral district or at-large elections was elected by what the constitutions persisted in calling "members." Some had reservation-wide elections for the principal officers like tribal chairman. Only Red Cliff Reservation used the term "chief," and that was a deliberate effort to maintain a pivotal political role for the seven hereditary chiefs recognized in Red Lake's 1918 constitution. Red Lake did not accept an Indian Reorganization Act (IRA) government. Most terms of office were two years, which contributes to instability and hinders government consistency.

The term "member" remains enshrined in usage today and conflates political status with race. The Indians should be described as citizens of nations that are sovereign under U.S. law. By calling citizens "members," usage creates an impression that being an Indian citizen is like being a member of some sort of honorary club, not a legal status. One does not call people "members" of the United States or members of Wisconsin.

All of the Chippewa constitutions required descent from enrolled band members to qualify for citizenship. Some used the term "blood quantum" and, like OIA, stipulated one-quarter blood quantum for membership. These terms merged race with citizenship, reflecting American racial consciousness. The OIA could do the math. Eventually, such requirements would eradicate the Chippewa completely. Several tribes moved to change citizenship requirements in the 1970s reform movements.

Historically, acceptance of immigrants was common in Chippewa bands. Individuals of European descent as well as Natives from other bands often became Chippewa. For instance, at one point there were numerous Dakota joining Chippewa communities. This led to creation of new clans to better integrate the Dakota. Absorbing foreigners had a long history for most American Indian tribes. Genetic composition was only part of the picture.

By the 1930s, the genetic composition of Chippewa communities was quite diverse. Band governments abandoned blood quantum in various ways as time progressed, but the issue remains divisive in the 21st century. White Earth Reservation recently convinced the Minnesota Chippewa Tribe to address the issue in a constitutional reform effort. Other tribes have dropped specific blood quantum requirements in favor of descent from a citizenship roll. For most Chippewa bands, the rolls drawn up for allotment provide the baseline for determining descent.

Some bands created a business council that was identical to the tribal council but had economic development duties made possible by the IRA. Business councils could tap into a revolving loan fund provided in the legislation. Business councils assumed some of the corporate duties previously exercised by the Office of Indian Affairs. Significantly, bands gained some control of their own funds and were granted the right to hire tribal attorneys without prior OIA approval.

The process of reinstituting band governments under new parameters did not always go smoothly. Suspicion about federal intentions was rampant. Representative government generated arguments about favoritism, corruption, and other conflicts endemic to elected governments. Squabbling over limited resources joined disagreements about political direction. In some cases, the OIA intervened to help sort out difficulties, raising more doubts among Chippewa people.

Expectations were higher than possibilities, and the Chippewa were not used to being allowed to make their own decisions after almost a century of federal colonialism. Most constitutions left the reservation Indian agent with veto power. Several Chippewa reservations had descendants of formerly independent bands thrown together and asked to become one band.

Political divisions often were rooted in historic and prereservation patterns. The OIA tended to discern divisions between "progressives" (i.e., those who had made most acculturative adjustments like to education and employment) and "traditionals" (i.e., those who tended to cling more steadfastly to language and religion and were less compliant with changes). Reservations large enough to have districts often had concentrations of traditional in one community and progressives in others.

Generally, the progressives tended to be mixed bloods, and the traditional tended to be full bloods. Blood terminology had long dominated American perceptions and usage to the extent that Chippewa people tended to embrace it, too. Ironically, by the 1930s and 1940s, the OIA considered nearly all Chippewa to be mixed bloods.

The New Deal's infusion of funds and its restoration of a form of tribal government did not restore tribal self-sufficiency. The iron hand of the Office of Indian Affairs kept control of individual Indian funds, tribal funds, federal allocations for reservations, and government jobs. Without resources and funds, many tribal councils were unable to control their lives. This contributed to Chippewa criticism of their reservation governments.

BAD RIVER RESERVATION: ONE EXAMPLE

Bad River Reservation within Wisconsin illustrates the reality of the continuing poverty of Chippewa Country. The stellar work of Edmund Danziger provides data gleaned from OIA records to flesh out the story. Other material is available in WPA oral history records.

Bad River adopted an IRA government in 1936. It was one of several reservations in the combined Great Lakes Agency after the 1920s. Grinding poverty, poor health, and a despoiled environment were common to all reservations, and Bad River was no exception. There were 235 families and 875 Bad River members living on the reservation. The OIA determined that 74 were full bloods.

In 1938, OIA records indicate that it was necessary for a Bad River average family to have an income of $282.56. This was based on the premise that seasonal or part-time employment combined with federal-state assistance and subsistence hunting and gathering would meet minimal standards. Many failed to meet this standard.

There was a health clinic, a visiting nurse, and a contract doctor, which helped account for improved health. Tuberculosis was substantially higher than that of the rest of Wisconsin's population, but there had been a decline in venereal disease. Other health problems caused by diet and exposure continued.

Bad River members had received 662 allotments, but by 1938 many had been sold for taxes or purchased outright by non-Indians after many Chippewa were declared competent to manage their own land. The allotments that remained were already being subdivided among many heirs and were often located in the swampy or sandy terrain that abounded throughout the overcut reservation.

Most Chippewa were clustered in Odanah near the Bad River and sloughs. Non-Indians acquired most of the Lake Superior shoreline. Rice fields had survived lumbering wastage, and fishing was abundant on the reservation. Hunting was problematical, but what the state insisted on calling poaching was an option despite Wisconsin's efforts to impose rigid game laws off-reservation. "Face fines or eat" was an easy choice.

Most of Bad River's houses were built around 1900 and were substandard. The primary community, Odanah, flooded each spring, which released raw sewage. Each house of about five rooms held 1.62 families and was valued by the OIA at $325. The average value of household goods was about $77 per household. There were 35 private vehicles for the entire reservation, but U.S. Highway 2 through the reservation was paved. Two bus lines went through Bad River. There was a well-used community center completed in 1937.

Schooling was available, and roughly 200 children attended in 1938. Odanah Rural School and Odanah State Graded School (formerly St. Mary's and staffed by nuns) served the reservation. The Catholic-run school had a dining hall, gymnasium, library, and shop. Its curriculum included music and fine arts. High school students were bused to off-reservation

Ashland, where they attended public high school or one of the Catholic High Schools, DePadua and St. Agnes. Attendance was spotty as children were needed for subsistence activities, racism was strong in Ashland, and Indian children were educationally disadvantaged. Twenty students were in boarding schools elsewhere.

To outside observers, little that was traditional Chippewa culture seemed to survive. Few retained fluency in Ojibwe, most wore what was termed "white men's clothes," and none wore moccasins. Federal and school staff saw little Midewiwin activity and considered that most Chippewa were either Catholic or Protestant. They saw only two or three powwows. The OIA had rigid, simplistic criteria defining Chippewa culture and was delighted to observe the demise of Chippewa cultural practices. They had no idea.

Reality was different. Being Chippewa might include quite a bit of acculturation, but uniqueness remained. The Chippewa saw things differently

COMMUNITY CENTERS IN CHIPPEWA COUNTRY

The New Deal provided support for building community centers in towns in Chippewa Country. Officials saw them as aiding in the transition from traditional culture, but they became something quite different than envisioned.

Traditional communities had larger buildings for Midewiwin and other ceremonies. They also used them for decision-making conferences reinforcing the value of consensus. Women's organizations grew to enculturate others in Chippewa ways. To the chagrin of officials, the new community centers were centers for cultural maintenance and consensus building about efforts to resist American assimilationist policy.

They evolved quickly into dance halls where both traditional and "white" dancing marked continuing Chippewa culture. Indian bands even played in American communities nearby. Socializing and decision making helped maintain a sense of community.

Louise Erdrich, the most widely known Chippewa author, described a community center in *The Round House*. Although its focus is on jurisdictional-caused tragedies, the Round House is a community center and she describes how it was the focal point of reservation life. Other authors have also described the centrality of the community centers. Most of her many books provide pictures of Chippewa Country at various historical times. *Love Medicine* is a masterpiece evoking reservation life over several decades.

Community centers are important parts of the story of the Chippewa.

and continued their tribal cultural practices. Ceremonies continued, children were named, dancing was widespread, and praying to Manitos continued. The large degree of retention of cultural practices was evident when the Chippewa Renaissance began in the 1960s and 1970s. The "old stuff" was widely demonstrated.

WORLD WAR II

World War II brought more changes to Chippewa Country. Not only did Chippewa volunteer in large numbers, but others left the reservation to work in war industries. Chippewa families and individuals have always participated in the larger communities of the United States, and this accelerated. Although they left for jobs, most Chippewa maintained their reservation contacts and a Chippewa identity.

The Indians were not segregated in the military or in civilian jobs as African Americans were. Often Chippewa were able to achieve ranks that allowed them to command white people. They also gained experience in leadership, saw how the rest of the world lived, and acquired skills that would prove useful back on reservations. Today, every reservation has a monument to its veterans and continues to honor them by having veterans carry the flags at the grand entry for powwows. Most see military service as a continuation of Chippewa warrior tradition.

Bad River Reservation's war experience was typical. The reservation had approximately 300 military-age

Thomas Whitecloud, a Chippewa from the Lac du Flambeau Reservation in Wisconsin, was a medical officer, first lieutenant, and parachutist during World War II, before becoming a poet and fiction writer. Many Chippewa volunteered for service during World War II, and others worked in war industries. (Corbis via Getty Images)

men and 116 volunteers. By 1943, another 129 had moved to work in war industries, often accompanied by the entire family. On-reservation activities included raising money for war bonds, growing food for market to allay the impact of rationing, sewing packets for soldiers, and even some letter writing.

Many Bad River Chippewa had moved from the reservation to small towns like Solon Springs and Ashland where they often comprised significant percentages of the population. Often these expatriates were better educated formally than reservation residents, and they too volunteered in large numbers. Some had joined the Wisconsin National Guard before the war as their $11 monthly training payments were significant family income. Some even became officers and NCOs before the war ended.

The war's benefits to Chippewa Country masked the legacy left by what Chippewa consider the failures of the U.S. trust responsibility. Health problems continued, the Office of Indian Affairs lost many of its personnel to the war effort, the Office of Indian Affairs budget was reduced, and the entire bureau was moved to Chicago. States continued to enforce their game laws on Chippewa regardless of treaties, and relief efforts by the state often shortchanged Indian communities. The CCC and WPA were canceled with much infrastructure left undone on reservations.

THE TERMINATION SPECTER: GETTING OUT OF THE INDIAN BUSINESS

Even as the war was continuing, a resuscitation of the assimilationist arguments that had prevailed before the IRA developed. Education was the first line of effort by those who wanted to "free the Indian" from the shackles of lingering tribalism. National OIA and educators used Indian participation in the war as indicating that Indians could be merged with non-Indians without trust protections. An organization called the American Indian Federation tried to get the IRA repealed as early as 1940, but John Collier pointed out their Nazi connections. However, their arguments against Indian rights resonated with many Americans.

In 1943, a Senate report questioned whether Indians were moving toward the goal of self-sufficiency that would terminate Indian guardianship. Representative Karl Mundt, of South Dakota, chaired an investigation of the OIA and announced: "The goal of Indian education should be to make the Indian child a better American rather than equip him to simply be a better Indian." Other congressmen just wanted to stop spending money on Indians.

Despite the ominous sounds from Washington and some states, the IRA combined with the impact of World War II to entrain a course difficult to derail. Tribal governments were a fact of life. A revived tribal emphasis on cultural values and practices, including freedom of religion, fueled American Indians in their determination to survive as tribal entities.

Among other achievements, Collier's commitment to tribal self-government and the enhancement of tribal culture had numerous spin-offs. Pan-Indian organizations developed and were encouraged. Western-educated Indians gained the knowledge and tactics to resist assimilation. In 1946, the Office of Indian Affairs was renamed the Bureau of Indian Affairs (BIA).

In 1945, John Collier succumbed to the increasing barrage of criticism from Congress and even within the Office of Indian Affairs and by some tribal leaders. He resigned, and soon Secretary of the Interior Harold Ickes followed. Assimilationists surged into the fore of Indian policy again. They developed a new tool to rid themselves of the trust responsibility: termination.

In 1946 tribal leaders founded the National Congress of American Indians (NCAI). Reservations were represented by tribal chairpersons in NCAI. Staff members became lobbyists advocating tribal positions. They testified to Congress, worked with BIA officials and staff, and guarded against antisovereignty legislation. By the end of the 1950s, Congress and the executive branch interacted with NCAI similarly to the way they interacted with associations representing states. Tribes gained a collective, U.S.-wide voice.

Following World War II, American ideology moved from the unifying cant of the New Deal and the drive for national unity of World War II to a narrower view of what government entailed. American Indians were affected by this change of national direction toward power to states, less federal involvement, and a strong commitment to melting pot theory. Abrogation of the trust responsibility called termination became official government policy.

The first objective of termination was to satisfy all legal claims that Indian tribes or groups of Indians had against the United States. Tribal leaders and even Collier had supported the idea of resolving outstanding Indian claims against the United States. Congress approved an Indian Claims Commission Act in 1946. Three commissioners were to hear claims of any Native American entity within the United States or Alaska.

Claims could be based on Indian perceptions of fraudulent U.S. actions on constitutional, treaty stipulation, mismanagement, agreements under duress, and any violation of "fair and honorable dealings." No limitations were in effect, but the United States could offset funds that had been used to help the claimant.

Unfortunately for justice, legal maneuverings dominated the hearings. Decisions often turned on fine points of law rather than following the canon of interpretation, which called for treating the claims of Indians with broad understanding. The Commission could only offer compensation.

Congress assumed a few years would settle all issues and authorized only monetary settlements, not, for instance, the return of fraudulently obtained land. This casual assumption was wrong. Congress granted extensions of time until 1978 when remaining cases were transferred to the Federal Court of Claims. Nearly all of the 176 tribes or bands notified of the program filed one or more claims. They all insisted they had been cheated. The ensuing 370 petitions of grievance were broken down into 670 dockets. Proceedings and records now occupy many board feet in the U.S. archives.

Most of the Chippewa reservation governments and even the nonfederally recognized bands of Michigan filed cases before the Indian Claims Commission. The Michigan bands received awards of $10.3 million. Several gained crucial information leading to their federal recognition in the 1970s. Chippewa bands from the core homeland therefore became the most recently recognized, long after their political descendants within Wisconsin, Minnesota, North Dakota, and Montana. The Pembina Band (Turtle Mountain Reservation) and the nonfederally recognized Little Shell Chippewa Band of Montana received their award of $237,127.82 in 1962. The Commission finding for the Minnesota Chippewa Tribe was $20 million. Wisconsin bands received individual awards.

Before the process ended, the U.S. liability to all Indian tribes was set at $818 million. The money was useful to the reservations, but most settled on distributing the awards per capita. Individual distribution of treaty funds extended back to prereservation days, and the BIA was supportive of per capita distribution as part of its continuing campaign to individualize Indians, not support tribal governments.

In the long run, the most significant impact of the Indian Claims Commission was the experience and knowledge gained by tribal leaders. They employed lawyers and utilized an array of experts to aid their causes. Anthropologists and historians working for tribes did the research and reported it. Tribal histories and oral histories were gathered from dispersed sources. Many Native Americans were able to learn the extent and continuity of their histories and societies and to discover what the U.S. government documents revealed.

In 1946, Congress reorganized and eliminated the standing committees on Indian affairs from both the House and the Senate. Ardent terminationists like Senator Arthur Watkins of Utah and Representative E. Y. Berry of South Dakota chaired the subcommittees that made Indian statutes and budgets. Other congressmen supported termination. too.

In 1947, acting BIA superintendent William Zimmerman testified to the Senate Committee on Civil Service. His announced goal was to reduce BIA costs, and he submitted three lists of tribes. The first group could be denied federal services immediately, the second could have minimal BIA supervision in a decade, and the third would need many years to prepare for freedom. He used tribal degrees of acculturation and state willingness to absorb tribes as criteria. Zimmerman submitted model termination bills for the Osage, Klamath, and Menominee.

In 1948 the Hoover Commission recommended that "assimilation must be the dominant goal of Public Policy." Commission staff concluded that "the basis for historic Indian culture has been swept away." The social programs maintained for Native Americans should just be transferred to the states.

The Commission and Zimmerman reflected the basic flaw in American Indian policy: the conflation of race and particular behaviors with the definition of Indian. In American assumptions, Indians looked like Indians and they acted like the Indians of precontact societies, or they were not "real." To the degree that they were not as expected, they were not Indians. If the current people who claimed to be Indian were not as Americans expected them to be, then they were not deserving of American assistance.

Throughout the 19th and 20th centuries, questions consistently arose about half-breeds who did not act like Indians. Policy makers and the public alike thought that if Indians changed and did not "live in tipis," they were not really Indians. Unlike African Americans who were colored if they even had one drop of African blood, Indians could be bred out of existence, and they could also cease to be Indians if they got college degrees, became lawyers, and lived in the modern era. Indians did not agree with this interpretation of what makes an Indian.

BIA records listed full bloods and mixed bloods as a matter of record. They also tracked whether or not "their" Indians "dressed white." Educated full bloods were suspected of not being Indian enough. Even Indians often bought into the conflation of race with political status. However, the law and even objective logic are something else. An Indian is a citizen of a polity, and the criteria for citizenship is a legal one.

After 1934, the right of federally recognized tribes to determine their own citizenship is embedded in the many tribal constitutions affirmed by the United States. The landmark *Martinez v. San Juan Pueblo* (1978) case recognized that the United States did not define what an Indian tribal citizen was; only the tribe had subject jurisdiction. The *United States v. Kagama* decision indicated that Indians were not a race, but rather their unique status derived from their historical, political relationship to the United States.

One of the dominant tropes in American culture in the period following World War II was a determination to resist Communism. The Cold War fixation still affects American political ideologies, but in the 1950s it was brought to a head. Anything that smacked of government ownership and control was attacked. The trust responsibility was often equated with socialism, and the state of Indians held up as proof that government control did not work. Evidence and causes were not part of the discourse.

On August 1, 1953, Concurrent Resolution 108 declared: "It is the policy of Congress, as rapidly as possible, to make the Indians within the territorial limits of the United States subject to the same laws and entitled to the same privileges and responsibilities as are applicable to other citizens of the United States and to grant them all of the rights and prerogatives pertaining to American citizenship." Indians and Indian groups "should be freed from federal supervision and control and from all disabilities specially applicable to Indians." In Indian country, it meant abolishing reservations and abrogating the trust responsibility. The BIA was slated for abolition. No Chippewa reservation was terminated, but Turtle Mountain and Red Lake were threatened with termination.

Two other approaches to eliminate the need for reservations directly impacted Chippewa Country. Public Law 280 transferred federal jurisdiction in criminal and civil cases to the states of Wisconsin and Minnesota. Three other states also received "280 jurisdiction," but they did not encompass Chippewa reservations. The law remains in effect and means that state police and courts penetrate reservations and impose state law in a reversal of federal laws that forbade state jurisdiction within reservations.

Red Lake Reservation was specifically spared state jurisdiction. Legislation excluded trust land from state control, confirmed treaty rights, and continued prohibition of state taxation of Indian lands or income on Indian lands. Chagrined state officials faced an unfunded mandate and the anger of Indians who were opposed to state interference. After 75 years a modus vivendi exists, but most reservation leaders would like to remove state jurisdictions.

Termination remained a threat through the 1970s but, aside from the psychological trauma of the threat, it faded. Within Wisconsin, the Menominee Reservation was terminated, and the debacle of termination formed a setting for Chippewa fears and concerns. The drive for termination lost its impetus in the face of concerted Indian opposition. The National Congress of American Indians (NCAI) brought together pressure groups from throughout Indian county and united with Democrats and others to resist termination. Lessons learned came into play as the country changed.

Only the Congress of 1952–1953 was dominated by terminationists. In 1954, Democrats returned to and maintained majority control of one or both houses. A few termination acts were passed, but soon terminated tribes were being restored to federal recognition if not to their lost lands and resources. Transfer of the Indian Health Service to Public Health Service from the BIA was a by-product of termination, but it was good for Indians. After a few years health began to improve on the reservation as Indians received services similar to those provided for other Americans.

RELOCATION TO THE CITIES

Another prong of the termination campaign was the relocation program. The Chippewa and other Indians were subsidized with one-way tickets to leave the reservations for urban opportunities. The BIA promised housing, employment assistance, and a better life for families. Reality was not quite what was expected. The Indians arrived in cities and soon found themselves in ghetto-like slums, often unemployed, and many became derelicts. Some did well and joined communities that had grown around World War II industries that continued. Significant Chippewa populations established a presence in the cities of Milwaukee, Minneapolis–St. Paul, Chicago, and Duluth-Superior.

Chippewa experience was similar to that of other urban minorities, but they could go home. Red Lake and other reservation governments encouraged their band citizens to return home and even opened offices in cities near the reservation to channel services to tribal members. Many returned to the reservations, while others moved back and forth from city to reservation as they had been doing for generations. Often, Native Americans felt the brunt of the criminal justice system, decrepit housing, dysfunctions like alcoholism, and discrimination. Urban Indians also participated in the growing demands for civil rights. Indian centers eventually grew access to influence.

The Chippewa had dodged another bullet by the 1960s. The political culture of the United States experienced a paradigm shift trumpeted by President Kennedy and given reality by the Great Society of Lyndon Johnson. Civil rights and a war on poverty resonated in Indian Country.

9

Self-Determination and Civil Rights

Tribal leaders' skills were honed in adverse conditions, and when the U.S. political culture changed to support multiculturalism and to declare war on poverty, Chippewa tribes and others leaped to take advantage of opportunities. The heady civil rights movement dominated by African Americans influenced urban Indians first but also spread to reservations.

Political leaders like tribal council members and an increasing circle of savvy, educated tribal officials tended to concentrate on ushering reforms through the system and the courts. Radically stimulated Chippewa utilized more flamboyant confrontational tactics. Often the two groups worked together, but they were sometimes in opposition. Indian groups fed off one another to mold a multifaceted pan-Indian approach.

In June 1961, more than 450 Indians from 90 tribes attended the American Indian Chicago Conference. After days of discussing Indian needs and concerns, the group issued a Declaration of Indian Purpose. The major thrust of the Declaration was a call for more Native American decision making, less paternalistic supervision by the BIA, economic development for reservations, and removal of anachronistic controls by the federal government.

This large gathering of young Indian leaders included many who would become officials in their tribes, college professors, and community developers. Many Chippewa were part of the conference and participants in a continuing drive for Indian self-determination.

At the same time, President John Kennedy was promising a sharp break with the policies of the Republican Party. He committed the government to consultation with tribes and promised no changes Indians did not support. Cultural practices would not be endangered by his presidency.

Kennedy's message was supported by the appointment of Secretary of the Interior Stewart Udall, an active advocate for Indian self-government, cultural integrity, and economic development. Udall built on an independent study that called for more tribal decision making by creating a task force on Indians that touted Indian involvement and economic investment to reverse the abject failures of the past. Chippewa leaders approved the new approach but were leery of new programs that might be a prelude to termination.

President Kennedy made tentative steps toward securing political rights for minorities and for addressing generations of poverty. After Kennedy's assassination, Lyndon Johnson pursued a "war on poverty" along with engaging the federal government in a campaign to realize the American dream for all. Legislation created the Office of Economic Opportunity (OEO) in 1964. Multiple programs offered a range of services to minority communities.

Tribal reservations were considered to be minority communities; certainly they were impoverished pockets of people, and they had community structures to meet OEO criteria for community action agencies. Tribes could finally create the infrastructure of governing by using OEO and other Great Society programs.

Tribal councils created community actions agencies (CAA) that served reservation needs. Funding for CAA programs brought an infusion of non-BIA funds onto the reservation. Unlike the past, tribal governments were encouraged to make decisions about how the money was spent. Indians were hired to run the programs for youth, economic development, infrastructure, and even paying tribal council salaries.

By 1968, $35 million went to 63 community action programs serving 129 reservations. Chippewa reservations became vast CAA operations. Simultaneously, BIA and Indian Health Services budgets increased as Indian commissioner Philleo Nash pushed the new focus of Indian policy into operations. In 1966, the first Native American commissioner since Ely Parker during the Grant administration succeeded the effective Nash. Robert Bennett, an Oneida, was from Chippewa Country in Wisconsin.

President Johnson made it clear that Indians were to be part of the Great Society. In a special message to Congress on Indians, he proposed "a new goal for our Indian programs: a goal that ends the old debate about 'terminating' of Indian programs and stresses self-determination; a goal that erases old attitudes of paternalism and promotes partnership self-help." He offered specific program plans and created a National Council on Indian Opportunity chaired by the vice president. Vice President Hubert Humphrey was a supporter of Indian governments in his home state of Minnesota and a friend of the Red Lake chairman, Robert Jourdain. Jourdain was a leading figure in creating the Tribal Chairmen's Association and a vociferous defender of tribal sovereignty.

Impressive as the gains made by Chippewa reservations in the 1960s were, consistency of access to funding and decision making was lacking. OEO funds did allow circumvention of BIA's stifling effects, as its members feared losing control. Tribes agreed and tried to make the fears come true.

Control of education and control of community development and government operations were needed. The Bureau of Indian Affairs had a track record of receiving funding for established programs and personnel lines. In 1970, President Richard Nixon got on the bandwagon of tribal self-determination.

Nixon made nine proposals to Congress. In combination, these amounted to a clearly stated continuation of the emphasis on tribal self-determination begun by Kennedy and implemented by Johnson. He called the policy "self-determination in a government to government relationship." Specifically, he called for Congress to renounce unilateral termination.

He wanted legislation to allow tribal governments to take over administration of BIA programs with the same funding as provided by Congress to the BIA if the tribes voted to do so. Other pieces of the proposal included tribal control of Indian schools, funding for economic development and health improvement, and establishing the position of assistant secretary for Indian affairs to provide clout for Indians in the Department of the Interior. All of the proposals did not become law immediately, but the die was cast. Nixon's embrace of self-determination demonstrated that both parties would reflect what Indian leaders had struggled to regain after 150 years: tribal sovereignty.

RED POWER AND THE INDIAN RENAISSANCE

The 1960s and 1970s were turbulent times throughout the United States. Chippewa Country was one of the centers for simultaneous efforts to secure tribal, governmental rights and to secure civil rights throughout the United States. At the same time a renaissance of emphasis on Native American cultures and religious restoration occurred. Minorities, even those like Indians who had a unique status, launched national campaigns to assure that their grievances would be heard and to try to obtain justice.

Many Indians started college in the postwar period, and Vietnam veterans joined them in their use of the GI Bill to pay for college. Increased educational funding allowed tribes to support their citizens in college. Urban Indian centers and prisons became breeding grounds for the growth of demands for civil protections from a racist society. Red Power was the symbolic term adopted by many different groups striving for recognition of Native American rights. It echoed and was influenced by Black Power.

The term was coined by Vine Deloria Jr., the author of *Custer Died for Your Sins* (1969). Deloria was also a leader of the National Council of American Indians (NCAI) organized in 1946 and the leading organization in the battle against termination. By the late 1960s, NCAI was the spokes organization for tribal governments. Its voting membership was representatives of reservation governments, not individuals. One reservation; one vote.

Red Power was a pan-Indian movement. National conglomerations of Native Americans made individual reservation-based efforts part of a larger whole. Intertribal leaders, organizations, lobbying efforts, and membership in organizations came from tribes and indigenous groups throughout the United States, sometimes Canada, and other indigenous communities. As the U.S. paradigm shifted to multiculturalism and was dominated by liberals, many non-Indians supported Indian causes.

Universities were often centers of change, and as liberals moved into government during the 1950s and 1960s, Native Americans received not only sympathy but powerful, focused support. Many universities initiated Indian studies programs as they were sponsoring programs like black studies and African studies. American higher education moved toward an inclusion activism. Often state legislatures provided additional funding for Indian programs in education, social services, and even business. State universities moved from being able to count the number of Indian students on one hand to having Indian numbers in the 10s and 20s.

Chippewa reservations joined others in organizations for changing federal Indian policies. The Chippewa organized and joined national organizations. Many moved to jobs in the federal bureaucracy where they influenced national changes. Perhaps disproportionately, the Chippewa moved to college teaching positions, and increasing numbers went to college where they became part of the national Red Power Movement. National Indian history and achievements were also the story of the Chippewa.

Alcatraz Island was occupied by Indian students from Oakland in November 1968. Indian occupiers offered to buy the island for $24 worth of beads. They would turn the vacant federal prison and island into an

Indian cultural and educational center. The United States tried to blockade the island but did not use force.

Alcatraz marks the beginning of militant demands and demonstrations in the Red Power Movement. National attention was riveted on the long-haired, young Indians and their radical demands by a supportive press and public opinion. Coincidently, the causes of Indian grievances received a sympathetic hearing throughout America. A great deal of discord developed among the occupiers, and their supplies began to dwindle; Indians trickled away until federal marshals removed the last few in June 1971.

As with most of the confrontational events, other Indians responded to the occupation differently. Some condemned the demonstrators for endangering what had been accomplished, some were indifferent because it was so far away, and some were heartened in their efforts to legitimize Indian rights by this visible action. Some thought the demonstration was too mild. These responses were similar to responses by other minority communities to the civil rights movement. All agreed that Indians needed justice.

At the heart of Red Power in Chippewa Country was a vibrant revival of Chippewa culture. Elders received renewed respect for their wisdom. Ceremonies such as those of Midewiwin and the Big Drum society increased in scope and frequency throughout Chippewa Country. Pan-Indian ceremonies like the plains-originated sun dance appeared in Chippewa communities, as did the Native American Church.

Powwows demonstrated a widespread commitment to maintaining the traditional dances. They became the central experience of American Indian existence for all of the many layers of Chippewa people. Tribal governments used tribal funds for reservation-wide powwows, and communities continued their own local powwows. The "powwow circuit" provided contests, associated cultural events, and interaction among Native Americans. Young men grew their hair long and wore symbolic adornment like chokers, ribbon shirts, beaded belts and vests, and head bands in pan-Indian celebration of being Indian.

Revival focused on ceremonial renewal. Language restorative efforts were fulcrums for renewing and invigorating the Chippewa story. Mundane practices such as naming ceremonies, intentional uses of traditional foods, prayer, and feasts, and an academic concentration on things Chippewa and Indian spread widely. The academic element affected all through changing school curriculums, valid academic research on such things as treaties and Indian law, and even the practices of traditional cultures. Being Chippewa was an exciting, perplexing, exhilarating, experience. In the midst of revival, the legacies of 150 years of colonial rule like poverty, paternalism, racism, and intra-reservation dysfunction were not ignored.

Differences about tactics and identity authenticity led to bitter divisions within Chippewa Country, but few disagreed with the goals of treaty rights restoration, sovereignty for reservation tribal governments, civil rights for off-reservation Native Americans, economic development, increased funding for reservation programs, and cultural integrity.

Professor Scott Lyons, a Leech Lake Chippewa, describes the dark side of cultural revivals as veering toward an intolerant fundamentalism. He notes that young fanatics of authenticity hastened to attack those they considered less than committed to the cause of an imagined purity of Chippewa practices and to expunging white colonialism. On Leech Lake Reservation, these "talibanishinaabe" claimed to know the only way to practice being Chippewa and decried mixed bloods, evidence of western education, and "inauthentic" ceremonies.

Ironically, these young people were often college educated, urban raised, and pursuers of a static culture that never existed. Divisions between neo-traditionalist culture cops and Chippewa who are more pragmatic pose problems on all reservations but paradoxically also stimulate continuing Chippewa cultural and political integrity. Chippewa culture is not static.

THE AMERICAN INDIAN MOVEMENT

As Red Power was being demonstrated spectacularly on the West Coast, the Chippewa based in Minneapolis–St. Paul decided to counter the pattern of police targeting of the Chippewa and other Indians and to demand the end of racial discrimination. The American Indian Movement (AIM) was created by Chippewas—Dennis Banks, Clyde Bellecourt, George Mitchell, and Eddie Benton-Banai—in 1968. Vernon Bellecourt and others soon joined. Their immediate task was to organize patrols to prevent police brutality, but enthusiastic adherents soon expanded AIM's goals and tactics.

AIM drew on the spirituality of traditional teaching thanks to the contributions of Benton-Banai and Mitchell. They also helped legitimize urban Indians while stressing reform on reservations as well as within urban environments. Soon AIM had the trappings of radicalism familiar in the 1960s and 1970s. They featured a one-fisted salute, wore red berets, and even got a flag. AIM chapters grew in cities where relocated Indians accumulated. Reservation communities saw demands for cultural restorations and for rapid political change. Native Americans from nearly all tribes joined the movement.

AIM members either led or participated in a succession of occupations and demonstrations across the United States. Dennis Banks became the most prominent of the Chippewa spokesmen of this quickly spreading association of Indians, but the Bellecourt brothers were not far behind. The National Youth Council (1961), Women of All Red Nations (1974), the International Indian Treaty Organization, the National Council on Indian Opportunity, and the Lakota Freedom Movement are some of several organizations that sprung up during the Red Power Movement.

In Wisconsin, AIM members were prominent in occupying Winter Dam, Wisconsin, and the abandoned Milwaukee coast guard station in 1971. They used the occasions to press the media to publicize treaty violations by the United States. Various other demonstrations occurred in colleges and towns throughout Chippewa Country. Many Chippewa joined enthusiastically as Red Power received national notice. Urban centers and reservation communities saw AIM members and adopted some of their goals.

The Trail of Broken Treaties in 1972 was sponsored by AIM members and joined by hundreds of Indians, some with tribal government support. They marched on Washington to demand reform and treaty rights. When the BIA and government agencies tried to ignore them, AIM radicals occupied the BIA headquarters and demanded congressional hearings. Stymied, many destroyed and looted the headquarters. Violence was nearly always eminent in mass demonstrations. Other AIM demonstrations included the capture of Plymouth Rock and of Mount Rushmore.

In February 1973, Native Americans occupied Wounded Knee, the site of the 1890 massacre often described as the event that ended Indian wars. Wounded Knee is on the Lakota Pine Ridge Reservation. The reservation and surrounding area was a center of controversy during the Red Power campaigns.

"Wounded Knee Two," as many call it, was the culmination of multiple streams: political corruption that denied Gerald One Feather election as tribal chairman, widespread anti-Indian violence in border towns, a vigorous cultural revival led by men like Fools Crow, political reform movements nationally, and the adoption of mass demonstrations by AIM. Dennis Banks was at Wounded Knee, but a Lakota AIM leader, Russell Means, became the spokesman most recognized. Indians and non-Indian supporters from all around the country flocked to Wounded Knee.

Federal marshals, tribal police, special deputies, BIA police, and a quasi-militia sponsored by the tribal government enforced a blockade. It was permeable enough to allow smuggling supplies. Gun salvos from armored personnel carriers were a feature of the federal response. Occupiers, many of whom were Vietnam veterans, shot back with rifles. Two people were killed during the 70-day occupation.

In May 1973, Fools Crow negotiated a surrender that guaranteed a hearing for Indian grievances and free exit of the occupiers. The United States pursued a campaign of criminal prosecution of AIM members over the next few years that weakened leadership because they were all in court. Despite federal efforts, only one, Dennis Banks, was convicted. He went to prison and then served his parole back on Pine Ridge.

Wounded Knee became the symbol of Indian demands for treaty rights. It was covered on national television and the media daily. As they searched for more stories, the press generated a great deal of information about the history, poverty, and unjust aspects of federal Indian policy. The traditional Indians like Fools Crow became heroes, and even AIM leaders who told reporters they were ready to die for sovereignty gained sympathy.

Dennis Banks continued to be a hero in Chippewa County among the younger people. Eddie Benton-Banai led in the development of curriculum materials for the Little Red School House in Minneapolis. His grandfather stories became basic texts for Chippewa schools. Vernon and Clyde Bellecourt worked to combine traditional cultural practices with government reform on and off reservations as did George Mitchell. All were prominent in the rest of Indian country, too.

Red Power is often credited with a barrage of legislation that Congress enacted during the 1970s. Indians were assisted by sympathetic, activist non-Indian reformers in Congress and the general public. Reform efforts within Congress involving tribal leaders led to significant changes in Indian policy and provided specific legislation. Many of the radical demands were already being developed as Red Power started demonstrating.

Perhaps the most important ally was Senator James Abourezk (Democrat–South Dakota), who chaired the Senate Select Committee on Indian Affairs. His support was crucial in creating the budgets and hallmark legislation supporting tribal sovereignty and self-determination. He was joined by a large number of other congressmen in support of changes. Civil rights groups in the larger society were supportive, too. His committee generated the Indian Child Welfare Act, the Tribal College Act, and a host of reforms.

INDIAN SELF-DETERMINATION/MEASURED VICTORY

The most significant piece of legislation since 1934 was the Indian Self-Determination and Education Assistance Act of 1975 (Public Law 93-638). True tribal self-determination and sovereignty began with implementation of this act on reservation after reservation. Without the power to assume control of resources and funds, self-determination would have been a hollow idea. Today's tribal governments exercising tribal sovereignty were enabled by PL 93-638.

The Act extended and widened tribal control of resources and policy making begun tentatively with the return of tribal governments as republics in the 1930s and expanded by OEO programs in the 1960s. Tribal governments were authorized to contract with the BIA and other federal agencies, like Indian Health Services and Department of Justice programs, to assume control of programs. Title II of the Self-Determination Act permitted tribal assumption of administration of the extensive BIA education system.

Contracting grew quickly. In fiscal year 1980, 370 tribes contracted $200 million worth of BIA programs. They received $22.5 million in funds to administer the programs. In 1981, 480 contracts were developed. Contracting requires the tribal government's authorization, and then the contract requires the tribe or school to meet statutory and procedural guidelines. Tribal agencies or reservation governments are responsible for hiring, setting policies within the contract framework, and assuring compliance. The BIA is reduced to an oversight role. In effect, the federal government became the funding source for tribal governments in most areas of government operations.

When it worked well, reservation life improved, Indians got jobs, and tribal governments set priorities and directions. When it didn't work because the tribe did not have the management and program delivery skills or because tribal politics interfered, problems arose. Chippewa Country was challenged to move rapidly from the paternalistic control of reservation governments to evolving functional, effective governments that would address the legacy of dysfunction left by a century of BIA rule. Internal disputes disrupted the transition on many reservations.

RED LAKE: POLITICS IN CHIPPEWA COUNTRY

The career of the powerful Red Lake chairman Roger Jourdain exemplifies the volatility of Chippewa Country during the campaign for self-government and reform. He succeeded the architect of the modern Red Lake government, Peter Graves. Jourdain performed on the national stage, drew on OEO programs to build his reservation, and secured a grip on nearly all patronage and economic development on the reservation. He generated controversy on Red Lake and in the larger society as one of Indian country's political bosses.

Jourdain pioneered Red Lake participation in state elections and politics by actively pushing voters and supporting or opposing non-Indian candidates. In rural, sparsely populated northwestern Minnesota, Jourdain's support was crucial to elected officials. He cultivated political friendships with senators, representatives, and state legislators. Jourdain cultivated alternatives to BIA officialdom.

Jourdain drew on housing and urban affairs money to build public housing on the reservation but evaded HUD regulations requiring cluster housing by declaring the whole reservation a housing district. Houses were built throughout the reservation as Red Lakers always had. He secured development funds for a general store on the reservation. Red Lake was the first reservation to issue its own license plates and to force the issue of recognition by Minnesota and other states.

Jourdain was a mover in the creation of the Minnesota Indian Affairs Council, a state government entity, and he helped organize the national tribal chairman's organization with federal funding. Naturally, he was a primary, influential supporter in the 1975 Indian Self-Determination and Education Assistance Act. He also worked on getting the Indian Child Welfare Act passed in 1978.

The most spectacular demonstration of Jourdain's power and of the melding of radicalism and tribal government actions might have been the 1966 boycott of Bemidji, Minnesota. The small city was at the center of several reservations and was the main market for reservation shoppers. It also had a significant resident Chippewa minority. Bemidji had a history of anti-Indian discrimination, and the flash point was created by racist rants against Indians on a radio show. Jourdain declared a boycott, withdrew Red Lake funds from Bemidji banks, and urged other reservations to join.

White Earth and Leech Lake Reservations quickly joined the boycott. After several weeks, the boycott was successful. The radio announcer left public office and the radio, a biracial committee was formed, and Bemidji elected officials implemented a number of reforms. Schools pledged cultural sensitivity and history courses. Jourdain's dominance at Red Lake seemed assured.

On Red Lake, opposition to Jourdain's highhanded control of the reservation life roused opposition among the hereditary chiefs, families other than the extended Jourdain family, and those he had attacked over the years. In 1979 Jourdain's fervent opponents occupied the Red Lake tribal offices, drove Jourdain off the reservation and burned his house, and launched attacks against Jourdain supporters.

The FBI is responsible for law and order on reservations, but in this crisis they simply withdrew. The violence was unabated by federal intervention. Eventually, Red Lakers themselves halted the violence, and Jourdain officially returned to be reelected several times. Opposition continued to bubble, and each election was contested more closely. The federal government paid compensation to Jourdain and to the tribe.

Gerald Brun defeated Jourdain in 1990. He disputed the results in tribal court. The judge he had appointed, Margaret Sealye Treuer, rejected the appeal. An era of one-man domination had ended. Red Lake elections changed officials regularly from then on as is the pattern in most of Chippewa Country. Only a few are reelected consistently.

Similar disruptions occurred on several Chippewa reservations as tribal governments matured and a new generation demanded more effective services to the whole reservation rather than just to political cronies and family. Chippewa leaders struggled to find a means long denied them for dealing with political differences. Local politics is personal and often family oriented. It is sometimes explosive.

Turmoil was often exacerbated by the young who favored a mythical cultural purity over the give and take of governance and the slowness of changes. "Culture cops," frustrated unemployed youth, and the dysfunctions of the BIA legacy kept many reservations in turmoil. Ironically, all Chippewa agreed on the goals of self-determination, economic development, cultural integrity and enhancement, and education, but the personal passions aroused interfered with the creation of common paths to the common goals.

THE INDIAN RENAISSANCE

Along with political changes, the eruptions of Red Power, and federal changes in policy, a Renaissance in American Indian arts and culture flourished. The Renaissance included the achievements of many Chippewa, but it was also a country-wide blending of Pan-Indian achievement sparked by American interest in Indian protests, embedded American ideas about noble savages, and Native Americans attracting national attention. Indians were memes symbolizing changes in American society. Native Americans were marketable.

Strictly speaking, the Indian Renaissance was a literary movement identified by Keith Lincoln, a literary critic. It quickly extended beyond just books. Lincoln described the Renaissance as focusing on the reclamation of Native American heritage, reevaluating earlier studies and novels with Indian themes, and demonstrating connections of the present with traditional culture. N. Scott Momaday won the Pulitzer Prize for *House Made of Dawn* (1968), which embraced each of the themes. Vine Deloria Jr.'s *Custer Died for Your Sins* (1969) was embraced by a generation of college faculty and students sympathetic to Red Power and committed to multiculturalism and redress for past grievances. Leslie Silko wrote about cultural connections to her tribal culture.

Louise Erdrich, of the Turtle Mountain Chippewa, is arguably the most well-known and celebrated Chippewa author. She has written novels, poems, essays, children's books, and has contributed to Chippewa cultural preservation. (Ulf Andersen/Getty Images)

Louise Erdrich, Gordon Henry Jr., and Gerald Vizenor wrote from different Chippewa experiences but were popular among the college educated in Chippewa Country. Erdrich's *Love Medicine* was entrenched in reservation realities mixed with allusions to Chippewa tradition. Each of these Chippewa authors worked beyond just their own tribes and extended the message of the movement to non-Indian audiences. They were not the only writers, just the most prominent.

The Renaissance encompassed art, and art was a means of communicating Indian themes and talent to non-Indians particularly. Among Chippewa artists, Norval Morriseau is considered the founder of the Woodlands style of painting. Patrick Desjarlait's modernizing of traditional images and brilliant colors spread Chippewa themes, too. Every reservation gave birth to its own artists and writers in the rush of creative expression.

Red Power and the Indian Renaissance have not disappeared. The Chippewa continue to use Red Power style confrontation in league with elected leaders as they try to influence national Indian policies. Artists and authors continue to publish works with the same themes but with even more attention to Indian audiences while still providing education and enjoyment to non-Indians.

TREATY RIGHTS AND THE COURTS

In 1959, Bad River Reservation's tribal council decided on a dramatic approach "to protect the members [of the band] from "unjust arrest by State

Conservation officials." The band stated: "IT IS HEREBY DECLARED, that a state of cold war exists between the Bad River Band of Chippewa Indians and the officials of the Wisconsin Department of Conservation, and that such state will exist until such time as the state of Wisconsin shall recognize Federal treaties and statutes affording immunity to the members of this Band from Stage control over hunting and fishing."

Chippewa communities had long complained about the indifference of the federal government to states ignoring treaty rights concerning off-reservation hunting and gathering. Beginning in the 1880s, Michigan, Wisconsin, and Minnesota had insisted that Indians must comply with their game laws. Some states even asserted that treaty rights had been abrogated when territories became states. As early as 1934 several Chippewa reservation leaders met in Hayward, Wisconsin, to complain about repeated violations of their rights.

At the heart of the Chippewa collective complaint were the treaties signed by Chippewa leaders. In each of the treaties, Chippewa leaders had insisted on retaining the rights to hunt, fish, and gather in the lands they were ceding to the United States. Article II of the 1842 Treaty with the Chippewa, better known as the Copper Treaty, stated: "The Indians stipulate for the right of hunting on the ceded territory with the other usual privileges of occupancy." Article V of the 1837 Treaty with the Chippewa promised: "the privilege of hunting, fishing, and gathering the wild rice, upon the lands, the rivers, and the lakes included in the lands ceded, is guaranteed to the Indians." Although the federal government had the responsibility as a trustee, they refused to defend the Chippewa against the states.

After Public Law 280 intruded state criminal and civil jurisdiction into states, they became more aggressive in arresting, fining, confiscating gear, and jailing Chippewa they considered poachers. After several incidents of arrest and some favorable federal decisions on treaty rights, Fred and Mike Tribble, Chippewa of Lac Courte Oreilles Reservation, were arrested in 1974 while ice fishing off reservation on ceded land. Lac Courte Oreilles Reservation filed in federal court on behalf of tribal members including the Tribble brothers, requesting the state of Wisconsin be barred from enforcing Wisconsin laws—a violation of treaty rights. Judge James Doyle ruled against the reservation and said their treaty rights had been abrogated in 1850 and again in 1854.

While the federal courts were considering the cases filed in Chippewa Country, struggles for treaty rights escalated into violence, state defiance of federal courts, and glaring publicity in Washington State. Judge Boldt decided that treaty rights entitled Indians whose tribes had signed the treaties to 50 percent of the salmon harvest and to being able to fish off reservations as they had historically. Washington State's appeals were rejected.

In 1983, a three-judge appeals panel reversed Doyle's decision on the Wisconsin case. The court said that the treaty rights were valid and Judge Doyle should rule further on the scope of tribal rights. Wisconsin's appeal to the Supreme Court was not heard, which let stand what is called the Voigt decision because the secretary of the Wisconsin Department of Natural Resources, Lester Voigt, was named in the case.

Earlier, the United States had represented Michigan-based Chippewa in defense of treaty rights and won. Minnesota's Chippewa tribes that had signed the treaties had their rights upheld in the 1990s. In all of Chippewa Country, the treaty rights to hunt and fish off reservation were upheld for those bands that had signed the original treaties.

In order to determine the scope of tribal treaty rights off reservation, Judge Doyle and later Judge Crabb oversaw a series of agreements between Wisconsin and Chippewa reservations. The same process proceeded in Michigan and later in Minnesota. As tribal citizens tried to fish according to rules approved by the courts, Wisconsin's sports fishermen and others opposed to treaty rights and Indians exploded into action.

Antitreaty groups organized to harass, threaten, campaign, and interfere with Chippewa fishermen. Opponents contrived to portray themselves as proponents of equal rights for all and against racist favoritism toward Indians. Eventually, the state of Wisconsin and the federal government intervened to prosecute the offenders against Indians to the point of confiscating resources from one antitreaty organization and jailing its leader. Wisconsin spent millions to protect exercise of Indian treaty rights.

The Voigt case and its aftermath led to uniting six tribes in Wisconsin, four in Minnesota, and three in Michigan to assure treaty rights. The Great Lakes Indian Fish and Wildlife Commission (GLIFWC) became the multitribal organization to implement Voigt decision compliance among the Chippewa. It answers to the tribal chairpersons of the member tribes and provides the scientific information necessary. GLIFWC acts as liaison with the states involved in determining the quantity of game and fish harvest, enforces tribal ordinances, and has become a force in cultural enhancement. It is the clearest, most effective demonstration of tribal sovereign partnerships for the good of all.

The use of federal court test cases is one of the many approaches tribes used and continue to use to assert tribal sovereignty. It is but one more aspect of the story of the Chippewa as domestic dependent but self-determining nations. Tribal leaders throughout Chippewa Country continue to press toward Bemadiziwin, the good life, which has been the goal espoused in the Chippewa story since time immemorial.

NOTABLE FIGURES

Dennis Banks (1937–2017), Nowacumig, or in English, Center of the Universe

The Los Angeles Times called Dennis Banks "one of the most famous Indians since Sitting Bull and Crazy Horse." Banks was one of the founders of the American Indian Movement (AIM) in 1968. His fame is based on his role in the turbulent 1970s when he was one of the two most prominent leaders of AIM along with the Lakota, Russell Means. The urban organization was a protest movement against police brutality in Minneapolis–St. Paul, where numerous Chippewa and other Indians were a disadvantaged minority.

AIM morphed into an organization supporting traditional religion under the guidance of the Mide grand chief Eddie Benton-Banai and either led or joined protests for tribal sovereignty and justice for Native Americans. AIM appealed to the growing young adult; urban American Indians and its signature berets and one-fisted salute appeared throughout Indian country. Older Native Americans and tribal elected leaders generally opposed AIM's radicalness and quickly triggered violence. Occupations were new to Indian country.

Banks, a Leech Lake Chippewa, was in the forefront of the Trail of Tears demonstrations in 1972, which brought Indians from all over the country to take Congress, the BIA, and the president to task for failing to provide justice to Indian country. As federal officials delayed, AIM supporters occupied the BIA headquarters, expelled the employees, and attempted to negotiate. In the process the headquarters were burgled and trashed. Files were taken and turned over to tribes and Indian advocates. Banks negotiated the withdrawal. Federal funds provided costs for Indians to return home, and amnesty was extended along with a promise to negotiate by President Nixon.

AIM brought its followers including prominent non-Indians to provide assistance to Lakota Sioux protesting Pine Ridge Reservation's border towns' police violence against Indians. In 1973, traditional elders and opponents of the tribal government invited AIM help. Demonstrations in Custer, South Dakota, deteriorated into violence by police against protesters who fought back, injuring two police officers and destroying two police cars. Fires were set at the Chamber of Commerce and county courthouse. Other demonstrations occurred in Nebraska and on Pine Ridge Reservation.

Banks became the face of Indian protest during the 71-day occupation of the Wounded Knee Massacre site on Pine Ridge Reservation. Hundreds of Lakota, AIM members, and supporters established a perimeter around the community. Federal officials and tribal police blockaded the occupiers. Occupiers secured weapons from the Wounded Knee Trading Post, which they looted. Federal marshals and tribal police were heavily armed.

Firefights were common, and flares lighted the skies to expose those trying to evade the blockade and bring in supplies and additional recruits. Eventually, Frank Fools Crow, the most prominent Holy Man of the Lakota, negotiated surrender after two occupiers were killed by federal fire and the church used as headquarters for the occupiers was destroyed by machine gun fire. The church was at the site of the mass grave of the Lakota victims of the 1890 massacre.

Banks was charged with conspiracy, assault, and theft after the occupation. A federal judge dismissed the charges because the federal government was guilty of misconduct. Historian Peter Matthiessen concluded that the FBI had fabricated evidence for this case and others as well. However, Banks was convicted in 1975 in South Dakota court for rioting and assault during the 1973 riots in Custer, South Dakota. Banks insisted his life would be in danger in prison, so he moved to California where Governor Brown refused to extradite him. Banks was supported by stars like Marlon Brando, Jane Fonda, and attorney William Kunstler. The Onondaga gave him sanctuary within New York.

Banks surrendered in 1984 and served one year in South Dakota. On parole, he returned to Pine Ridge, where he worked as a drug program counselor until he could return to his Leech Lake Reservation home. He continued to work in drug counseling and built a rice and maple sugar business. Banks continued speaking about Indian issues and advocating Chippewa spiritualism. Many AIM members moved from confrontation to working with tribal government, supporting social service programs, and moving into economic development as the years passed. Banks was a member of the board of trustees of Leech Lake Tribal College. He remained a hero to many, including those returning to traditional religion and a disruptive symbol for others.

His memoir, *Ojibwa Warrior*, was coauthored by Richard Erddoes. He traces his problems to being sent to a boarding school at a young age, joining the air force, and descending into the common despair of so many Indians. Alcohol and drug abuse led to prison when he attempted a robbery. After being exposed to Chippewa spiritualism, he converted to militant activism and became one of the founders of AIM. Once he abandoned activism to work for economic development in the 1990s, he acted in a few movies as did fellow AIM member, Russell Means. He had at least five wives and about 20 children who gave him about 100 grandchildren.

Like so many of the Red Power activists, Dennis Banks contributed mightily to the sense of pride in being Chippewa. He contributed in many ways to his community, his tribe, and Indian country. This is the legacy of AIM and of Dennis Banks.

Chippewa Authors: Louise Erdrich, Gerald Vizenour, and Anton Treuer

The Chippewa are not limited to reservations, and many of the major contributors to Chippewa culture and knowledge are comfortable in the worlds of cities, academe, and the larger society. They are not expatriates in any sense because they retain ties to specific Chippewa communities and to extended families while they pursue careers in the larger society reflective of their Chippewa roots. As Gerald Vizenour might say, it is a means of survivance, using the term he coined. More than half of Chippewa people live other than on their home reservations. Home may be a place, or it may be an identity. Each of the three included here have made significant contributions to the story of the Chippewa. They are representative and not the only ones, and the present generation is producing even more fictional and scholarly authors. They also represent a kind of elite within Chippewa Country because of their good fortune in being educated in Ivy League schools and having the families that enabled their achievements.

Louise Erdrich (b. 1954) has received the most acclaim in literary circles, where she has won awards since 1984 when *Love Medicine* won the National Book Critics Award. She has won the National Book Award for fiction and been a Pulitzer Prize finalist. Erdrich was born in Minnesota and grew up in Wahpeton, North Dakota, well away from her reservation, Turtle Mountain. Her mother was Chippewa and her father German-American, but they taught at an Indian school and kept ties with their home reservation. She and her siblings were educated off reservation, and most have professional careers. Erdrich readily draws on her mixed-blood heritage and integrates it into her fiction that tends to revolve around a reservation she created, a thinly camouflaged Turtle Mountain. She is prolific, and nearly all of her writings integrate Chippewa characters with non-Indian characters and include multiple references to Chippewa themes, history, and spiritual knowledge.

Erdrich has six children and was married to Michael Dorris until 1997. She has published many books, including the five-book series for children called the Birchbark series with the first one named *The Birchbark House*.

It begins with a girl on Madeleine Island and continues the story through the girl's experiences as Chippewa life changes and of her descendants across Chippewa Country. The series effectively provides knowledge of traditional culture and Chippewa history, which can be entertaining and a means of enculturation for Chippewa youth. *The Round House* examines the contemporary problem of legal jurisdictions that permit the abuse of Indian women to continue. An interesting aside is her work that involves her non-Indian roots like *The Master Butchers Singing Club* in 2003. *Love Medicine* remains her signature book because of its use of Chippewa metaphor alluding to the creation narrative. The Nanapush family is clearly meant to allude to Nanabozho, and the story spins off into descriptions of reservation life and experiences. Erdrich was formally educated at Dartmouth and Johns Hopkins. She owns Birchbark Books, a store specializing in Indian literature and Native American crafts, and sponsors a foundation that publishes books.

Gerald Vizenour (b. 1938) was born on White Earth Reservation. His mother was Danish-American and father was White Earth Chippewa. His father was murdered when he was a boy, and he grew up in Minneapolis for the most part. His postgraduate education was at Columbia and Harvard, but he returned to first Lake Forest College near Chicago and then to be the founding faculty member of Native American Studies at Bemidji State University. There was also a period after he completed military service where he was director of the American Indian Employment Center in Minneapolis. He was an activist in the period 1964–1968. He worked as a reporter for the *Minneapolis Tribune*, particularly on American Indian issues. Vizenour did not have much sympathy for what he considered the posturings of AIM and the self-seeking efforts of Dennis Banks and Clyde Bellecourt. He served Chippewa Country by teaching and writing within a burgeoning Indian studies movement in higher education—a movement he would satirize in his work. He became a professor of Indian studies at the University of Minnesota–Minneapolis and then moved to the University of California–Berkeley.

Vizenour's work can be described as postmodern Indian literature, haiku, and even Anishinaabe traditional, but it is uniquely Vizenour. His first work was *Wordarrows: Whites and Indians in the New Fur Trade* while he was working in the Indian community in Minneapolis. Since then he has published academic essays, novels, poetry, edited collections, and other works. During a lengthy academic career he founded and edited the American Indian Literature and Critical Studies Association and journal. He was influenced by Jacques Derrida and Jean Baudrillard. His works are often dystopian and pursue the theme that Indians as one people was invented by European invaders. To Vizenour, Indian survival is based on resistance to colonialism and the structuring of Indians as others. He coined the term "Survivance" to describe Indian continuing existence. According to at least one critic, he utilizes irony and Barthesian jouissance in his works. In *The Heirs of Columbus* (1992), Vizenour created a Columbus who was actually Mayan and was just trying to get home. In 2006, Vizenour published a book of poetry, *Bear Island: The War at Sugar Point*. *Shrouds of White Earth* won the 2011 American Book Award. All of his work is informed by his Chippewa knowledge and background and can form a point of pride, reference, and modern cultural authenticity for the Chippewa people.

Anton Treuer (b. 1969) is representative of the current generation of Chippewa who are combining formal education and traditional Chippewa culture in their lives as a means to contribute to Chippewa survival and continuation. Treuer was born in Washington, DC, the son of an Austrian Jewish holocaust survivor and a White Earth Chippewa mother who became the first Native American female lawyer in Minnesota and a tribal judge. He was educated at Bemidji High School near his reservation where he lived while his mother pursued her career in law and on the bench. Then he went to Princeton and the University of Minnesota, where he received his PhD. He moved to Bemidji State and is a faculty member in the department inaugurated by Gerald Vizenour. Treuer has contributed to the story of the Chippewa in three ways: academic publications, work to reinvigorate Ojibwemowin through publications and work with language immersion camps and programs, and as an assistant in both medicine dance and drum ceremonies. His biographical study of the assassination of Hole in the Day and his history of the Red Lake Nation are examples of the kind of work that the story of the Chippewa needs to continue evolving. Other Chippewa academics like Scott Lyons, David Treuer, Therese Schenk, Brenda Child, Erik Redix, and many others are fleshing out the story. The Chippewa have always been willing to benefit from the work of non-Chippewa, and this continues in works by scholars of Ojibwe history and culture.

10

The Story of the Chippewa Continues

As the 1980s and 1990s passed, Chippewa Country settled into its new world of what might be termed embattled self-determination. The struggle to regain and exercise treaty rights and sovereignty continued, but as a series of jurisdictional disputes not that uncommon in interstate arguments. Challenges to existence are faint but important memories. States wanted more control of Chippewa Country, and reservation governments wanted less. The federal government tried to support Chippewa self-determination and provide technical assistance, and at the same time, guard state interests. Statutes, court cases, political posturing, and even return to demonstrations marked the efforts of each of the "sides."

Normalcy now meant that states accepted tribal sovereignty while still disputing its extent. Normalcy allowed reservations to concentrate on the business of trying to govern well, settle internal disputes with civility, and continue a measured separatism within the United States. It also meant expanding the institutions of government to replace what the BIA had usurped over the years. Courts, social services, schools with elected school boards, infrastructure, roads, and garbage collection are the stuff of normalcy. Dealing with dysfunctions in society fueled by the many anomalies of jurisdiction and shortages in resources is also part of normalcy in the continuing story.

Tribal efforts to govern well have benefited by interactions with other polities like the states and local governments even to forming intergovernmental MOUs and binding agreements. The Great Lakes Indian Fish and Wildlife Commission (GLIFWC) is an example of cooperative tribal-controlled interactions for the benefit of states and local communities. It supervises Chippewa compliance with the Voigt decision, which requires interaction with the state on enforcement in fishing, hunting, and gathering. It has launched scientific programs monitoring natural resources that meet tribal and state needs for understanding threats and opportunities in the environment.

It has also drawn on cultural resources to operate programs for reservation youth on maintaining the environment in culturally sensitive ways. Its quarterly publication, *Mazina'igan,* presents scientific news about the environment of the Great Lakes and always contains lessons, stories, and language instruction pieces. It is widely distributed throughout the United States. GLIFWC is staffed by tribal members and non-Indians working for the Commission to meet its goals. It has become a major force in environmental circles.

Other cooperative agreements include working with non-Indian-founded environmental groups and with pan-Indian organizations. These agreements and actions demonstrate the increasing sophistication and skills of tribal communities. Self-determination has been a powerful avenue for Chippewa achievements.

The overarching need in all of Indian country is economic development. The federal government and numerous task forces have identified the poverty of reservations and the absence of resources for a stable economy as a key problem. Native Americans told the government this for generations, too. Since the 1970s, tribal governments have attempted to do what the federal government had failed to do since it had taken away the tribal economies and resources earlier.

Tribal governments throughout Chippewa Country pursued federal funds, as state governments did, in order to support economic growth. The federal approach had been short-term stimulus grants or tax breaks for private businesses to operate on reservations, but these did not work once the tax breaks were withdrawn because the businesses like moccasin factories and craft works were, at best, marginal. Tribes tried to invest in the tourist trade they had been workers in for generations. Some experienced mild success with the ventures. For instance, Grand Portage Reservation drew on the tourists who ventured to the rebuilt fur trading post and the fishing and camping along Lake Superior to fill a motel they built.

The problem with these federally assisted steps was that they did not address the large unemployment of reservations in a quasi-private economy. They just nibbled at the problems and did not generate capital for economic development. One welcome by-product of contracting allowed by self-determination was that government employment soared on reservations. Tribal governments (not the federal government) are the largest employer on every reservation. Individual Chippewa pursued education and training to fill jobs above the lowest level for the first time since reservations were created.

Tribes like Red Lake Reservation continued to supervise their logging and fishing industries. The fishing industry experienced a major setback when Red Lake was overfished by commercial fishermen exploiting the state-controlled portion of the lake. State fishermen accused the band of overfishing, but data indicated otherwise. Cooperation with Minnesota has led to a return to commercial fishing on Red Lake. Other tribes used federal funds to develop fisheries and manage their own resources. Court battles led the way to making rice fields productive for commercial development again. The chip-away method of economic development did work but did not generate enough capital for effective, continuing development.

CASINOS IN CHIPPEWA COUNTRY

In 1987, the Supreme Court held in *Cabazon Band of Indians v. California* that tribes could offer gambling at casinos on trust land and the state could not regulate the tribes. The state could not tax the tribes and could not enforce laws about gambling on reservations. Tribes around the country realized that this could be a lucrative way around their absence of significant resources. Several tribes near urban areas had lucrative gaming in bingo already, so the market was available. In Chippewa Country, reservation governments began discussions with entrepreneurs to finance casino building and management and solve the absence of capital on reservations problem. Mille Lacs Reservation was first.

One year after the *Cabazon* decision, Congress responded to the anguish of states with the Indian Gaming Regulatory Act. Principled congressmen, prodded by Indian tribes and pressure groups, did protect tribal sovereignty partially but yielded to state pressure in significant ways. The law created a federal Indian Gaming Commission to regulate tribal casinos. A key provision was that a reservation casino required a tribal government–state compact. The compact would spell out the terms of operations for the tribal casino and had to be approved by the Gaming Commission.

Congress intended to pressure states into good faith negotiations by authorizing tribes to sue states, but this provision was taken out by a court decision that the Eleventh Amendment prevented the federal government from taking away state sovereign immunity from suit. States could dictate terms of compacts because tribes had no recourse. Tribes were used to state interests being favored over tribes.

Tribes were faced with states that could control whether or not they would be able to even have casinos. States have a veto power. In Chippewa Country and in most other areas, states negotiated what they considered reasonable agreements. From a Chippewa governmental perspective, Minnesota negotiated a fee for administration but was less restrictive than other states. Michigan insisted on larger payments from the tribes and often disputed placement of casinos. Wisconsin insisted on a revenue sharing that covered expenses they felt the state incurred because of the presence of casinos, and Wisconsin limited the duration of compacts with the tribes.

Each of the states argued that casinos were taking revenue from the states in some way because casinos were on trust land within the states. They contended that tribes should compensate the states, counties, and municipalities for additional traffic to get to the casinos and for a projected increase in crime. Congress agreed.

Tribes contended that they were sovereign and that the states' positions were illogical. If, for instance, Michigan built a highly successful casino near the Wisconsin line, Michigan did not have to compensate Wisconsin for lost revenue or traffic damages when Wisconsin citizens drove to Michigan. Congress disagreed. At least in Chippewa Country, the states did not prohibit gambling entirely within their borders as states could, according to the *Cabazon* decision. The *Cabazon* court insisted that tribes had to comply with state's moral cultures, but if a state allowed gambling, tribes had the right, too.

Despite their objections, tribes accepted state demands for revenue from the casinos and to other provisions. The Indian Gaming Commission pressured states to be reasonable, given the premise that tribes had to compensate states. For the Chippewa, the requirements set by Congress were reminiscent of the way their timber, fishing, and land were taken by states. Chippewa reservations have authorized casinos, governed by state-tribal compact and supervised by the National Indian Gaming Commission.

None of the Chippewa Country casinos create the profits and wealth equivalent to the well-positioned, small population tribes in Connecticut and California. These high-income casinos have become the symbol of tribal gambling, but they are an anomaly. Chippewa casinos as a whole operate in the 3–8 percent profit margin common in most of Indian country.

Leaders agree that the most important by-product is jobs for tribal members followed by investment in the community. Chippewa people are not rich. Income levels both per capita and per household remains at less than the average in the states. The goal of tribal casinos is not to maximize profit but to improve the reservations. Casinos are owned by the tribe, and this places elected officials in charge. Individuals do not get rich either.

Chippewa casinos have attracted enough revenue to transform each of the reservations. One tribal chairman commented: "we are players now." He was referring to the clout that capital generated by the casino gave the band. A Chippewa leader at Bay Mills Reservation, the site of the Chippewa victory over the Iroquois nearly 400 years earlier was happy to say: "Any tribal member who wants to work can have a job." Chippewa leaders have not been able to say this since reservations were created.

Other leaders have pointed to the management experience gained, the reduction in citizens needing relief, lower unemployment rates, the pride generated in a tribally run business, the respect gained from nearby community members, and the flexibility casino revenue provides in community options. Although there are some Chippewa who complain about casino revenue being misused and about various other practices, most support casinos and see their benefits.

Capital is the ingredient missing in Chippewa Country. Casino revenues provide funds that can generate benefits to the entire reservation. Even when the federal government increased funding for programs on reservations, there was no investment capital available. Chippewa governments have made a variety of choices.

Some have used profits just to maintain government services not funded by Congress as part of the trust responsibility. Some have contributed to community projects like new roofs for senior citizen centers, services to senior citizens, and various support groups dealing with the dysfunctions that remain constant in all communities. Some have used tribal funds to help influence government actions or support tribal colleges. Some have chosen "per caps" that provide what amounts to capital gains for individual tribal citizens. Others have used funds to create trusts. The key is that tribes get to decide what to do with the profits.

Most of the tribes have used casino funds to spin off other tribal businesses. Some reservations got their first grocery stores and gas stations, while others have provided loans to tribal members starting their own businesses. Start-up capital remains in short supply on reservations because land cannot be used for collateral, and most of the natural resources were taken in the robber baron era.

On the whole, casinos have been a positive influence on reservations. Most citizens and government leaders know that being dependent on a single business, especially one that can be affected by changes in the larger economy, is not the best option for continuing to build nations. Given available resources, it is the best option right now. The alternative is a return to the grinding poverty of the past. With casinos, marginal niche pieces of a tribal economy like fishing, hunting, guiding, tourism, ricing, and even art can diversify sufficiently to continue tribal growth.

Negative predictions about Indian casinos including those in Chippewa Country have not happened. States, foundations, tribal gaming associations, and the National Indian Gaming Commission have monitored tribal casinos since 1988. Organized crime has not penetrated Indian casinos, gambling addiction has not grown, a few Indians have not stolen the money, corruption in tribal government has remained at the pre-casino levels, and Indian tribes have not been exploited by unprincipled non-Indians.

Communities near reservations have demonstrably profited from the presence of casinos. State and local areas receive more funds than the Chippewa reservations do. Even in Chippewa Country, the majority of employees are drawn from the surrounding non-Indian communities. Supportive wholesalers and suppliers of everything from machines to paper towels have expanded their businesses. The spin-off and multiplier effect is particularly important because the reservations usually are located in economically depressed areas. Given the sparse populations, casino impact is especially important.

Casinos are not without their critics. Many in the larger society have reacted to casinos. They also condemned restoration of tribal fishing, hunting, and gathering treaty rights. They are aided in their claims by confusion about the legal rights of tribes as "domestic dependent nations" being conflated with Indians as a race. The opposition quickly takes on a racist tone in the many organizations that have sprung up, just as in the antitreaty groups. They complain that Indians are getting an unfair advantage over white people or middle-class people. The arguments are specious but can generate backlash against justice. Tribes have to fear the plenary power of Congress.

Other critics complain that Indians are abandoning their culture. To the extent that tribes make money and individual Indians have jobs and Indian leaders pursue economic development, they are judged as "non-Indian" profiteers. Supposedly, Indians are supposed to adhere to the trope of poor Indians suffering in dignified, spiritual poverty. Some Native Americans, like the Chippewa writer Marty Firerider, assert the Chippewa pursuit of economic development is an abandoning of tribal values of sharing and spirituality. "Gaming has brought in the dominant culture's disease of greed."

Another Native American, Sherman Alexie countered, "I've heard it said that Indians should not be involved in high-stakes gambling because it tarnishes our noble heritage. Personally, I've never believed in the nobility of poverty." Tribal leaders and proponents of casinos and economic development point out that money can support the continuation and enhancement of traditions, cultural wisdom, values, and practices.

Some critics complain that tribes should not receive funding from the federal government because they do not deserve it. State opponents point to the profits made by tribes as unfair and claim the tribes should share. Most of the compacts do require tribes to pay supporting funds to various state governments, and often states take a percentage of profits just as they do from other businesses in the state.

Unfortunately, many Americans think that some tribal members are not "real" Indians because they are mixed blood. Here again is the conflation of race with political status. Current president Donald Trump echoed what many Americans accept. He remarked on the absence of Indian-ness of Pequots to frame his opposition to tribal casinos while he was creating casinos in Atlantic City.

An interesting aside is that the combined profits and individual employee salaries generate more federal taxes than the budget of the Bureau of Indian Affairs. Indians are funding themselves. State tax revenue is enhanced by employees' salaries and casino purchases. The generation of capital investment seems to be good for states, federal, and tribal coffers.

CONTEMPORARY CHIPPEWA COUNTRY

Tribal leaders and most of the people are aware of the continuing realities of Chippewa Country. Given that Chippewa reservation populations extend from Michigan to Montana, conditions vary greatly. Chippewa communities are similar to those around them. Sometimes even the people, Chippewa and non-Chippewa, resemble one another whether on or off reservation. Most Chippewa have European surnames; most are French. The Chippewa dress the same as the general population and certainly have similar aspirations. We all want Bemaadiziwin with 21st-century characteristics.

Despite the diversity in Chippewa Country, it remains possible to describe Chippewa Country through generalizations with the stipulation that they do not apply to all reservations or people. Of course, this is true in describing the non-Indian populations and governments of the five-state area of Chippewa Country.

The demographics of Chippewa Country are in flux, but the legacy of history remains. Tribal governments and Chippewa people are working to improve their nations, but the task is monumental for the more than 100,000 Chippewa who write their story. It is easiest to begin with the negative aspects remaining in Chippewa Country. All of the tribal governments would agree with the generalizations, and federal studies have long confirmed the negatives of Chippewa existence.

Poverty is the central feature of Chippewa communities, as a legacy of the past 170 years or so of reservation life. Most of the dysfunctional aspects of Chippewa demography flow from poverty. The population is younger than the general American population due to a high birthrate and shorter life spans. The Chippewa are less healthy than most Americans because of poverty and generations of poor health care. Diseases remain a problem as diabetes and heart conditions are worse than their larger society counterparts. Infant mortality is also higher.

Unemployment and underemployment have always been a problem. Despite the economic gains symbolized by the casinos, rates of 35–65 percent are common if one counts adults not employed. Without the safety net provided by trust responsibility funding of programs, tribal services, and health care, unemployment and its consequences would be worse. There are few private sector businesses on reservations and no large-scale employers excepting government and the casinos. Small businesses are springing up with the assistance of tribal funds, and the future appears better.

Education levels reflect characteristics of poverty as well. The Chippewa graduate from high school at about a 65 percent rate. Chippewa students do not go to college and postsecondary schools at a rate as high as their neighbors. This has changed steadily as several tribes have built tribal colleges, which often vault students into other higher education institutions, or students can complete all they need on reservations. Tribal colleges are available in all of the states within Chippewa Country and have graduated hundreds of students, mostly at the associate degree level, since the 1980s. State universities have improved their acceptance of Native American students consciously, and several have worked with tribal colleges supportively.

Single-parent households are common, which generates neglect of one kind or another despite culturally based kinship networks. Given the fragmented nature of families in the 21st century, maintaining tribal family support is fraught with difficulties. This is particularly true given high rates of drug and alcohol abuse common in all impoverished communities. There are too many breaks in continuity of family amid the struggles of day-to-day existence. Housing is in short supply even as tribes leverage federal housing funds that are not enough to cover needs adequately. Many Chippewa live in substandard housing and are crowded into multiple family units.

Health care is available through the Indian Health Service as part of the trust responsibility and as continuing payment for land, as agreed in the 19th century. Funding is always short as is true of public health throughout the United States. Most of the reservation governments have contracted to administer their own services. Not only are tribes able to make decisions about how to administer health services, but they are can tap into medical insurance funds available to tribal members as to all Americans. Several of the reservations supplement shortfalls in health funding with casino-generated subsidies.

Crime rates on reservations are high because of poverty and the gaps in enforcement created by the federal government. The root of the problem in enforcement is that tribes are not able to police their reservations. Even for tribal citizens, all felony level cases have to be prosecuted by federal courts. Federal prosecutors decline a great many cases, particularly domestic crimes, because they do not want to or do not know how to interact with tribal communities. Neither the FBI nor the federal district courts have offices on any reservation in Chippewa Country.

In the Public Law 280 states of Wisconsin and Minnesota, county police are generally responsible for pursuing crimes concurrently with tribal police. However, studies indicate that the sheriff offices do not generally provide the same coverage on reservations as they do off reservation. They are further hampered by being outsiders to reservation communities. Federal delegation of jurisdiction to states was not accompanied by federal funding, which adds stress to county and state funding.

During the 21st century, reservations have experienced an explosion of drug-related trafficking and abuse. Gangs and drug distribution organizations have found that reservations offer a "free ride" because of conflicting jurisdictions that expect the federal government to manage drug crimes and prohibit tribes from doing it. It is easy to set up meth labs in rural areas and even easier if they are on reservations where many cannot be prosecuted because they are not Indians or because the federal and state governments choose not to. Some cooperative arrangements among the law enforcement agencies have helped, but tribes have many complaints about task force responses run by state or federal police.

Non-Indians on reservations are not subject to arrest or prosecution by tribal legal systems. If land on the reservations belongs to non-Indians, tribal police have no jurisdiction. If two non-Indians commit a crime on privately owned land, the tribe has no jurisdiction, and if it is on trust land, the federal government has jurisdiction except in the PL 280 states not tribal courts, the general pattern has been to exclude tribes from civil cases within reservations that include non-Indians or non-Indian land. Even tribal zoning and other regulations often cannot be enforced on reservations because the land is owned by non-Indians who do not affirmatively consent to tribal jurisdiction.

The complexities of jurisdiction because of what is called "checkerboarding," where nontribal citizens own land on reservations, make effective governing difficult. On the criminal side, federal laws like the Violence Against Women Act have allowed tribal prosecution of intimate partners of Native Americans on trust land. The restrictions still make it difficult, but the Act is the first step in extending tribal jurisdiction over non-Indians within reservations. The price for tribes is that they have to comply with standard federal court procedures, thus surrendering their ability to have tribally determined justice. Self-determination is much hedged in by federal laws and court decisions.

Chippewa Country governments and communities are intimately concerned with developments beyond reservation boundaries. Environmental concerns are an example. Chippewa traditional culture stressed the responsibility of humans to interact respectfully with all living things, including inanimate beings. This value is held dear throughout Chippewa Country, and individuals and tribal governments have responded with efforts to protect their environments.

Plans for oil pipelines through reservations and for mining near reservations have been met with concerted opposition, including demonstrations by individuals, sometimes supported by tribal governments, by tribal government law suits, and sovereign actions. Existing pipelines were not approved by tribes, and they are concerned with leaks and other dangers. Tribes have some jurisdiction because of Environmental Protection Agency regulations and the Clean Water Act, which equate reservations to states in jurisdiction and power.

Michigan-encircled tribal governments launched opposition to pipelines on legal and public fronts in 2017 and 2018. Bad River Reservation blocked railroad transportation of nuclear material across their lands, and tribal citizens occupied the tracks. Lac Courte Oreilles has provided leaders for antipipeline, protective rice field actions, and tribal exercise of treaty rights off reservation. Red Lake Reservation government has ordered a Canadian pipeline company to remove all existing pipelines from the reservation because they were never authorized by the tribe or the federal government. Suggestively, a deal between the company and Red Lake foundered because of doubts about federal action required by the deal.

Members of the Bad River Band of the Lake Superior Chippewa Tribe protest a proposed strip mine, Ashland, Wisconsin, May 31, 2014. Chippewa governments and citizens often take part in protests and court actions to protect their lands. (Jim West/Alamy Stock Photo)

Many of the Chippewa reservations have developed their own environmental programs that often are proactively supporting the environment. The Great Lakes Fish and Wildlife Commission that developed after the Voigt decision is one of several consortia of tribes that works hard to provide scientific data and support for regenerating the natural environment. These consortia often work with states and federal forest service to coordinate sustainable harvest of resources, not just fish.

Throughout Chippewa Country governments have become more responsive to reservation needs. As with governments throughout the United States, efficiency and effectiveness are uneven across Chippewa Country and from year to year. Sometimes Chippewa elected officials and bureaucracy make questionable decisions. Given the limited resources available, conflicts over allocations can become rancorous. There is enough discontent that turnover in elected officials is common.

Chippewa leaders have even betrayed the public trust on occasion but not at a higher level than public officials in the states. One joke on a Chippewa reservation was: "If you want to visit the former chairperson, you have to go to a federal prison." Others accuse tribal governments of favoritism

> **THE GREAT LAKES INDIAN FISH AND WILDLIFE COMMISSION**
>
> The Great Lakes Indian Fish and Wildlife Commission (GLIFWC), formed in 1984, provides nature resource management, conservation enforcement, public information services, and legal and political analysis in regard to treaty hunting, fishing, and gathering rights for 11 tribes in Minnesota, Wisconsin, and Michigan. The GLIFWC is an example of the exercise of tribal sovereignty in the current atmosphere of self-determination and demonstrates how responsible federal support can be combined with tribal rights to interact positively with states for the common good. It also exemplifies how a tribally supported organization can reinforce and enhance traditional values and culture. GLIFWC's existence and contributions are the result of more than a century of Chippewa efforts throughout Chippewa Country and follow complex and tortuous legal efforts by various Chippewa bands and people.

to their relatives and political supporters. Dissidents want the tribal government to listen to their version of what is needed and to ignore others. The reality is that tribal governments are subject to the monitoring oversight of the BIA because of contracts. Tribal casinos are monitored by tribes, the National Indian Gaming Commission, and states. Other programs are accountable to the federal government. Complaints often have some basis in tribal actions.

Despite problems and even some outright law breaking and corruption, nearly all tribal government officials, both elected and hired, are working conscientiously. Because they are human, they make good decisions and bad decisions. Fortunately for Chippewa people they are able to make these decisions in an atmosphere of continuing growth in efficiency and effectiveness based on stability.

One area that all tribal governments pursue is economic development. The casinos are graphic evidence of tribal efforts despite BIA opposition at first, and numerous efforts to promote industry, employment, and development are common. As with many businesses, many fail, and this stirs turmoil.

The reality is that only the tribal governments have the funds to contribute to economic development. Few Chippewa have capital to create businesses and lay the foundation for growth. Few have the acumen and success of Famous Dave's Barbeque, founded by Chippewa and tribe member, Dave Anderson. Tribal ownership and tribal investment are the continuing future in Chippewa Country. Part of the hope is that eventually individuals will be able to create more than just small businesses that employ only immediate family at best.

All tribal governments are confronted with one issue that is part of their unique status: what is a tribal citizen? Identity may be the most written about subject by Native Americans and non-Indians alike. It is a convoluted issue involving appearance, alleged blood-given personality traits, and behaviors.

Americans in general and Chippewa too have a legacy of equating race with being an Indian. Thomas Jefferson echoed many western Europeans when he discussed what made an Indian. He wondered how much white blood it took to extirpate Indian blood. He and others finally agreed that someone with seven-eighths white blood was white and therefore someone with one-quarter or more Indian blood was Indian. One should remember that blood was thought to convey behavioral traits that could not be overcome. Hence, the one-drop rule for African descended people.

Being Indian automatically meant behaving in certain, "uncivilized" ways. Throughout the 19th century and beyond, the BIA has adhered to the commitment that one had to have one-quarter or more Indian blood quantum to qualify as Indian, and anyone less did not deserve to be called Indian. Americans are confused by Indians who do not look and act Indian.

As reservations were established, the fact of being Indian was emphasized in nearly all government reports. Many treaties, including those with Chippewa, provided separate treatment for Indians (meaning full bloods) and what was termed generically as "half-breeds." These mixed bloods were deemed a corruptive influence on Indians because they had the worst characteristics of both races. BIA and others contrived to discredit mixed bloods and saw only full bloods as deserving. Efforts to exclude mixed-blood Indians from any payments or treatment as Indians were constant.

When the allotment act was passed, tribal rolls had to be drawn up by BIA staff to determine who was a tribal member who could receive land from the tribal estate. On White Earth Reservation the "scientific" determination of Chippewa-ness included using phrenology. Phrenologists believed they could tell how Indian someone was by feeling bumps on their heads. The result of judgments like this meant that often members of the same family were excluded, while others were considered real Indians.

Accusations of white people claiming to be Indian abounded throughout Indian Country. Later, mixed bloods who were allowed to remain on tribal rolls and take allotments were often required to convert the land to private property because their white blood made them intellectually competent. Many lost their land as a result, particularly in Chippewa Country where interethnic mixing had been going on for 300 years.

When tribes were allowed to restore tribal government in the 1930s, the idea of blood quantum had become sufficiently entrenched that even Indians accepted it. Given the divisions within tribes on levels of acculturation and a perceived difference between traditional full bloods and the questionable Indian-ness of mixed bloods, tribal constitutions generally accepted the idea of needing one-quarter Indian blood in order to be included on tribal rolls.

Culturally, this was nonsense. Chippewas had always considered even the completely non-Indians who married into the community to be relatives and, if living in tribal communities, to be "real" Chippewa. As time passed, the mixed-blood offspring married other Chippewa and lived as Chippewa. Aside from some usual joking, no one said you are not Chippewa because your great-grandfather was a Frenchman. Intermarriage with other tribes was common, too, and no one really was concerned about parentage—how one acted and lived was the determinant.

Scientifically, this was nonsense, too. But blood quantum became and remains a part of Indian life. "How much Indian are you?" is a question that has real implications for Chippewa people. One aspect of the problem is that non-Indian acceptance of tribal citizenship is necessary for maintaining sovereignty; the general American public and many lawmakers continue to see Indian as a race, and race membership is required to be accepted by the outside world.

Another facet of the problem of identity is to figure out what sort of behavior is required to be Chippewa. Like the blood quantum problem, this is both an internal and an external issue. Since the Red Power Movement and the Indian Renaissance, traditional cultural behaviors have been espoused by many, including tribal governments. Sometimes this means that those who do not belong to a Drum or Mide lodge are victims of a kind of fundamentalist frenzy where a few claim for themselves the right to declare who is "authentic."

Many reservations have been divided over the issue, some quite bitterly. Ironically, cultural purity was never required in traditional times. The Chippewa readily embraced their fellow Chippewa who converted to Christianity, and marriage outside the tribe was encouraged. "Foreign" religious ceremonies like the sun dance, the big drum, the Native American Church, and the multiple Christian religions took their place along with Midewiwin.

At the same time, nearly all Chippewa value the traditions of the past. Nearly all tribal governments insist that Chippewa culture be taught in contracted tribal schools and pressure public schools to do the same.

Government-sponsored tribal powwows are annual events because they are seen as public displays of commitment to being Chippewa. Several reservations and reservation schools support language immersion programs.

Lac Courte Oreilles Reservation adopted Ojibwemowin as the official government language in 2015 as symbolic of their commitment to the value of what makes a person a Chippewa. Much of the traditional cultural practices have been revived throughout Chippewa Country. Tribes have translated their names from English, and tribally significant symbols abound throughout the reservations.

Externally, non-Indians expect Chippewa to behave in what they construe as the way Indians should behave. They should revere the earth and be poor. They should hunt and fish for subsistence, harvest rice for personal use, and do so traditionally. They should speak their language and, above all, they should "look" like Indians. Feathers and beads are de rigueur, too. Chippewa leaders often play the culture card to insist on their rights. The Chippewa are generally aware that federal recognition can be withdrawn, and the United States can abandon the trust responsibility and even eliminate reservations.

The reality of being Chippewa is a bit different from the idealized characteristics constructed by the Chippewa and Americans. According to tribal enrollment figures, nearly all Chippewa are mixed bloods. The degree of Indian blood is difficult to maintain at the one-quarter levels because you can't marry your cousins and Chippewa populations are small. Indians across the United States marry non-Indians at a higher rate than any other ethnic group. In terms of blood quantum, Chippewa are breeding themselves out of existence, as some have put it.

Many Chippewa are coalescing around the idea that blood quantum should be abandoned. Tribes have the right to amend their constitutions and to change the blood quantum requirement in favor of the idea of descent. Descent from ancestors on tribal rolls is already a basis for tribal membership, but today the idea is to simply be direct descendants regardless of incoming intermarriage over the years. White Earth Reservation has adapted its constitution, but the Minnesota Chippewa Tribe must allow it. As of 2018, a referendum has been scheduled. In Michigan, descent has been enacted. The idea is spreading.

Most Chippewa do not speak Ojibwemowin. Efforts to restore the language have been made but have not resulted in widespread usage. Ceremonies are attended by most Chippewa, but they usually belong to Christian churches for their weddings and funerals at least. Churches on reservations are numerous, and each has its adherents. Knowledge of tribal history is encouraged, and the hope among many is that continuing to emphasize culture will provide the glue that holds 21st-century Chippewa reservations intact.

More than half of all Chippewa do not live on reservations or nearby border communities. Every city in Chippewa Country has a Chippewa community. Urban Chippewa often intermarry, become part of pan-Indian communities, and use English. As they become adults, urban Chippewa go to school, get jobs, and variously practice their traditional behaviors. Most do retain ties and make visits "home" with frequency.

Part of the traditional creation narrative addresses the future. After he had completed his work of identifying all things and their functions as well as restoring the earth to the Chippewa, Nanabozho withdrew. Some say he became a rock and can bring you to where he abides on the shores of Lake Superior. Nanabozho promised to return if Chippewa existence were on the brink of extinction. He has not returned yet.

It is also said that the future of the Chippewa is tied together with the survival of wolves. If they disappear, so will the Chippewa. Wolves are endangered, but they have rebounded, and they still exist. So do the Chippewa.

The story of the Chippewa continues as it has for centuries. The Chippewa adapt by bringing in new ideas, practices, people, and even aspirations. It is a safe bet that the story will continue.

Bibliography

Andersen, Chris. *"Metis": Race, Recognition, and the Struggle for Indigenous Peoplehood.* Vancouver, BC: University of British Columbia Press, 2014.

Anderson, Gary C. *Kinsmen of Another Kind.* Lincoln, NE: University of Nebraska Press, 1997.

Bellfy, Phil. *Three Fires Unity: The Anishnaabeg of the Lake Huron Borderlands.* Lincoln, NE: University of Nebraska Press, 2011.

Benton Banai, Edward. *A Mishomis Book.* St. Paul, MN: Red School House Graphics, 1975.

Bieder, Robert E. *Native American Communities in Wisconsin, 1600–1960: A Study of Tradition and Change.* Madison, WI: University of Wisconsin Press, 1995.

Birmingham, Robert A., and Leslie E. Eisenberg. *Indian Mounds of Wisconsin.* Madison, WI: University of Wisconsin Press, 2000.

Bishop, Charles A. *The Northern Ojibwa and the Fur Trade: An Historical and Ecological Study.* Toronto, Canada: Holt, Rinehart, and Winston of Canada, 1974.

Blair, Emma H., ed. and trans. *The Indian Tribes of the Upper Mississippi Valley & Region of the Great Lakes As Described by Nicolas Perrot* et al. vol. I. Originally published 1911. Lincoln, NE: University of Nebraska Press, 1996.

Carpenter, Leah. "Tracking the Land: Ojibwe Land Tenure and Acquisition at Grand Portage and Leech Lake." Unpublished dissertation, University of Arizona, 2008.

Child, Brenda J. *Holding Our World Together: Ojibwe Women in the Survival of Community.* New York: Viking Press, 2012.

Child, Brenda J. *My Grandfather's Knocking Sticks.* St. Paul, MN: Minnesota Historical Society Press, 2014.

Cleland, Charles E. *Rites of Conquest: The History and Culture of Michigan's Native Americans.* Ann Arbor, MI: University of Michigan Press, 1992.

Clifton, James A. "Wisconsin Death March: Explaining the Extremes in Old Northwest Indian Removal," *Transactions of the Wisconsin Academy of Science and Letters,* 75 (1987), pp. 1–39.

Copway, George. *The Traditional History and Characteristic Sketches of the Ojibway Nation.* London: Charles Gilpin, 1850.

Danziger, Edmund Jefferson, Jr. *The Chippewas of Lake Superior.* Norman, OK: University of Oklahoma Press, 1979.

Danziger, Edmund Jefferson, Jr. *Great Lakes Indian Accommodation & Resistance during the Early Reservation Years, 1850–1900.* Ann Arbor, MI: University of Michigan Press, 2009.

Densmore, Frances. *Chippewa Customs.* (Orig. 1929.) St. Paul, MN: Minnesota Historical Society Press, reprint 1979.

Dewdney, Selwyn. *The Sacred Scrolls of the Ojibway.* Toronto, Canada: University of Toronto Press, 1975.

Dickason, Olive P. *Canada's First Nations.* Norman, OK: University of Oklahoma Press, 1992.

Doerfler, Jill, Niigaanwewidam James Sinclair, and Heidi Kiiwetinepinesiik Stark, eds. *Centering Anishinaabeg Studies: Understanding the World through Stories.* East Lansing, MI: Michigan State University Press, 2013.

Eid, Leroy V. "The Ojibwa-Iroquois War: The War the Five Nations Did Not Win," *Ethnohistory* 26, 4 (Fall 1979): 297–324.

Ellinghaus, Katherine. *Blood Will Tell: Native Americans and Assimilation Policy.* Lincoln, NE: University of Nebraska Press, 2017.

Fixico, Donald L. *An Anthology of Western Great Lakes History.* American Indian Studies Department, University of Wisconsin–Milwaukee, n.d.

Fletcher, Matthew L. M. *The Eagle Returns: The Legal History of the Grand Traverse Band of Ottawa and Chippewa Indians.* East Lansing, MI: Michigan State University Press, 2012.

Foster, Martha H. *We Know Who We Are: Metis Identity in a Montana Community.* Norman, OK: University of Oklahoma Press, 2006.

Goddard, Ives. "Central Algonquian Languages," in *Handbook of North American Indians,* XV, pp. 583–587. Washington, DC: Smithsonian Institution, 1978.

Great Lakes Indian Fish and Wildlife Commission. *A Guide to Understanding Ojibwe Treaty Rights.* Odanah, Bad River Reservation: Great Lakes Indian Fish and Wildlife Commission, 1998.

Hallowell, A. Irving. "Northern Ojibwa Ecological Adaptation and Social Organization," (orig. 1976) in *Contributions to Anthropology*, pp. 333–350. Chicago: University of Chicago Press, 1976.

Hallowell, A. Irving. "Ojibway Ontology, Behavior, and World View," (orig. 1960) in *Contributions to Anthropology*, pp. 357–390. Chicago: University of Chicago Press, 1976.

Hallowell, A. Irving. "Ojibway World View and Disease," (orig. 1963) in *Contributions to Anthropology*, pp. 391–448. Chicago: University of Chicago Press, 1976.

Hickerson, Harold. *The Southwestern Chippewa: An Ethnohistorical Study*. Menasha, WI: American Anthropological Society, 1962.

Hickerson, Harold. *The Chippewa and Their Neighbors: A Study in Ethnohistory*. New York: Holt, Rinehart and Winston, 1970.

Hultkranz, Ake. *Belief and Worship in Native North America*. (Edited with an introduction by Christopher Vecsey.) Syracuse, NY: Syracuse University Press, 1981.

Institute for the Development of Indian Law. *Treaties and Agreements of the Chippewa Indians*. Washington, DC: Institute for the Development of Indian Law, n.d.

Johnston, Basil. *Ojibway Heritage: The Ceremonies, Rituals, Songs, Dances, Prayers and Legends of the Ojibway*. Toronto, Ontario, Canada: McClelland and Stewart, 1976, reprint 1990.

Kohl, Johann. *Kitchi-Gami: Life among the Lake Superior Ojibway*. Lascelles Wraxhall, trans. St. Paul, MN: Minnesota Historical Society, orig. 1860, reprint 1985.

Lancaster, Daniel. *John Beargrease: Legend of Minnesota's North Shore, 1858–1910*. Duluth, MN: Holy Cow Press, 2008.

Landes, Ruth. *The Ojibwa Women*. Introduction by Sally Cole (orig. 1938). Lincoln, NE: University of Nebraska Press, 1997.

Lyons, Scott R. *X-Marks: Native Signatures of Assent*. St. Paul, MN: University of Minnesota Press, 2010.

MacLeod, D. Peter. "The Anishinabeg Point of View: The History of the Great Lakes Region to 1800 in Nineteenth-Century Mississauga, Odawa, and Ojibwa Historiography," *Canadian Historical Reveiw*, 83, 2 (1992): 194–210.

McClurken, James M. *Our People, Our Journey: The Little River Band of Ottawa Indians*. East Lansing, MI: Michigan State University Press, 2009.

McDonnell, Michael A. *Masters of Empire: Great Lakes Indians and the Making of America*. New York: Hill and Wang, 2015.

Meyer, Melissa L. *The White Earth Tragedy: Ethnicity and Dispossession at a Minnesota Anishinaabe Reservation, 1889–1920*. Lincoln, NE: University of Nebraska Press, 1999.

Miller, Cary. *Ogimaag: Anishinaabeg Leadership, 1760–1845*. Lincoln, NE: University of Nebraska Press, 2010.

Murray, Stanley. "The Turtle Mountain Chippewa, 1882–1905," *North Dakota History* 51 (1984): 14–37.

Nichols, Roger L. *Indians in the United States and Canada*. Lincoln, NE: University of Nebraska Press, 1998.

Norgaard, Chantal. "Beyond Folklore: Historical Writing and Treaty Rights Activism in the Bad River WPA," in *Tribal Worlds: Critical Studies in American Indian Nation Building*. Brian Hosmer and Larry Nesper, eds. Albany, NY: State University of New York Press, 2013.

Norgaard, Chantal. *Seasons of Change: Labor, Treaty Rights, and Ojibwe Nationhood*. Chapel Hill, NC: University of North Carolina Press, 2014.

Peacock, Thomas, and Marlen Wisuri. *Ojibwe Waasa Inaabiida, We Look in All Directions*. Afton, MN: Afton Historical Press, 2002.

Pevar, Stephen L. *The Rights of Indians and Tribes*, 4th ed. New York: Oxford University Press, 2012.

Prucha, Francis P. *The Great Father: The United States Government and the American Indians*, abridged ed. Lincoln, NE: University of Nebraska Press, 1986.

Quimby, George I. *Indian Life in the Upper Great Lakes, 11,000 B.C. to A.D. 1800*. Chicago: University of Chicago Press, 1960.

Rasmussen, Charlie O. *Oibway Journeys: Treaties, Sandy Lake & the Waabanong Run*. Odanah, WI: Great Lakes Indian Fish and Wildlife Commission Press, 2003.

Redix, Erik M. *The Murder of Joe White: Ojibwe Leadership and Colonialism in Wisconsin*. East Lansing, MI: Michigan State University Press, 2014.

Ritzenthaler, Robert E. "Southwestern Chippewa," in *Handbook of North American Indians*, XV, pp. 743–759. Washington, DC: Smithsonian Institution, 1978.

Rogers, E. S. "Southeastern Ojibwa," in *Handbook of North American Indians*, XV, pp. 760–771. Washington, DC: Smithsonian Institution, 1978.

Ross, Hamilton N. *LaPointe: Village Outpost on Madeline Island*. Madison, WI: State Historical Society of Wisconsin, 2000.

Schenck, Theresa M. *"The Voice of the Crane Echoes Afar": The Sociopolitical Organization of the Lake Superior Ojibwa, 1640–1955*. New York: Garland Publishing, 1997.

Schoolcraft, Henry R. *The American Indians, Their History, Condition and Prospects, from Original Notes and Manuscripts*. Buffalo, NY: George H. Derby, 1851.

Sleeper-Smith, Susan. *Indian Women and French Men: Rethinking Cultural Encounter in the Western Great Lakes*. Amhearst, MA: University of Massachusetts Press, 2001.

Stark, Heidi Kiiwetinepinesiik, "Marked by Fire: Anishinaabe Articulations of nationhood in Treaty-Making with the United States and Canada," in *Tribal Worlds: Critical Studies in American Indian Nation Building*. Brian Hosmer and Larry Nesper, eds. Albany, NY: State University of New York Press, 2013.

Tanner, Helen, ed. *Atlas of Great Lakes Indian History*. Norman, OK: University of Oklahoma Press, 1987.

Treuer, Anton. *Ojibwe in Minnesota*. St. Paul, MN: Minnesota Historical Society, 2010.

Treuer, Anton. *Warrior Nation: A History of the Red Lake Ojibwe*. St Paul, MN: Minnesota Historical Society Press, 2015.

Trigger, Bruce G. *Natives and Newcomers: Canada's "Heroic Age" Reconsidered*. Montreal, Canada: McGill-Queen's University Press, 1986.

Vecsey, Christopher. *Traditional Ojibwa Religion and Its Historical Changes*. Philadelphia: American Philosophical Society, 1983.

Warren, William W. *History of the Ojibway People*, 2nd ed. (Edited and annotated by Theresa Schenck.) St. Paul, MN: Minnesota Historical Society. First edition, 1885.

White, Richard. *The Middle Ground: Indians, Empires, and Republics in the Great Lakes Region, 1650–1815*. New York: Cambridge University Press, 1991.

Witgen, Michael. *An Infinity of Nations: How the Native New World Shaped Early North America*. Philadelphia: University of Pennsylvania Press, 2012.

Index

Note: Page numbers followed by *f* indicate photographs.

Abourezk, James, 172
Adena-Hopewell culture (Ohio Valley), 5
AIM (American Indian Movement), 170–171, 179
Ajijawk (far calling bird), 28
Alcatraz Island, 168–169
Alcohol usage, 78, 100, 120, 163, 180, 192
Alexie, Sherman, 191
Algonquian language, 4, 6, 18, 41, 66
Algonquians, 42, 46, 48
Allotment Act (1887), 121
Allouez, Claude, 62
American agents: appeals to, 97; in Chippewa and Dakota Country, 93, 94; functions of, 99; Madeline Island and, 113; payment withholding by, 101; White Earth reservation and, 119–120
American/Canadian attitudes toward Indians, 88–89
American-English settlers, 76, 79

American Fur Company (1822), 84, 90–91, 112
American Indian Chicago Conference (1961), 126
American Indian Defense Association, 147
American Indian Federation, 158
American Indian Movement (AIM), 170–171, 179
American military forces in 1800s, 93
American racism, 88
American Revolution, 79
American usage of tribal names, 29
Amherst, Jeffery, 72–73, 75
Amherst, Lord, 81
Anderson, Dave, 196
Anglo-French Wars (1740–1763), 65
Animal totems or symbols, 27
Anishinaabeg (Anishinaabe), 6, 8, 28–29, 41, 67, 111
Anishinaabewaki (land of the Chippewa), 1, 41
Annual cycle of movement, 10–11

Aqua-Plano communities, 5
Archaic-Boreal societies, 5
Armstrong, Benjamin, 109, 126
Arthur, Chester, 142
Ashiniwin (Stone Child), 144
Astor, John Jacob, 90
Auineau, Jean-Pierre, 63
Ayers, Frederick, 135

Baaga'dowe (baggataway) (Lacrosse), 74, 114
Bad River Reservation (Wisconsin), 110, 115, 154–155, 157–158, 176–177, 194
Balfour, Henry, 72–73
Band ogima, 15–16
Banks, Dennis (Nowacumig), 170–171, 172, 179–181
Baraga, Frederic, 113, 114
Basque whalers, 42
Basswood tree, 9
Battle of Fallen Timbers (1795), 82, 96
Battle of Iroquois Point (1662), 50
Battle of Sugar Point, 132, 137
Battle of the Monongahela, 68
Battle of the Thames (1813), 83
Battle of Tippecanoe (1795), 83
Baudrillard, Jean, 182
Bay Mills band, 107
Bear clan, 14, 26, 27
Beargrease, John (Grand Portage Chippewa), 130
Beargrease Dogsled Race, 130
Bear Island (Vizenour), 183
Beaulieu, Paul, 138
Beaver Wars (1641), 48, 51
Bellecourt, Clyde, 170, 171, 172
Bellecourt, Vernon, 170, 171, 172
Bemaadiziwin (the good life), 17, 21, 22, 23, 26, 32, 33, 191
Bemidji, Minnesota, 174
Bennett, Robert, 166
Benton-Banai, Eddie, 170, 172, 179
Berry, E. Y., 160

BIA. *See* Bureau of Indian Affairs
Biaushwa II, 63–64
Biauswah, 34, 79
Big Drum Society, 31–32, 136, 169, 198
Big Marten (Kechewaubishash), 64–65
Birchbark, 8–9, 31–32
Birchbark House, The (Erdrich), 181
Bizahiki (Great Buffalo, or Buffalo), 109–110, 111, 114, 126–127
Blackbird, Andrew, 6, 84
Blizzards and famine in winter, 11
Blood quantum issues, 197–198, 199
Body soul, 37
Bonnin, Gertrude, 145
Bottineau, John, 142
Boundaries, tribal, 17–18
Bow and arrow, 25
Braddock, Edward, 68
Brando, Marlon, 180
Brenner, E. W., 142
Briggs, George, 127
Bright Eyes, 145
British (English): as allies of the Chippewas and Ottawas, 73–74; British-Canadian Indian policy, 85–86; colonists, 46, 54; Fort William Henry and, 70; fur trade pattern, 52; growing power of in 1700s, 66–67; reservations and, 42–43; as traders, 42; Treaty of Paris and, 81–82; in War of 1812, 82–83
Brown, Orlando, 107
Brule, Etienne, 46
Brun, Gerald, 175
Bugonaygeshig (Hole in the Day) (Leech Lake Pillagers), 130, 131–132
Bureau of Indian Affairs (BIA): Chippewa working for, 129; as Indian Service/Department, 94; leases and, 134; mixed-blood issues

and, 197; records of epidemics, 130; relocation programs, 163; renamed in 1946, 159, 160; reservation land leasing and, 103; tribal assumption of BIA education system, 173
Burgoyne, John, 81
Burke, John, 142
Burkhead, Oscar, 132
Business councils, 153–154

CAA (Community Actions Agencies), 166
Cabazon Band of Indians v. California (1987), 187, 188
Cabot, John, 42–43
Cadillac, Antoine de la Mothe, 51
Cadotte, Michel (Madeleine), 111, 112, 113
Cadotte family, 77, 78, 112–113
Canada: British and, 83, 85; Chippewas in, 86, 89; deportation of metis to, 143; French sovereignty in, 46; Red Power and, 83; Red River Valley and, 91–92; Turtle Mountains, 140; U.S. border with, 87
Cannibalism, 19
Canoes, birchbark, 4, 8
Carlisle Indian School, 152
Cartier, Jacques, 43
Casinos, 187–191
Catholic Drexel sisters, 135
Catholic missions, 113–114, 135, 141
Cavelier, Sieur de la Salle, René-Robert, 51
Cayuga tribe, 17–18
CCC (Civilian Conservation Corps), 151, 158
Century of Dishonor, A (Jackson), 145
Champlain, Samuel, 46
Cherokee Nation v. Georgia (1831), 94, 95
Chibiabos (Ghost Rabbit), 24
Chiefs (ogimaag), 13, 14, 15

Child, Brenda, 133, 183
Children of intermarriages, 58
Chippewa, history of: in the 18th century, 55–57; adjusting to 19th century changes, 88–91; areas of Chippewa Country ceded to the U.S., 101; as balance of power between European governments, 80; in battles between French and British, 66–67; changes after 1815, 85–87; controllers of fur trade center, 52; first contact with Europeans, 46; struggles during first third of 20th century, 129–130; support of British in War of 1812, 82, 83; treaties with United States, 91–93; in Wisconsin and eastern Minnesota, 115
Chippewa communities: adaptability of, 10–11; conferences, 79–80; education levels in, 192; health care in, 193; losses in the 1900s, 105; poverty as central feature, 90, 123, 192
Chippewa Country: boundaries of, 1, 19–20; ceded to the U.S. by 1900, 101; center shift in 1800s, 55; decision making by consensus, 13–14; doubling of, 55, 63, 86–87; economy of, 78–79; as ethnic group in Michigan, 1; land ownership, 19–20; population of in 1600, 6; self-determination and, 185; tribal governments in, 149; vegetation and climate of, 4
Chippewa Country map ca. 1800, 2
Chippewa men in the Civil War, 103
Chippewa National Forest, 122
Chippewa religious beliefs: afterlife, 37–38; as animist, 36; dreams and the great migration, 36; flexibility of, 32; healers, 38; lack of need for consistency, 23; legalized in 1933, 136; in Michigan, 103; origin

Chippewa religious beliefs (*cont.*) tradition, 23–24, 33; small creatures and children as saviors, 26; worldview of illness, 21

Chippewa tribes: hunting territories, 13, 20; roles of men and women in decision making, 7, 8; as sovereign nations, 1; torture of enemies, 19; tribal council governments, 152–153; values in creation and prophetic narratives, 26; westward migrations, 28–29

Chippewa women: American traders and, 83; in fur trading system, 57; new kinship matrices with Frenchmen, 57; as rice harvesters, 13; as warriors, 17, 34; women's council, 17

citizen vs. member, 153

Civilian Conservation Corps (CCC), 151, 158

Civilization Act (1819), 97

Civil rights movement, 165

Civil War, Chippewa men in, 103

Clair, Arthur St., 82

Clan (doodem) membership: in the 1820s, 86; autonomous bands and, 27; immigrants, acceptance of, 153; multiclan communities, 12; original clan names, 14; patrilineal, 26–27

Clapp, Moses, 122

Clapp Act (1906), 122

Clean Water Act, 194

Climate challenges, 4

Clovis technology, 5

Cole, Sally, 7

Collier, John, 147, 151, 158, 159

Colonialist mentality, 7

Columbian Exchange, 42

Commerce Clause in U.S. Constitution, 93

Community Actions Agencies (CAA), 166

Concurrent Resolution 108 (1953), 162

Coolidge administration and offer of citizenship, 146

Copper Treaty (1842), 177

Copway, George, 6

Corte, Gaspar, 42–43

Coureurs de Bois (Runners of the Woods), 53

Crane clan, 14, 16, 26, 27

Crane guides, 28

Creator culture hero, 24–25

Cree tribe, 18, 63

Crow Dog, 118–119

Cultural truths, 32–33

Custer Died for Your Sins (Deloria), 168, 175

Dakota Sioux, 61–65

Dakota tribe, 6, 18, 20, 32, 55, 153

Dakota wars, 63–65, 79, 86, 115–116

Danziger, Edmund, 154–155

Davis, Charles, 143

Dawes Severalty Act or Allotment Act (1887), 102–103, 123

Declaration of Indian Purpose, 165

Deer clan, 14, 26

Deer hunting, 13

Deganawida, 17, 48

Delaware tribe, 72

Deloria, Vine, Jr., 168

DePeyster, Arent Schuyler, 80–81

De Rigaud, Pierre, 69

Derrida, Jacques, 182

Desjarlait, Patrick, 176

Dewdney, Selwyn, 31–32

Diseases and epidemics: captives and, 19; as caused by Manitos, 38–39; destruction of entire villages, 43–44; diabetes and heart conditions, 192; fry bread (Indian bread) and malnutrition, 130; glaucoma and tuberculosis, 125, 130; smallpox epidemics, 43, 70

Djessakids, 36
Doctrine of Discovery, 43, 93, 94
Dole, William, 116
Doodem membership. *See* Clan membership
Dorris, Michael, 181
Doyle, James, 177, 178
Dutch traders, 42, 43, 46, 48

Eagle clan, 26, 27
Eastman, Seth, 10*f*
Elders and spiritual power, 36
Eleventh Amendment, 188
English. *See* British
Environmental Protection Agency (EPA), 194
Epidemics. *See* Diseases and epidemics
Episcopalians, 135
Erddoes, Richard, 180
Erdrich, Louise, 156, 176*f*, 181–182
Erie Canal, 84
Erie tribe, 18
Eshkebugescoshe (Flat Mouth), 92*f*, 104
Europeans: assumptions about women, 57; belief in right to govern pagans, 43; Chippewa reaction to, 47; confusion over boundaries, 20; as disease carriers, 43; misinterpretation of Chippewa pleas, 35; power struggles between, 43; religious proselytizing, 44–45
Ewing, Thomas, 107

Falls, Albert, 147
Famous Dave's Barbeque, 196
Feast of the Dead, 37–38
Feasts as celebrations, 35
Fillmore, Millard, 109, 110, 114, 127
Firerider, Marty, 190–191
Fish clan, 14, 26, 27
Fishing industry, 8, 12, 178, 187

Flat Mouth (Eshkebugescoshe), 92*f*, 104
Fletcher, Alice, 10
Fonda, Jane, 180
Fond du Lac, 62
Fools Crow, Frank, 171–172, 180
Fort Duquesne, 68
Fort Michilimackinac, 69, 72–73, 74–75, 82, 83
Fort Orange (later Albany), 48
Fort Oswego, 69
Fort Pontchartrain, 51
Fort Totten, 142
Fort William Henry, 69
Four Winds, 24, 33
Fox tribe, 6, 8, 18, 58
Fox Wars (1690–1736), 58–60, 61
Franco-English treaty (1632), 46–47
French: claim of the entire Mississippi watershed, 51; closing and reopening of fur trade, 53, 54; dependency on Indian allies, 55; forts as trading centers, 54–55, 62; guns and, 46; in Louisiana, 59; maps and, 46; seen as equals by Indians, 60; traders, intermarriage with Chippewa women, 42, 54, 57, 83
French and Indian War (1754–1760), 54, 65, 67–68, 76
French Catholics, 45
Friends of the Indians, 102
Frontenac, Onontio, 62
Fry bread (Indian bread), 130
Funeral services, 37–38
Fur trade: channels for, 79; Chippewa participation in, 56; fur traders, 42, 48, 50, 82; kinship network and, 79; new society around fur trading posts, 58; as source of wealth for Indians and Americans in 1820s, 91; women's functions in, 56–57

Gage, Thomas, 74–75
Gender role flexibility, 7, 9, 17
George Washington's War, 82
GI Bill, 168
Giiskitawa (Joe White), 130, 131
Gitchee Manitou, 22, 23, 30–31
Gitchi-anishinaabeg, 15
Glaciers, prehistoric, 4
Gleska, Sinte (Rosebud Sioux), 118
GLIFWC (Great Lakes Indian Fish and Wildlife Commission), 178, 186, 195, 196
Goddard, Ives, 6
Gold Rush (1849), 98
Gomes, Estevao, 42–43
Grand Medicine Society. *See* Midewiwin
Grandmother (Nokomis), 25
Grand Portage, 55, 78
Graves, Joseph, 138
Graves, Peter, 125, 136–138, 173
Great Buffalo (Bizahiki), 109–110, 111, 114, 126–127
Great Depression, 147, 151
Great Flood, 25–26
Great Lakes Indian Fish and Wildlife Commission (GLIFWC), 178, 186, 195, 196
Great Lakes trade, 77
Great Law of Peace, 17–18
Great Peace conference (1701), 52
Great Society programs, 166
Grenville, George, 75, 76

Half-breeds. *See* Metis
Handbook of North American Indians (Goddard), 6
Harmar, Josiah, 82, 96
Harrington, D. B., 135
Harrison, William Henry, 83
HBC (Hudson's Bay Company), 52–53, 63, 77, 82
Heirs of Columbus, The (Vizenour), 183

Henry, Gordon, Jr., 176
He Who Was Spoken To (Medweganoonind), 134, 135
Hiawatha, 17, 48, 139
Hicks, Josiah, 131
HoChunk (Winnebago), 5, 6, 8, 18, 55, 116
Hole-in-the-Day (Bugonaygeshig), 34, 116, 120, 130, 131–132
Homicide, 15
Homosexuality, 34
Hoover, Herbert, 146
Hoover Commission, 161
House Made of Dawn (Momaday), 175
Howard, Edgar, 147
Hudson's Bay Company (HBC), 52–53, 63, 77, 82
Humphrey, Hubert, 167
Hunter-gatherers, evolution of, 6
Hurons: in Chippewa Country, 6, 8; conflict with Iroquois, 48, 49; Franco-Huron alliance, 46, 47; intertribal discussions with, 73; villages, 18

Ickes, Harold, 159
Illness caused by Manitos, 38–39
Incest, 26
Indian bread (Fry bread), 130
Indian Child Welfare Act, 172, 174
Indian Claims Commission Act (1946), 159–160
Indian Defense Association, 147
Indian Gaming Commission, 187, 188
Indian Gaming Regulatory Act, 187
Indian Health Service, 163, 192
Indian possessory interest, 94
Indian religion, legalization of, 136
Indian Removal Act (1830), 97
Indian Renaissance, 32, 167–170, 175–176, 198
Indian Reorganization Act (IRA), 139, 144, 147–148, 149, 151, 158–159

Indian right of occupancy, 94
Indian Rights Association, 146, 147
Indian schools, 90, 124–125, 167
Indian Self-Determination and
  Education Assistance Act (1975),
  172–173, 174
Indian Service police, 102, 132
Indian Service schools, 101–102, 124
Indian Territory Act (1830), 97
Indian title, 94–95
Indian Women and French Men
  (2001), 57
Intercourse acts (1790), 96
Intermarriages, children of, 58
International Indian Treaty
  Organization, 171
IRA (Indian Reorganization Act),
  139, 144, 147–148, 149, 151,
  158–159
Iroquois: Algonquians and, 46, 48;
  battle in 1655 with Chippewa,
  49–50; Battle of Iroquois Point
  (1662), 50; English and, 43; fur
  trade and, 48; Iroquois
  Confederation and League, 17, 48,
  49; shatter zone, 49
Iroquois Wars (1641–1701), 48–55, 59,
  66, 111

Jackson, Andrew, 97
Jackson, Helen Hunt, 145
James II, 52–53
Jaunay (missionary), 74
Jessakids, 36, 39
Jesuits, 30
Jogues, Isaac, 46
*John Beargrease: Legend of Minnesota's
  North Shore* (Lancaster), 130
Johnson, Lyndon, 163, 166–167
*Johnson and Graham's Lessee v.
  McIntosh*, 94–95
Johnson-O'Malley Act (JOM), 152
Johnson v. McIntosh (1823), 94
Johnston, Basil, 30–31

Joliet, Louis, 51
JOM (Johnson-O'Malley Act), 152
Jones, Peter, 6
Jones, William, 132
Jourdain, Robert, 167, 173–175

Kechewaubishash (Big Marten),
  64–65
Kennedy, John F., 163, 166
Keweenaway band, 107
King George's War (1740–1748), 54,
  66
King William's War (1689–1697), 54
Kunstler, William, 180

Lac Courte Oreilles Reservation, 149,
  177, 194, 199
Lacrosse (Baaga'dowe), 74, 114
Lac Vieux Desert band, 107
Lake Mohonk Conference,
  145–146
Lake Superior Chippewa Tribe,
  106, 110–111
Lakota Freedom Movement, 171
Lancaster, Daniel, 130
Landes, Ruth, 7
Langlade, Charles, 67, 69, 70, 74–75,
  78, 81
La Pointe de Chequamegon, 29
La Pointe Village (Madeline Island),
  106, 114
Lea, Luke, 108
Leech Lake Reservation, 86, 132, 170,
  174
LeSeur, Pierre, 62
Lincoln, Keith, 175
Little Shell (Chippewa), 141–142, 143,
  144, 149, 160
Little Turtle (Miami), 82, 96
Little Wind (Nodin), 134–136
Loon clan, 14, 16, 26, 27
Louisiana Purchase, 97
Love Medicine (Erdrich), 156, 176, 181,
  182

Lusson, Duluth Saint, 48–49
Lyons, Scott, 133, 170, 183

Machilimackinac (Great Turtle Island), 28, 41, 62
Mackinac Island (Michigan), 28
Madeline Island. *See* Mooniingwanekaanig
Major Crimes Act (1885), 102, 119
Mandua fight with Chippewa, 29–30
Manitos: ceremonies of propitiation and gratitude, 23; Chippewa Country and, 32–33; creation of Chippewa world, 22–23; in dreams, 25, 28; elders and, 36; gifts of to particular clans, 27; gratitude to, 26; as guardians of living things, 22–23; harvest festival, 12, 13; illnesses and, 38–39; lack of hierarchy, 23; maple sugar and, 9; Midewiwin and, 31; music and, 9–10; ogimaag and, 16; pipe ceremony and, 26; prayers to, 35; precreation existence of, 21; relationship with, 15; worldview and, 21
Maple tree sap, 9
Maps, Chippewa Country ca. 1800, 2
Marquette, Jacques, 46, 51, 62
Marriages: in Chippewa tradition, 14–15; within clans, 26; with European fur traders, 140; between French and Chippewa, 54, 57; mixed-blood children as interpreters, 58
Marshall, John, 93, 94–95, 129
Marten clan, 14, 26, 27, 30
Martinez v. San Juan Pueblo (1978), 161–162
Master Butchers Singing Club, The (Erdrich), 182
Matthiessen, Peter, 180
McCumber, Porter, 142, 143

McCumber Agreement and Commission, 142, 143
McDonnell, Michael, 76
McKinley, William, 132
Means, Russell, 171, 179, 181
Medard, Paul, 46
medicine men, 27f
Medweganoonind (He Who Was Spoken To), 134, 135
Megis shell, 28
member vs. citizen, 153
Memeska (Miami), 67
Menominee tribe, 6, 8, 18, 162
Mercer, William, 136
Meriam, Lewis, 146
Metis (mixed-blood): American Fur Company and, 90–91; children of Indian-French marriages, 54; as cultural brokers, 58; as fur traders, 63, 82, 83, 91; as husbands, 56; Michif language, 77, 140; in Montana, 144; in Red River Valley, 77–78, 91, 140–143
Miami tribe, 18
Michelet, Simon, 122
Michel's Island, 111
Michif language, 77, 140
Michigan: admitted to the U.S., 87; casinos and, 188–191; game laws and, 177–178; opposition to pipelines in, 194; state of, 107
Michilimackinac (Great Turtle) straits area, 28, 55, 70, 71–72, 80
Midewiwin (Grand Medicine Society): in the 1960s, 169; Christianity and, 30–32; Dewdney, Selwyn, and, 31–32; as epicenter of Chippewa culture, 30; geographic extent of, 30; Manitos and, 30–31, 32; Midewiwin scrolls, 9; Mooniingwanekaanig and, 112; origin of, 62; as priesthood, 36
Migratory pauses, 28
Mille Lacs Reservation, 64, 187

Minnesota: admission to the U.S. (1819), 87; casinos and, 188–191; fishing regulations during WWI, 137–138; game laws and, 177–178; Public Law 280 and, 162, 177–178, 193–194
Minnesota Chippewa tribe, 107, 149, 153, 160, 199
Minnesota Indian Affairs Council, 174
Mishebeshu, 22, 25, 26, 33
Missionaries, 45, 55, 89–90, 112, 124, 135
Mississauga, 51
Mississippian cultural influences, 5
Misty Past, 21, 22
Mitchell, George, 170, 172
Mixed bloods. *See* Metis
Mohawk tribe, 17–18
Montcalm, Louis-Joseph, 69, 70
Mooniingwanekaanig (Madeline Island): center of interactions after French and Indian War, 55; as center of modern Chippewa population, 28, 29; as cultural and trading center, 79; as epicenter of Chippewa society, 61–62, 79, 111, 112; Odanah, town of, 113–114; southwestern Chippewa and, 30
Moorhead, Warren, 122–123
Moose Dung (Moozoomoo), 116, 117, 133, 134
Morrill, Ashley, 117
Morriseau, Norval, 176
Mudjeekewis (Warrior Sun), 24
Mundt, Karl, 158
Murder of Joe White, The: Ojibwe Leadership and Colonialism in Wisconsin (Redix), 131
Muskrat, 26

Naming practices, Chippewa, 34
Nanabozho: birchbark and, 8; dual nature of, 25; fight with West Wind, 24–25; maple sugar and, 9; most powerful Manito, 22, 33; in oral tradition, 6; pipe ceremony and, 45; promise to return, 200; Turtle Island and, 26, 28
Napoleonic Wars, 85
Nash, Philleo, 166
National Association on Indian Affairs, 147
National Congress of American Indians (NCAI), 159, 163
National Council of American Indians (NCAI), 168
National Council on Indian Opportunity, 167, 171
National Indian Defense Association, 146
National Indian Gaming Commission, 190, 196
National Youth Council (1961), 171
Naudowewigoning (Place of Iroquois Bones), 50
NCAI (National Congress of American Indians), 159, 163
NCAI (National Council of American Indians), 168
Nelson, Knute, 122
Nelson Act, 121–122, 134
Neolin (Delaware), 72, 82
Neutral tribe, 18
New Deal, 151–152, 154, 156, 159
Nicollet, Jean, 46
Nixon, Richard, 167, 179
Noble savage concept, 7
Nodin (Little Wind), 134–136
Nokomis (Grandmother), 25
Non-Chippewa writers, colonialist mentality of, 7
Norrgard, Chantal, 133
Northern Lights, 38
Northwest Company, 63, 78, 82, 112
Northwest Ordinance, 96
Northwest War, 82
Nowacumig (Banks, Dennis), 170–171, 172, 179–181

Odanah (Wisconsin), 155–156
Office of Economic Opportunity (OEO) (1964), 167
Office of Indian Affairs (OIA): assimilationist bias of, 151; business councils and, 154; Collier and, 147; control of programs and funds, 153; efforts to eradicate Native American religions, 145; enforcement of laws after 1883, 143; membership requirements, 153; Odanah and, 156; progressives vs. traditionals, 154; Red Lake fisheries and, 138; schools and, 136, 143, 152; after World War II, 158;
Ogimaag (chiefs), 13, 14, 15
Ohio Valley: center of Adena-Hopewell culture, 5; English as threat to, 68–69; in French and Indian War, 72; invaded by American forces, 96–97; new villages in, 66; Quebec Act and, 76
OIA. *See* Office of Indian Affairs
Ojibwa Warrior (Banks and Errdoes), 180
Ojibwe language, 29, 156
Ojibwemowin, 26, 35, 53, 199
Oklahoma Indian Welfare Act, 147
Old Crossing Treaty (1863), 117, 133, 141
Oneida tribe, 17–18
Onondaga tribe, 17–18
Onontio (French Governor General), 60, 62, 66
Ontario Peninsula, 51
Oskabewis (messenger), 16–17
Ottawa (Trader) tribe, 20, 28, 41, 65–66

Palco-Indians, 5
Pan-Indian organizations, 71, 126, 159, 165, 168
Parallel verticality, 17
Parker, John, 69

Pays d'en Haute, 66
Pembina Band, 106, 116, 117, 133, 139–141, 160
Pemmican, 13, 141
Phrenology, 197
Pickawillany, 67–68
Pierre, Paul St., 62
Pine Ridge Reservation, 171, 179, 180
Pine Tree Treaty, 114
Pipe ceremony, 16–17, 24, 26, 34, 35, 44–45
Place of Iroquois Bones (Naudowewigoning), 50
Plains Chippewa, 28, 29
Plains Wars, 103
Plant crops, 8
Poison removal, 36
Polygamy, 14–15
Pontiac's War (1762–1764), 71–77
Population of Indians in U.S. in 1910, 145
Portage sites, 4
Potawatomi (Keepers of the Fire), 28–29, 41, 73
Powwows, 139, 169, 199
Presbyterians, 135
Price, Hiram, 119
Prisoners as adoptees or slaves, 19
Problem of Indian Administration, The (Meriam Report, 1928), 146
Proclamation Act (1763), 76
Progressivism, 118, 145
Prophetstown, 83
Protest against strip mine, 195f
Protestant missionaries, 45–46
Proto-Chippewa hunter-gatherers, 6
Prucha, Francis, 96
Puberty rites, 33
Public Health Service, 163
Public Law 280 states (Wisconsin and Minnesota), 162, 177–178, 193–194
Pukawis (Son Who Breaks), 24
Pukwudinniewag, 22

Quebec Act (1774), 76
Queen Anne's War (1702–1713), 54

Racism, 124
Radisson, Pierre, 46
Ramona (Jackson), 145
Ramsey, Alexander: closure of mission schools, 135; demand for Chippewa removal, 107–109, 114; demand for reduction of Indian land, 115; Red River Valley and, 116–117; White Earth Reservation and, 119–120
Raymbault, Charles, 46
Red Cliff Reservation, 110, 115, 153
Red Cloud, 145
Redix, Erik, 131, 133, 183
Red Lake Band (Chippewa), 138
Red Lake Fisheries Association, 152
Red Lake Reservation (Minnesota): 1889 land trade, 121; Canadian pipeline and, 194; as cultural center, 86; Dakota Wars and, 115–116; excluded from 1934 confederation, 107; license plates and, 174; lumber industry and, 134; Old Crossing Treaty and, 117–118; overfishing and, 187; Pembina Band and, 106; rejection of IRA, 148–149, 153; relocation to cities, 163; state jurisdiction and, 162; surrender of land to U.S., 103; taken from the Dakota, 132–133
Red Power movement, 167–171, 172, 176, 198
Red River Valley, 116–117, 140
Red River Valley Metis culture, 77–78, 91, 140–143
Refugees, 48
Relocation program, 163
Reservations: agents and Courts of Indian Offenses, 102; as checkerboards, 103, 123, 194; Chippewa negotiations for, 98; constitution in Minnesota, 138; drug trafficking on, 193; federally recognized Chippewa tribes, list of, 3; inconsistent enforcement of treaties, 101; manifest destiny and, 88–89; percentage of Chippewa not living on reservations, 200; treaties and boundaries, 98–100, 106; unemployment in, 187. *See also specific reservation names*
Rice, Henry, 114, 134
Rice, wild (mahnoomin), 9, 10, 29
Rice Gatherers, 10f
Rice harvests, 13
Riel, Louis, 141
Robber barons, 145
Rocky Boy Reservation (Montana), 143–144
Roosevelt, Franklin, 147
Round House, The (Erdrich), 156, 182
Runners of the Woods (Coureurs de Bois), 53
Rupert's Land, 53

Sacred stories, 11
Sandy Lake tragedy (1850), 97, 108, 126
Sauk tribe, 18, 55
Saulteurs, 46
Schenk, Therese, 183
Second Hundred Years' War, 54
Seneca tribe, 17–18
Seven Years' War (1756–1763), 65
Shaking tent ceremony, 36
Shamans, 14, 17, 27f, 34, 36, 38
Shawnee Prophet (Tenkswatawa), 82, 83
Shawnee tribe, 72
Shrouds of White Earth (Vizenour), 183
Sidestreaming, 7
Silko, Leslie, 175
Single-parent households, 192
Sitting Bull, 145

Sky Woman, 23–24
Sky world, 37
Sleeper-Smith, Susan, 57
Smallpox epidemics, 43, 70
Snakes tribe, 52
Social Gospel crusades, 145
Songs, 9–10
Son Who Breaks (Pukawis), 24
Spirit keepers, 34–35
Stamp Act (1763), 76
Standing Bear, 145
St. Clair, Arthur, 96
Steenerson Act (1904), 122
Stone Child (Ashiniwin), 144
Straits of Mackinac as trade crossroad, 79–80
Sugarbushes, 12, 17
Summer and fall activities, 12
Sweat lodges, 34, 39

Taylor, Zachary, 107, 126
Tecumseh (Shawnee), 83
Ten Cent Treaty, 143
Tenkswatawa (Shawnee Prophet), 82, 83
Three Council Fires, 18, 28, 41
Thunder, Otto, 138
Thunderers (Thunderbirds), 22, 23, 26, 33
Tobacco as gift, 35
Tobacco tribe, 18
Trail of Broken Treaties (1972), 171
Trail of Tears, 98, 179
Traveling soul, 37
Treaty of 1837, 106
Treaty of 1854, 149
Treaty of Greenville, 96–97
Treaty of LaPointe (1854), 110, 114–115
Treaty of Paris, 81–82
Treaty rights, ignored by states, 177
Treuer, Anton, 133, 134, 136, 183
Treuer, David, 183
Treuer, Margaret Sealye, 175

Tribal boundaries, 18
Tribal Chairmen's Association, 167
Tribal citizen, 197
Tribal College Act, 172
Tribble, Fred, 177
Tribble, Mike, 177
Tricksters, 24
Trump, Donald, 191
Turtle Island, 26, 28
Turtle Mountain Reservation: created in 1882, 103, 142; Little Shell and, 144; Pembina Band and, 106, 117, 133, 139–141, 160; population of, 143; threatened with termination, 162; traders in, 112; treaty negotiations in 1862, 100
Turtle Mountains (North Dakota and Manitoba), 28, 30, 86
Tuscarora tribe, 48

Udall, Stewart, 166
United States: Doctrine of Discovery and, 43, 93, 94; fur trade and, 90–92; incorporating tribes into American system, 101–102; manifest destiny and, 88–89; Native Americans and U.S. expansion, 85–87; treaties between 1785 and 1902, 92–93, 94–95
Universities and Indian studies programs, 168
Upper Great Lakes drainage basins, 1
Upstreaming, 7
U.S. Constitution Commerce Clause, 93
U.S. v. Kagama (1886), 119, 162

Vecsey, Christopher, 30, 35
Verendrye, Baptiste Gaultier de la, 63
Verendrye, Pierre Gaultier de la, 62, 63
Veterans, monuments to, 157
Vicenti, Francis, 92f, 104
Village (odanah), size of, 12

Violence Against Women Act, 194
Vision quests, 34
Vizenor, Gerald, 176, 181, 182–183
Voigt, Lester, 178
Voigt decision, 178, 186, 195

Waabibines (White Thunderbird), 133
War in intertribal relations, 12, 13, 18–19
War of 1812, 82, 83, 85–86, 88
War of Austrian Succession (1744–1748), 65
Warren, Lyman, 112–113
Warren, Truman, 112–113
Warren, William, 6, 64, 65
Warrior Nation (Treuer), 133
Warrior Sun (Mudjeekewis), 24
Washington, George, 68
Waskish, Minnesota, 138
Watkins, Arthur, 160
Watrous, John, 107, 108, 109, 110, 114
Waugh, John, 142
Wayne, Anthony, 96–97
Wendigos, 11–12, 36–37
West Turtle Mountain Chippewa, 106–107
West Wind, 24, 26
Wheeler, Burton K., 147
Whipple, Henry, 117, 120
White, Joe (Giiskitawa), 130, 131
Whitecloud, Thomas (Chippewa), 157f
White Crane, 111
White Earth Reservation: in 1867, 103; blood quantum requirements, 153; boycott of Bemidji, 174; constitution of, 199; creation of, 98; establishment of, 119–123; phrenology and, 197
White Earth Tragedy, The (Meyer), 119
White Thunderbird (Waabibines), 133
Wigwams, 9
Wild rice (mahnoomin), 9, 10, 29
Willows, 8
Wimitigoozhig, 42
Winnebago (HoChunk), 5, 6, 8, 18, 55, 116
Winonah, 24
Winter communities, 11, 55
Winter stories, 39
Wisconsin: admission to the U.S. (1854), 87; casinos in, 188–191; fishing rights controversy, 177; policy vs. tribal police, 193; Public Law 280 and, 162, 177–178, 193–194; reservations in, 106
Witchcraft, 36
Wolves, 25, 200
Women of All Red Nations (1974), 171
Woodland Era, divisions of, 5
Worcester v. Georgia (1832), 94
Wordarrows (Vizenour), 182
Works Progress Administration (WPA), 151–152, 158
World War I, 146
World War II, 157
Wounded Knee, 171–172, 180
WPA (Works Progress Administration), 151–152, 158
Wyandots, 49, 50, 51

Za, Zitkala (Sioux), 145
Zimmerman, William, 161

About the Author

Gregory O. Gagnon, Bad River Band of the Lake Superior Chippewa, began collecting episodes in the story of the Chippewa from his grandmother, Josephine Baker Bresette Gagnon. She filled his boyhood with traditional stories and oral histories. Collection continued as he went through life. College degrees including a PhD from the University of Maryland provided more information, and many Chippewa people contributed pieces of the story. Dr. Gagnon moved from college administration on Pine Ridge Reservation to an Indian Studies Department at the University of North Dakota, where he taught Chippewa history and courses in tribal government and federal policy. He gained more knowledge as a consultant and visitor at several reservations: Lac Courte Oreilles, Leech Lake, Red Lake, White Earth, and Bay Mills. Now retired, he teaches American Indian law at the Loyola College of Law in New Orleans. He returns to reservations to learn more.

Other parts of the story received emanate from the generations of academic scholars and published Native Americans who have researched and written about the story of the Chippewa. Many of these are mentioned in the book. Dr. Gagnon's rendition of the story is not possible without the monographs of his colleagues—both Chippewa and non-Chippewa. His interpretations and conclusions drawn from the work of others are his own, and none of them are responsible for his mistakes.

The author offers this part of the Chippewa story in a good way.

www.ingramcontent.com/pod-product-compliance
Lightning Source LLC
Chambersburg PA
CBHW070410100426
42812CB00005B/1701